# VEERAPPAN

# VEERAPPAN

## India's Most Wanted Man

*Sunaad Raghuram*

An Imprint of HarperCollinsPublishers

FIRST U.S. EDITION

*Designed by Cassandra J. Pappas*

Library of Congress Cataloging-in-Publication Data

Raghuram, Sunaad.
    Veerappan : India's most wanted man / Sunaad Raghuram.
       p. cm.
    Originally published: New Delhi : Viking, 2001.
    ISBN 0-06-621063-1
    1. Vårappan. 2. Wildlife smuggling—India. 3. Criminals—
India. I. Title.
HJ7890 R34 2001
364.1′8—dc21

                                                2002021100

02   03   04   05   06   BVG/QM   10   9   8   7   6   5   4   3   2   1

*To all those brave men and women who lost their lives*

*in the hunt for Veerappan.*


*To my in-laws Chitte and Podnolanda Ramakrishna*

*for always being there for me.*

# Contents

# Acknowledgments

PUTTING TOGETHER THIS BOOK entailed meeting and interacting with a lot of people. And not one of them was reluctant to help. It was very fulfilling as a journalist to experience their generosity in sharing information, and their honest concern for the future of the project. I am deeply indebted to all of them, far too many to name.

While I am not in a position to name all my sources for the book, I would like to express my heartfelt gratitude to:

My friends Madan Vrishabendra Murthy, H. C. Lakshmi Kantha, Arun Mallaraje Urs, Laiqh Ahmed Khan, Keshava Murthy, and Dr. Sunil Dutt, who played such a major role in keeping me going despite daunting odds;

M. J. Chandra Shekar, who allowed me to torture-drive his prized 1967 Fiat on the impossibly treacherous tracks deep inside Veerappan territory as we went scouting for information;

My childhood mates Srinivasa Padaki, Seshadri Babu, Prakash Somashekariah, Dr. Sudesh Kumar, Dr. Madhu Gowda, Harsha Gowda, Satish Kikkeri, and H. R. Jagadeesh for all their concern and good wishes;

M. R. Shivu for his magnanimity in allowing me a virtual free run of his office computers, Internet, e-mail, et al., in the process of writing this book; and to everyone at P. K. Tech India Pvt. Ltd., for being so good to me;

M. B. Shiv Kumar and Shankar Prasad, who never once refused to answer my late-night calls about technical problems with my computer;

My lawyer and childhood friend Sridhar Chakke, who helped me with the legal aspects of writing this book;

Inspector General of Police (Southern Range) M. K. Srivastava for making time for me;

Superintendent of Police Gopal Hosur, for willingly sharing his experiences as an STF officer;

Inspector "Tiger" Ashok Kumar, a fine officer, without whose help this book would not have been completed;

Vijay Kumar Gogi, Deputy Conservator of Forests, Chamarajanagar, for readily agreeing to meet me and letting me in on extremely vital aspects of the personality of his good friend DCF Srinivas, who died tragically at the hands of Veerappan;

Forest jeep driver Anwar Pasha for his warmth and the elaborate meal he cooked for me in his house late at night;

Foresters Siddiah and Krishniah, and guard Andani, who narrated their chilling experiences in Veerappan country and so patiently answered all my queries late into the night, unmindful of the swarming mosquitoes, in a "lightless" guesthouse deep inside the Kollegala forests;

Venkate Gowda of Hanur, a fellow journalist, for rare insights into the story and for introducing me to Muthuram;

Muthuram, for the most startling bits of information on Veerappan, and for his hospitality;

Advocate A. M. Mallikarjuniah of Kollegala, who provided me with vital information, especially on the area in which the narrative is set;

Advocates Umesh, Manjunath, Venkatraje Urs, and especially A. K. Ramakrishnan for their help and their warmth;

Kattera Naniah for putting me in touch with his friend Dr. Krishna Murthy, who came up with a perfect sketch of Veerappan's terrain;

Dr. Krishna Murthy himself, for racing against time for my sake and finishing the job so well;

My dear friend P. V. Giri, for all his uplifting e-mails in spite of his maddeningly busy schedule;

Abdul Kareem and his son Jameel Ahmed for their encouragement;

My neighbor Sridhar, a clerk in the Mysore court, who spoke to advocate Mallikarjuniah on my behalf;

My good friend Prakash, a senior reporter with a Bangalore-based Kannada TV channel Suprabhata, whose concern for the project made him spend long hours in his studio, playing an endless succession of tapes relating to the Veerappan story;

Ravi Udaya, Senior Manager, State Bank of India, and his colleagues Prasanna and Arun for their enthusiasm and interest in my work;

Jayapriya Vasudevan, friendly and ever-smiling consultant of Jacaranda Press, for taking the idea to Penguin and making it all happen;

Sudeshna Shome Ghosh, my extremely efficient and methodical editor, who ever so unobtrusively took out the unwanted and incomprehensible facets of my writing "genius!"

And to my untiringly focused commissioning editor, V. K. Karthika, for putting the book together in its final form.

# Introduction

KOOSE MUNISWAMY VEERAPPAN, fifty-four, is India's most wanted man. The reward for getting him, alive or dead, is four million rupees. He and his gang are alleged to have poached more than a hundred tuskers in the past twenty-five years. It is estimated that they have also taken sandalwood worth tens of millions of rupees from the rich forests of the districts of Mysore, Chamarajanagar, Dharmapuri, Salem, Periyar, and the Nilgiris on the Karnataka–Tamil Nadu border.

According to available records, Veerappan and his gang have committed 119 murders in the two states. Among those killed are thirty-two police officers and ten forest officials of various ranks. There are 134 cases registered against Veerappan and his men, ranging from murder, extortion, *dacoity*, and kidnapping to indulging in terrorist acts. While fifty-nine cases have been registered in Karnataka, seventy-five are pending in Tamil Nadu. These are the known cases. It is widely believed that scores of murders committed by the bandit deep inside the forests have gone unreported over the years because of the villagers' fear of incurring his wrath.

It was in the year 1988 that I first became interested in knowing more about the phenomenon called Veerappan. As a postgraduate student at Mysore University, I befriended a postman named Krishna Naik. In December of that year, we were sitting in the cool shade of a banyan tree in the campus one day, chatting idly, when Naik began to reminisce about his childhood days spent in the enchanting wilderness of his native Kollegala taluk, about thirty-five miles from Mysore.

In the course of his stunning description of life on the fringe of the forest, Naik mentioned Veerappan. He described him as a forest bandit who was looked upon with awe by villagers in the Malai Mahadeshwara (MM) Hills area, of which Kollegala is a part. "I don't know much about his life. All I know is that he has visited my grandfather's house once or twice, late at night, and asked for food to be served to him and his gang members," said Naik. My curiosity was aroused. But before I could ask him any questions about the mystery man, he had taken off on his rickety bicycle, to deliver more letters.

On January 20, 1989, I hopped on to my scooter after breakfast and headed for Kollegala, en route to MM Hills. All I had was 180 rupees, money enough to buy a couple of gallons of gasoline and some basic foodstuff to eat during my two-day sojourn in the forest.

The road from Mysore to Kollegala must rank as one of the worst in the country, even to this day. Bumping over potholes, some the size of craters, and avoiding getting in the way of oncoming buses and lorries would tax even a professional stunt driver. It took me over two hours to cover a distance of thirty-five miles.

Entering the dusty little town, I stopped at a roadside tea stall. As I stretched myself on a charpoy and ordered a cup of tea, I noticed a middle-aged man sitting nearby. I engaged him in conversation, and found him friendly enough. But the moment I broached the name of Veerappan, his demeanor toward me turned to cold indifference. He muttered something before shuffling away, without even giving me a second look.

This little incident intrigued me. It also strengthened my resolve to get to know more about the man called Veerappan. I continued on to Gopinatham, a little village known to be Veerappan's birthplace. My arrival there seemed to be of no interest or consequence to anybody. Except for one man. He was sitting outside his small thatched house, smoking a *beedi*. As my scooter halted in front of him, he gave me a long, quizzical look. Moments later, he smiled, and I knew that I had found refuge for the night. His name was Sambhandam.

I told Sambhandam that I was an ardent devotee of Lord Mahadeshwara and had visited the temple on the hill, before deciding to explore the area a bit more. He seemed suitably impressed with my credentials as a "pilgrim." Perhaps my beard and the spot of vermilion on my forehead gave strength to my claim. He allowed me to spend the night in his little house. Before we turned in, Sambhandam talked to me of life in the heart of the forest, especially around Gopinatham. Veerappan's name cropped up often in the narration.

Twelve years have gone by since that night, and my fascination with the subject of Veerappan has not waned one bit. Subsequently, I met more people in the village and in the neighboring areas, talked to police and forest officers in the region, and tried my best to unearth as many details as I could about the man who has reigned outside the law for over two and a half decades. My intention in writing this book is not in any way to lionize Veerappan, but to provide a narrative that puts him in context, and explore the many aspects of his life and relationships. I have taken years to sift through papers, photographs, and archival material to cull what I think are the significant moments of his criminal career. Several details and episodes have had to be left out, primarily because they could not be satisfactorily verified, and reports and rumors have constantly had to be tempered with caution, but in the end, I hope I have produced an account that is as close to reality as possible.

# VEERAPPAN

# Prologue

From atop one of the craggy summits of the Malai Mahadeshwara (MM) Hills in the state of Karnataka in southern India, the narrow pothole-ridden road that curves and weaves through the green vegetation of the dense jungle looks like an enormous mythological serpent slithering along aimlessly.

The sun slowly slides into the far end of the western horizon, bathing the sky in orange-bronze reflections. Twilight falls on the vast expanse of trees and shrubs below, and the place begins to echo with the nocturnal sounds of the jungle. A peacock takes off shrieking from a short stump, like a blazing comet darting into space. A great cluster of bamboo heaves and sways in the cool breeze that wafts in from the mountain ranges to the north. The branches groan, as if unable to withstand their own weight. Just below this heaving mass stands a lone tusker, majestic in his solitude. His curved ivory tusks glisten in the shimmering moonlight like two sharp swords.

A few yards away, on a slightly elevated ridge, a tall man with ripcord muscles and a wiry frame focuses his deep-set eyes on the elephant, unmindful of the flies buzzing around. He slithers forward over the grass, a country-made double-barreled gun in his grasp, carefully inching closer to the edge of the rock shelf, toward the unsuspecting creature. Normally the elephant would have sensed the intruder in its vicinity, but today the strong breeze is blowing away from it, and the scent of the man goes undetected. He slides up further, emboldened by the unconcerned demeanor of the animal below, his gun cocked and ready to fire. When he judges the distance to be right, he gets to his feet in one swift move, picks up a small pebble, and hurls it in the direction of the tusker from behind. The slight sound is enough to make the great beast veer around, startled. Quickly, and with cruel precision, the man aims his battered weapon and fires. The bullet hits the elephant on its temple, just above the right ear, the only place where a clean shot will kill almost instantly. The animal lets out a shrill, earsplitting scream. The second bullet, aimed more hastily, strikes it somewhere on the side of the head. The elephant runs crashing through the bamboo for about two hundred yards before collapsing. The jungle all around resonates with the panicky cries of the langur and the alarm calls of the sambhar as they scatter in fright. The hunter has found his mark yet again as one more beast has fallen victim to his greed.

A few shadowy forms materialize from the jungle to salute the killer. Armed with sharp axes, the men start work on the mammoth creature, hacking till the two gigantic tusks can be removed. The once majestic pachyderm is slowly reduced to a grotesque mass of torn flesh. Bluebottle flies, some the size of small beetles, begin to buzz around the carcass feverishly.

Two hours later, bloodied and exhausted, the men load the huge tusks still dripping with blood into gunny bags and disappear into the jungle as noiselessly as they had emerged.

# PART I

# I

## History of Mayhem

Nearly seven thousand square miles of lush and almost impenetrable jungle covers the districts of Chamarajanagar and Mysore in the state of Karnataka on one side and the districts of Nilgiris, Dharmapuri, Erode, and Salem in the state of Tamil Nadu on the other. The jungle is an integral part of the Western Ghats, one of the hot spots of biodiversity in the world.

The terrain for the most part is undulating, with a seemingly endless succession of high mountains that stretch from north to south. Denkanikota, Pennagaram, Baragur, Guttielathur, Talamalai, and the eastern slopes of the Nilgiris in Tamil Nadu, and Biligirirangana Betta, Edayarahalli, Mahadeshwara Malai, Chikkailur, Hanur, Dhangur, Kowdalli, and Doddasampige in Karnataka form one the largest chunks of thick, unbroken forest in the Indian subcontinent, and they teem with a rich variety of wildlife. The jagged hills, the deep gorges, the vast valleys, and the thick undergrowth combine to make it an area that is not just inhospitable but almost inaccessible.

It is a forbidding place for the unsuspecting. Hundreds of animals roam the mostly dry deciduous forests of teak, rosewood, sandal, mathi, and honne trees, and at night the sounds they make can chill the heart of those uninitiated in the ways of the jungle. There is the distant plaintive call of a fawn being grabbed by a hungry tiger; the shrill trumpeting of an elephant herd near a water hole; the guttural sawing of a panther from atop a tree; the grunting of a wild boar digging for roots in the dark; the rustle of leaves as a gaur moves into a clearing. For a human being, negotiating this undergrowth can be exhausting; sometimes, chopping through the lantana bushes and other vegetation with a machete is the only way to fight through.

Gopinatham, a tiny hamlet of about a hundred dwellings which takes its name from Lord Krishna, nestles inconspicuously amid this rugged expanse. It's a stone's throw away from MM Hills, about sixty miles from the dusty little town of Kollegala, and home predominantly to a community known as the Padiacchi Gounder. Basically cattle grazers, the Gounders eke out a livelihood by herding cattle and trading milk as well as meat. Some of them have small landholdings on which they grow millet and corn, the yield from which is directly proportional to the largesse of the rain gods, who invariably play truant, especially at the time of sowing. The forests around have also been home for centuries to scheduled tribes like the Soliga, Irula, Betta Kuruba, Jenu Kuruba, and Mullu Kuruba. Members of these communities subsist on the collection and sale of minor forest produce like fruit, honey, tamarind, bamboo shoots, and a variety of berries and nuts. The tribes have been given special permission to use the resources of the forest because this has been their only source of livelihood for generations. Hunting is strictly forbidden in the reserved forest territory.

Also found in the area are communities identified as "backward" castes, such as the Tambadi Lingayat, Vokkaliga Gounder, Malaivellala Gounder, Kuruba, Parivara, Shetti, Lambani, and Golla. These communities are for the most part homogeneous, culturally and linguistically, and are found on both sides of the border. The language spoken is predominantly Kannada, and the tribals speak a dialect of the language. The Padiacchi and the Malaivellala Gounders, though, trace their ancestry to Tamil Nadu and are conversant only in Tamil.

Approximately sixty years ago, in the 1930s, a man named Muniya Gounder migrated to Gopinatham from his village of Kothanagere, in the Mettur taluk of Salem district in Tamil Nadu. His ancestral land was submerged after a dam was built across the Cauvery River, close to Mettur. Forced to vacate the place of his forefathers, Muniya Gounder began to look for another home, and eventually decided that Gopinatham would be an ideal place. So he found a small piece of land to till and some cattle to graze, and moved in.

Like most interior villages in India, Gopinatham had its share of illiteracy, superstition, poverty, and hunger. Tucked away in the confines of the jungle, it was a place where practically no developmental work had been initiated by the government, and for most of its inhabitants, especially the new migrant family of Muniya Gounder, life was more drudgery than pleasure. Muniya Gounder, along with his two sons, Koose Muniswamy and Kirya Ponnuswamy, toiled under the relentless sun all day, tilling land and grazing their meager collection of cattle and sheep. Occasionally they managed to supplement their income by charging a small fee to graze the cattle of a few other villagers.

In this harsh land, where even the young did not dare to dream, Koose Muniswamy's wife, Punithayamma, gave birth to three sons: Koose Madiah, Koose Veerappan, and Arjunan. Born on January 18, 1952, Veerappan soon showed himself to be the smartest of the boys. He was a precocious child, and as he grew older he proved to be an excellent marksman. He could fling a stone effortlessly and with fine-tuned precision to bring down a bunch of tamarind fruit dangling high up in the branches, much to the awe and delight of his friends. Very soon, he and his two brothers were assisting their father in hunting langur in the nearby forests—langur meat being an occasional and much needed supplement to their meager diet.

The three young boys soon started illegally cutting and smuggling bamboo out to the local craftsmen, who converted it into artifacts for the market. On one of their forays into the jungle, in early 1965, forest guards in the Kollegala division cornered them. Madiah and Arjunan escaped, but Veerappan was caught and a case was registered against him in the Ramapura police station. A local villager known to Veerappan's father stood surety for his bail. This was Veerappan's first brush with the law.

The young Veerappan's spirit of enterprise did not go unnoticed. A pair of eyes had been watching him with interest for a long time.

Poacher and smuggler Sevi Gounder was a man who understood the importance and value of forest wealth amid the gut-wrenching poverty, and in the young Veerappan he recognized a spark, a dash of daredevilry that he knew he could groom to his benefit. A native of the neighboring hamlet of Karangalur, a few miles from Gopinatham, Sevi Gounder had chosen to live outside the framework of the law. Although he owned a sizable tract of land on which he grew sugarcane and turmeric, he had begun in the 1960s to poach elephants in the vast forests around Gopinatham, along with his gang of local youngsters, for whom this was a lucrative if bloody avocation. He slowly took the young, impressionable village boy under his wing, teaching him how to shoot elephants with the minimum risk. Veerappan, with his natural talent as a marksman, did not take long to learn. Sevi taught his protégé to handle a gun and encouraged him on his way into the smuggling and poaching world, and was meanwhile shrewd enough to ensure that one of his own sons became a judge in a court in Tamil Nadu.

Under Sevi Gounder's tutelage the eighteen-year-old Veerappan quickly realized the prestige that came with carrying a gun, and the effect it had on the others around him. The simple village folk, who had hardly any exposure to the outside world, began to treat him with respect. His exploits with the gun, especially his shooting dead a huge tusker at almost point-blank range in the forests near Hogenekal, were talked about with an admiration and awe that slowly turned to fear and fawning subservience. Confident in his growing power, Veerappan became bolder and more imaginative in his attempt to increase his sphere of influence. Working with Sevi Gounder, he had already discovered nature's incredibly rich potential for creating wealth. There were thousands of sandalwood trees growing in the jungles, and hundreds of bull elephants roaming the area with their valuable tusks of ivory.

Sandalwood and ivory have been the most desired commodities of these forests for centuries. The use of ivory in India can be traced back to more than four thousand years. Traditionally, ivory has been used for crafting ornaments and for making commonly used objects like combs, scales, rods, batons, kohl sticks, containers, caskets, pins, hooks, and even toys. Ivory pendants and amulets are still considered sacred and are supposed to protect the wearer from evil.

The steady demand for ivory and sandalwood in the markets of Karnataka and Tamil Nadu ensured that their value only increased as time went by. The local handicrafts industry, based mainly in Mysore, a five-hour drive from Veerappan's main operational area, supplied both regional and international markets, and brokers were not difficult to find. Moreover, in the desolate stretches of stark jungle, there was little danger of running into policemen or law enforcement officials of any sort.

Ivory trading in India was restricted even as early as 1873, when the colonial British regime established a law known as the Madras Act, to prevent the indiscriminate killing of wild elephants and protect their natural habitat. In 1912 the law was made applicable to the entire Indian territory. But the Wildlife (Protection) Act of 1972 was the first comprehensive legislation for control and management of wild animals and their habitat.

Although trade in wild animals and their products was banned by this act, Sevi Gounder was undeterred. He regularly fed the ivory market through conduits mainly in Kozhikode and Tiruvananthapuram, in Kerala, sometimes using Kochi and Trissur as midway storage points. Veerappan and his brother Arjunan had worked out ways to get past the forest check posts along the route. One of their methods was to hire a lorry, place the tusks on top of the driver's cabin, and cover them with tarpaulin. Since the lorry's hold was empty, nobody bothered to check it, and invariably they would drive away without getting caught. The valuable tusks were then taken to Kerala, and from there they made their way to Mumbai, eventually to land in major carving centers such as Jaipur, Udaipur, Agra, Varanasi, Murshidabad, and Delhi.

Ivory is traded in basically two forms: raw and worked. Whole tusks or those cut into pieces are known as raw or unworked ivory. Ivory that has been converted into artifacts is considered finished or worked. Markets for both raw and finished ivory lie mainly in the Far East. In the 1980s, Hong Kong was the single largest market, although later Japan and Singapore became significant end markets as well. The Japanese market, for instance, buys up large quantities of ivory to make "henkos" (name-seals) and kimono drawstring beads. From Mumbai, consignments are also smuggled in Arabian dhows to the Middle East, and from there to Far Eastern destinations.

Sevi Gounder's "labor" fetched him anywhere between approximately seven hundred and nine hundred rupees per pound of ivory. New manufacturing techniques using electric lathes enabled the mass production of ivory carvings, which along with a rising demand in the Far East led to an increase in elephant kills. Sevi and his men, including Veerappan, prospered.

By the mid-1970s the jungles of MM Hills were also being systematically robbed of their glorious sandalwood trees. It was not hard to find labor to cut and ferry the valuable wood. In a place where one full meal a day was difficult to come by, villagers, under the watchful gaze of Veerappan and his band of young men, began to volunteer in droves. A day's work fetched them thirty rupees, a truly princely sum by their reckoning. Every pound of sandalwood sold earned their enterprising supervisor thirty-odd rupees.

Now that he had money, the attitude of the villagers toward Veerappan became even more worshipful, and he played the role of demigod to perfection. With his newfound money he bought himself a lorry, and he and his youngest brother, Arjunan, would often stop to offer a lift to the villagers on their way to work or home. In the far-flung villages in and around the jungles, where automobiles were an unheard-of luxury, this gesture earned for Veerappan the sobriquet of savior. But his notoriously volatile temper also gave him a nickname: Molaga, or "Chili" in the local Tamil language.

Sevi Gounder continued his pillage of ivory until 1975 when he finally "retired." Although he was a known criminal, against whom the police of both Karnataka and Tamil Nadu had filed several cases, he was never convicted, because of lack of evidence. He lived in his native Karangalur until his death, in 1996, at the age of eighty.

FOR OVER A CENTURY, the villages in the region where Veerappan lived, including the small settlements of Hanur, Ramapura, Kowdalli, Palar, Gopinatham, Meenyam, Hoogyam, Nallur, and a few others in the jungle belt, had been known for their disregard for the law. Their sheer remoteness from the nearest post of civilization ensured that no police or forest officer ever made the arduous trek to the wild forest land. In the days before the jeep became a popular mode of transport, the daunting prospect of riding horseback for miles on end, amid the ever-present threat of wild elephants, put off even the most committed of officers.

In fact, the town of Kollegala, thirty-five miles to the northeast of the royal city of Mysore, has long been known as a dangerous area where violent looting and robbery are common. According to legend, it was home to a demon named Kahola in the Puranic times. In more recent memory, bandits have been known to waylay caravans belonging to traders and pilgrims on their way through the jungle to the temple of Lord Mahadeshwara and make away with valuables.

A British officer who served in the area in the 1890s reportedly complained to his superiors that the people in these parts had a tendency toward militancy and showed scant regard for forest laws. Intrusions into the forest were common, and poaching of animals and smuggling of wood were regular occurrences. Murders and extortions also took place with alarming regularity.

The near total absence of policing meant that disputes were usually settled in favor of the physically stronger man, often with the help of machetes or wooden clubs. It is widely believed that the progenitor of this tradition of violence was a bandit called Mumpty-vaayan. A native of Mechcheri, Mumpty-vaayan operated with impunity in this region in the early decades of the twentieth century, and died at the age of thirty-six. Physical descriptions of him, at least in the local narratives, lionize the man and his body. Mumpty-vaayan was said to have had a frame over six feet tall, with arms and legs that resembled tree trunks, and a monstrous mustache that reached almost up to his temple. He had an appetite to match, and could devour an entire deer raw. His upper lip protruded slightly, and a deep scar stretched from the corner of his right eye to his right earlobe. His real name was Selvaraj, but the villagers nicknamed him Mumpty-vaayan, meaning "the man with a mouth like a shovel."

The young Selvaraj's father had an ongoing feud with one of his neighbors. Matters came to a head one night when the neighbor assembled a group of eight relatives, waylaid the old man, and murdered him. He then tied the body to a tree close to the main road in the village as a warning to others not to meddle with him or his family. In revenge, Selvaraj, with the assistance of his brother and five other men, broke into the house of his father's murderers and hacked all nine of them to pieces with woodchoppers.

The murders created a sensation in the area. Most of the villagers were aware of the sequence of events, so it wasn't long before the relatives of the murdered discovered the identity of the murderers. The police caught three of the men involved, and they were convicted and finally hanged. But Selvaraj, his brother, and the two other men who had escaped conviction went into hiding.

The relatives of the murdered men continued their search for Selvaraj, and one day they got lucky. Selvaraj's brother had befriended the wife of a local tailor, and he and the other fugitives had moved into the tailor's house. The aggrieved husband leaked this information, and one night the hut in which they were sleeping was set on fire. Selvaraj's brother and his lover were burned to death. But the others, including Selvaraj, miraculously escaped. The police rushed to the village and arrested the men who were responsible for the murder. Two of them were sent to the gallows.

Selvaraj, dispossessed of all his belongings, went into hiding in the jungle nearby. He had no means of earning a livelihood and he was certain that the police would swoop down on him the moment they sighted him. It was then that he decided to adopt robbery as a means of sustenance. As the years went by, he became a dreaded bandit, known to rob the rich in order to feed the poor. His victims were invariably the wealthy landlords, businessmen, and shopkeepers in the surrounding areas, ranging from the eastern portion of Kollegala taluk into Salem district, up the Doddahalla River, and across the mountainous range to the outskirts of Pennagaram town.

By now he was known more commonly as Mumpty-vaayan than as Selvaraj. He rarely emerged from the forest, and the villagers supplied him with rations in return for the money he gave them. The police did not get any credible information about his whereabouts as they could find no one to help—such was his popularity. The only people who hated him were his victims: the rich.

Mumpty-vaayan's method of looting was quite simple. He would gather information about landlords and merchants in the area from the ever-obliging villagers. He would then descend in the dead of the night and knock on their doors. With a knife and a twelve-gauge gun staring them in the face, there was little room for escape.

Another of Mumpty-vaayan's regular activities was to extract money from timber smugglers. These illegal operators usually earmarked a tree of good girth deep inside the jungle and started hacking it after sunset. They would take lorries to the spot to load the felled timber and make a quick getaway before daybreak. Mumpty-vaayan would wait until the lorries were about to start, then appear near the driver's cabin and demand fifty rupees—the price for his silence.

It was said that Mumpty-vaayan's annual earnings from his criminal activities in those days was in the region of 25,000 rupees. In fact, it was probably at least twice that, for he invariably looted money and valuables from those who, on account of the nature of their activities, found it impossible to approach the police. Compare this figure to the twenty rupees that was the average monthly salary of a government employee during those days.

Mumpty-vaayan believed in working alone. He didn't trust anybody. This was one of the major reasons his free run was possible. Those who saw him say he always wore a khaki uniform with a huge leather cartridge belt strapped across his shoulder. A huge knife dangled from a belt around his waist, and the twelve-gauge gun was a standard accessory. Sometimes he even wore a green turban, much like a forest guard of that time.

If Mumpty-vaayan had one weakness, it was women. He was known to have more than one mistress, as well as a wife who lived in Mechcheri, about nine miles from the Mettur dam. In their attempt to capture him, the police decided to keep a strict watch on this house, but Mumpty-vaayan was too clever for them. Once he came disguised as a woman, and the policemen found out only long after he had left. But they continued to keep watch. A few weeks later, after sunset, they saw a shrouded figure approaching the house. Certain that it was Mumpty-vaayan, they pounced on the figure, knocked it to the ground, and fastened handcuffs on the wrists and ankles. But much to their embarrassment and to the great amusement of the scores of villagers who had gathered around, the figure turned out to be in fact a woman. She not only tricked the police but also revealed that it was Mumpty-vaayan who had sent her to fool them.

Mumpty-vaayan obviously derived pleasure from making a laughingstock of the police. He once went to a police station in broad daylight, disguised as a mendicant in a dirty-looking loincloth, without a trace of hair on his head or face, and begged for food. The irritated constables on duty gave him something to eat before shooing him away. After a while they found one of their tiffin carriers missing. Two days later, the missing item was found in front of the gate of the police station. There was a note inside from the bandit thanking them for lending it to him!

The police were incensed by this incident. A posse of three hundred policemen was sent into the jungle, in batches of fifty, to bring the bandit to book. As the policemen huffed and puffed through the difficult terrain searching for Mumpty-vaayan, he calmly walked into the village of Pennagaram and made himself comfortable inside the tent of a traveling cinema to watch a film. He sat through half of the show, then barged into the box office and pocketed the evening's collection. The cashier begged him not to take the money, pleading that he wouldn't be able to convince the owner that it was Mumpty-vaayan who had robbed the cash. Nobody would believe him if he said the wanted outlaw had walked into a crowded cinema hall and put himself at risk. Mumpty-vaayan was sympathetic, and thoughtfully scribbled a note certifying that it was he who had taken the money and not the cashier. He also gave a five-rupee note to the hapless man, telling him to buy himself a decent meal at the local hotel before he gave the news of the robbery to the owner of the cinema tent.

Around this time, a guard working in Salem jail was dismissed from service for some impropriety. He returned to his home in Pennagaram a very disgruntled man. He heard about the exploits of Mumpty-vaayan and decided that if there was one way of getting reinstated, it was by nabbing the bandit, dead or alive. He spread the news that he was keen to work as an informer for Mumpty-vaayan and could give him regular information about rich landlords and businessmen in Salem. The bandit fell for the bait. Through a conduit, he met the former guard. It was decided that they would meet again the following night at 10 p.m., under a particular tree at a place called Panapatti inside the jungle, seven and a half miles from Pennagaram, so that they could come to an understanding.

The jail guard was excited. He rushed to the police station and informed the cops about his rendezvous with Mumpty-vaayan. The police decided to swoop down at exactly 10:30 p.m. They also promised him that the guard would be reinstated in his job. At 10 p.m. the following night, the two men met as planned. As they sat talking, Mumpty-vaayan heard the clanking of iron from inside the former jail guard's shirt pocket. "What is that strange sound?" he asked. Even before the man could mumble an answer, the bandit knew that it was a pair of handcuffs. The police had given these to the guard to secure Mumpty-vaayan.

The bandit immediately realized that the meeting was a ploy to nab him. He leaped on the man ferociously, throwing him to the ground. A silent tussle ensued. Mumpty-vaayan was about to choke his adversary to death when he heard the roar of the approaching police van. He took out his knife and in one stroke severed three fingers from the right hand of his potential trapper. The man writhed in pain, screaming. Blood spurted from the injured hand. In a flash, Mumpty-vaayan vanished into the darkness.

The bandit became very careful after this incident. He was not seen in his usual haunts for nearly four months. He had moved to the faraway towns of Dharmapuri and Krishnagiri, where he robbed shops.

Mumpty-vaayan announced his return to his old haunts in quite a dramatic manner. Perhaps taking advantage of the lull in the bandit's activities, the superintendent of police (SP) had taken his family on a picnic to the picturesque Hogenekal Falls in the area and had parked his jeep a few hundred yards from the falls. As the senior police officer lazed with his family, Mumpty-vaayan appeared on the scene. But this time, all he did was scribble in chalk on the sides of the jeep, in Tamil, that he was the raja of bandits.

By the beginning of the 1940s, Mumpty-vaayan's notoriety was at its peak, and he had become a challenge to the British administration in the area. The British government in India announced a handsome reward—five hundred rupees plus five acres of land—for anyone who could bring him in, dead or alive. But there were no takers for the offer; bounty hunters, having heard of the man's deeds, were far from eager to pit their skills against his.

At this juncture, quite strangely, Mumpty-vaayan's depredations actually began to lessen with each passing month. For almost a year, nobody heard of him. The villagers as well as the authorities wondered where he had gone and whether he was alive at all. It turned out, to everyone's shock and disbelief, that Mumpty-vaayan had had an amazing change of heart. He had become a mendicant and lived near the famous temple town of Madurai, answering only to the name of Om Krishna. Then one day, Mumpty-vaayan met his nemesis. He had decided to visit one of his concubines near Mechcheri. The woman, in deadly collaboration with her brother and a member of the local Koose family, poisoned his food. The unsuspecting robber-turned-mendicant realized a little too late that it would be his last meal. It is said that the woman was forced to poison Mumpty-vaayan by her brother, who was in grave debt and wanted to get his hands on the reward that Mumpty-vaayan carried on his head. Incidentally, one of the members involved in the treacherous conspiracy was none other than Veerappan's own father, Koose Muniswamy, who was known to have regularly supplied rations to Mumpty-vaayan.


VEERAPPAN'S SUCCESS in exploiting the forest resources spawned in its wake other gangs of young unemployed men who sought to follow his example. There was frenzied activity in the jungles with groups of men working day and night, cutting down trees and stacking logs of sandalwood. The birth of rival smuggling gangs resulted in the extension of their sphere of activity up to the Thithimathi forests in Kodagu district, approximately 150 miles away; Sangama and Mekedatu in Mandya district; and Muthatti in Bangalore district, along the Cauvery basin. The distant drone of a jeep somewhere on the circuitous mud road leading up the hills would signal the arrival of a middleman, who would cart away the loot after making due payments. The forest bled under the onslaught as the gangs became more and more prosperous.

Veerappan quickly realized that this newfound avocation of his fellow men was a direct threat to his reign over the jungles. At some point he seems to have decided that enough was enough, and action had to be taken quickly and effectively. He chose a beautiful full-moon night for the implementation of his plan. On January 4, 1989, Veerappan invited the entire village to party with him, ostensibly to bring about a rapprochement between him and the members of a rival gang with whom he had lately been having constant run-ins. The five young men, Aiyyan, Aiyyan Dorai, Gunashekar, Muthukumar, and Dhanapal, were suspicious to begin with, but when Veerappan talked to them of peace, they saw no reason to doubt him. "Let's be friends for life. Where is the need for antagonism when there is so much for all of us to have?" The villagers around them swayed to the heady taste of locally brewed alcohol. There was plenty to eat and drink, and a smile on every face. Drums throbbed in the background and the young men danced.

As the night wore on, Veerappan's opponents let their guard down, persuaded that he was genuinely contrite. Choosing his moment, Veerappan suggested a final gesture of reconciliation, saying to the five men, "You touch my feet and I shall touch yours." They readily agreed. Followed by the others, Veerappan slowly made his way to the center of the village square, where an ancient banyan tree stood. There he halted. Then he turned to look at his young adversaries and nodded. As if on cue, all five bent to touch his feet.

Without warning Veerappan whipped out a gun from under his shirt and with a shout of rage, fired at the five men. Defenseless and caught completely unawares, they went down without a chance. Their bodies slumped to the ground under the tree, and there was blood everywhere, soaking the earth red. The sound of the gunfire brought festivities to a sudden shocking end. Pandemonium broke out as men and women ran helter-skelter, dragging their children to safety. In a matter of minutes the village square was empty. All had vanished into the confines of their small huts. Veerappan, still shouting profanities, was swaying like a man possessed. "Anyone who tries to cross me will meet the same end. It is for all of you to heed my warnings," he screamed. For a moment, as though to calm himself, he stretched out at the base of the banyan tree. Then abruptly, with renewed anger, he picked up a hatchet and proceeded to chop the bodies into pieces. He then paraded the mutilated bodies in a bullock cart around the small village, reinforcing his warning to the villagers before flinging the bloody pieces into the Palar River, which flowed nearby. It was the most heinous crime ever committed in the history of the small village, and one that the villagers say they will never be able to erase from their memories.

After this chilling mass murder, nobody dared to even raise his head when Veerappan walked past. He continued to plunder the forest wealth with the active connivance of forest officers whose silence he bought with regular bribes. Most of the forest guards were poor and ill-paid, taking home a salary of less than one thousand rupees, and there was little motivation for them to resist the easy flow of cash. But there was one man in the forest department who chose not to toe the poacher's line. He was a guard named Monniah, a strapping young man from Somwarpet in Kodagu district, who did his duty without compromise. In mid-August 1989, he intercepted a lorry smuggling sandalwood belonging to Veerappan near the Palar checkpost and had the driver arrested. The lorry with its valuable cargo was seized.

Veerappan was furious. Systematically, he plotted revenge. For days he gathered information about Monniah's movements and daily activities from his own source within the forest department—a guard who had helped him before on several occasions. From the guard he learned that Monniah was in the habit of feeding the fish in the nearby Palar River. Every evening, he would walk up to the middle of a bridge that spanned the river and throw puffed rice into the water. On September 4, 1989, toward evening, Veerappan took position behind a tree near the bridge. As Monniah walked back after his appointment with the fish, Veerappan opened fire with a muzzle-loader, killing him on the spot.

With these two crimes, Veerappan had made it clear to the villagers as well as to the local government that he was king—and thus started one of the bloodiest chapters in the history of modern lawlessness.

## 2

## Ambush at Hogenekal

By the end of the 1980s, "Sandalwood Veerappan" had established himself as the biggest poacher and sandalwood smuggler in the long stretch of forests adjoining Karnataka and Tamil Nadu. His gang numbered nearly a hundred. Often villagers in the forest areas surrounding Meenyam in MM Hills range silently witnessed Veerappan transporting lorry loads of sandalwood, with his gang members seated menacingly on top of the sandalwood pile, holding guns. The forest and police personnel in the area were hopelessly outnumbered by the marauders. There was a severe shortage of weapons and vehicles to patrol the huge expanse of forests, and the lack of a cohesive operational plan hampered policing efforts.

The forest belt where Veerappan had established himself was also home to nearly one thousand quarries. Mysore Minerals Limited (MML), a state government undertaking, had around two hundred quarries in the Chamarajanagar belt. The Ministry of Mines and Geology under the state government had also leased its lands to private entrepreneurs, who paid a tax of 12.5 percent on the turnover and a royalty of two thousand rupees per cubic meter (about one and a third cubic yards) of granite extracted. Quarrying was also done on patta lands—private ancestral properties held by villagers—which were leased to businesses.

Commercial quarrying in these parts began in 1977. Until then, only the Mysore royal family mined granite on a small scale, for personal use. The black granite found in abundance in Chamarajanagar, MM Hills, Palar, PG Palya, Bandipalya, Gumballi, Yeragumballi, Chengadi, Ponnachi, Hanur, Jellipalya, and Hoogyam is considered among the best in the world, and there is a huge demand for it in countries such as Taiwan and Japan, which export it to Europe and the United States. The price of one cubic meter of rough granite extracted here was in the range of $1,600 to $2,200 in the international market. During the 1980s, when quarrying was at its peak, all the quarries put together extracted nearly four hundred cubic meters of rough granite every day, which meant that the daily turnover was anywhere between twenty million and thirty million rupees. The demand from foreign buyers was so great that quarry managers were known to collect huge advances from them after giving them receipts, stuff wads of currency notes into gunny bags, and count them at leisure, after the clients had left. In all, the stone industry here currently provides jobs to nearly 25,000 workers, with an overall turnover running into tens of millions of rupees.

Veerappan began toward the latter half of 1989 to extort money and explosives from the quarries. Gelatin sticks used to blast huge granite boulders in the quarries soon began to find their way into his hands. These he later used to make crude bombs with which he could terrorize policemen on their beats. The quarry managers and owners were helpless to resist whenever Veerappan sent word or went personally to collect explosives. The Karnataka government under Chief Minister (CM) S. Bangarappa, sensing the potential danger, banned quarrying on government as well as patta land in June 1991 in these parts, despite a huge loss in taxes to the exchequer. Work came to a halt almost overnight. It was a deathblow to the multimillion-rupee granite industry. Yet in the face of the industry representatives's solidarity, demonstrated by a procession of six hundred lorries to the Vidhana Soudha in Bangalore, the government upheld the ban.

The quarry owners and their workers suddenly found themselves idle.

The owners twiddled their thumbs helplessly even as investments worth hundreds of millions of rupees went to waste, and thousands of workers were reduced to penury. Most of them left the area for good, while a few took up low-paying menial jobs in the surrounding villages and towns.

By the beginning of the 1990s, Veerappan was being looked upon as the most dreaded criminal at large in the country, and the governments of Tamil Nadu and Karnataka finally awakened to the threat he posed. Soon the sound of gun battles between police forces and his gang became familiar in the forest ranges. Every now and then, there would be an "encounter" that left people on both sides injured or dead. The area was becoming increasingly dangerous for common folk to live in.

Whereas the police were hindered at every step by the unfamiliar terrain, Veerappan's greatest asset was his intimate knowledge of the jungle. By the 1990s, he had also started accumulating sophisticated weaponry—as was proved by an incident on January 23, 1990. A patrol party led by the inspector general (IG) of the forest cell of the Karnataka police was making its way in a convoy through the Silvekkal forests. As it reached a spot near a spreading karadi tree, one of the officers noticed that the road ahead looked like it had recently been dug up. At the IG's command the convoy stopped just before the point where the loose soil became visible. Gingerly, a few constables knelt down to examine the ground. They found themselves staring at crude landmines planted inside pits. A bomb expert was quickly summoned from Coimbatore and six landmines were defused. This was the first inkling the police had that the balance of power in the jungle had shifted.

UNPERTURBED BY THE DISCOVERY of his plan, Veerappan continued to forage. Pitching camp in the interior depths of the MM Hills range, he bided his time. Every morning at daybreak, he and his men would bathe and offer worship to their most precious possession: their guns. Then they would chalk out the agenda for the day. The nights were spent in the open, with gang members taking turns at keeping vigil, guns on the ready, beside a fire that burned all night. The man on sentry duty would signal an alarm, if required, in the form of an animal or bird call.

Veerappan always selected an elevated place with adequate tree cover to spend the night, for the obvious advantage the height afforded him for tracking police movement. Veerappan himself always slept a little away from the rest of the gang. He was known to be a light sleeper who retired late and rose early. The men slept inside makeshift plastic tents on rainy or misty nights. Otherwise, they generally slept scattered between trees and rocks, but never inside caves. Campsites were also never located in valleys where the men could be trapped easily, and were always in the vicinity of a water source—but not closer than half a mile, or they would have had to contend with wild animals, and perhaps even police personnel who might use the water hole. As a rule, the gang never stayed in one place for more than a day or two. The key to their survival lay in shifting camps and confusing the police.

Their food consisted mainly of rice and dal, cooked on a makeshift three-pointed stone platform, in aluminum vessels. Supplies were regularly procured from villages around the jungle. Veerappan's method was to target the head of a family and, at gunpoint, order that rations be supplied immediately. The petrified villagers would always oblige. Sometimes Veerappan would take hostage one of the numerous cattle grazers in the pattis and *doddis* (cattle pens) deep inside the jungles while the others hurried to the nearest village to do his bidding. They would be instructed to dump the rations at a predesignated spot where an unimportant member of the gang would pick them up. Veerappan himself would never venture anywhere near the spot, for fear that the ration supplier would be trailed by the police. But the bandit never forgot to pay the suppliers handsomely. Often he paid as much as one thousand rupees for a few pounds of rice and dal.

When the tedium of the menu got to the gang members, either a sambhar or a langur, plentiful in the area, would be shot for dinner. Every time they killed an animal for food, slivers of the excess meat were dried, salted, and packed in bags for future consumption. Though they camped in elevated spots, Veerappan's standing instruction to all his gang members was to do the cooking only in some suitable depression in the vicinity. This precaution was taken to ensure that the smoke from the fire did not alert the police.

The gang had an interesting method of snaring animals. Veerappan is said to be a fantastic mimic, and he would imitate the mating call of a langur. Within minutes, at least one or two creatures would materialize from between the tree branches to investigate the source of the call, only to be shot dead. The bandit is also adept at imitating the sounds of an elephant. He appears to know the various tones an elephant uses in different circumstances, ranging from a shrill trumpet to a low, deep, guttural moan. In fact, many times, when confronted by a herd, Veerappan has been known to drive it away by mimicking the panic-stricken cries of a baby elephant.

On February 13, 1990, an incident took place that reinforced Veerappan's image as a dangerous outlaw who recognized few limits. It was 6:30 in the evening, and twilight had set in the Garkekandi area. Veerappan waited behind a pile of rocks along with fifty of his gang members for a vehicle to come along the road. Eventually two buses, one belonging to the Jeeva Transport Corporation of Tamil Nadu and the other to the Karnataka Road Transport Corporation, drove into view, one behind the other. When they were close enough, Veerappan leaped down from his perch, waving his gun, and shouted, "Get off the bus, all of you. Don't make a sound." As the frightened passengers tumbled out, he turned to one of his gang members, demanding a can of kerosene and a matchbox.

Before anyone could react, he had splashed kerosene on the buses and struck a match. The two vehicles burst spectacularly into flames. Then, while the passengers stood around numbly, Veerappan and his followers systematically deprived them of all their money and valuables. Shouting warnings and firing into the air, the gang disappeared into the darkness of the night with approximately four thousand rupees in cash.

Soon after this incident, the police arrested eleven members of the gang in the Andipallam forests. A month later, as if to avenge the arrest of his men, Veerappan cornered two forest guards patrolling the Baragur forests at a place called Koilnatham, and assaulted them with belts and iron rods. He ranted as he hit them, "If you think you can cow us down by making arrests, this is what you'll get. Go and tell your officers that they cannot afford to take things for granted. We will not take their authority lying down." The men, bleeding profusely, were let off with a warning that they should never be seen in the area again.

One of the main reasons the police of Tamil Nadu and Karnataka couldn't get anywhere near Veerappan was the unwillingness of the two states to cooperate. Veerappan would often commit an offense in the jungles of one state, then escape into the jurisdiction of the other. The police forces in the two states, beset with internal wranglings and ego clashes, could not bring themselves to launch joint operations. And Veerappan was too shrewd to stay in one place for too long, especially after committing a crime. The police were soon reduced to sporadic pursuits driven by a few committed officers.

In the ranks of the Karnataka police, based in Mysore, one such man was SP Bipin Gopalkrishna. He was a flamboyant officer who apart from his love for showmanship understood his role as the head of a police force whose jurisdictional ambit coincided with Veerappan's range. In the early hours of April 7, 1990, Bipin was traveling in the direction of MM Hills, eighty-five miles from Mysore. He had been informed that Veerappan and his gang had been sighted in the precincts of the temple town a few days earlier. Not one to miss an opportunity to capture the poacher, Bipin launched a combing operation in the area with a handpicked team of subinspectors (SIs). The team included officers Ramalingu of Mysore's F2 traffic station, Jagannath from the Vidyaranyapuram station, Chandrappa from the Krishna Raja station, Krishne Urs from the nearby town of Krishna Raja Nagara, and the ever-enthusiastic Dinesh, stationed at MM Hills. Before setting off for the forest, Bipin gave his men a pep talk, emphasizing the importance of their mission.

As soon as he reached MM Hills after a five-hour journey, Bipin went into a closed-door meeting with Narasappa, the deputy superintendent (DSP) of the Chamarajanagar subdivision. Bipin's idea was to split the team into two batches and start scouring the area. One party would advance from the Tulsikere side and another from the Kokkabare end. He realized that the pressure and momentum of the chase had to be unrelenting so that Veerappan could be put on the defensive. Narasappa nodded in agreement to his superior's strategy. He too had warned his officers of the difficulty of the task and told them not to become disheartened if the operation did not yield any positive results. The important thing was to persevere.

Toward evening, all the subinspectors reported for duty at MM Hills. Chandrappa had brought along additional personnel: one of his trusted constables, Mallanna. The men spent the night restlessly, thinking about the big operation slated for the next day. There was no doubt that Veerappan had to be nabbed before he got completely out of control, and with a capable officer like Bipin Gopalkrishna heading a team of highly motivated men, there was no reason why the mission should not be a success.

On April 8, Bipin divided the team into two batches as planned, and they began the combing operation even as the sun was beginning to rise over the hills. The MM Hills range is vast and densely forested, so it was not an easy task. The police teams, armed with rifles, searched the region methodically. Starting from the Tulsikere area, they went around the interior forest hamlets, including Indiganatha, Parsalnatha, Tekane, Doddane, Kokkabare, and Kombdikki. But there was no clue to Veerappan's whereabouts. Toward evening, the police party returned to base, disappointed but not disheartened. The same evening, Bipin decided to go back to Mysore. "I don't think it's necessary for me to stay on in MM Hills," he told Narasappa, "but we should not give up. It's just a matter of time before we land the big catch. You guys have done a good job by keeping up the tempo. I want you to keep going in the same manner." Narasappa and the subinspectors saluted as the white Ambassador carrying Bipin began its descent down the hill. They were staying on for another day.

The next day, toward noon, Narasappa too left MM Hills after sending a wireless message to the Chamarajanagar circle inspector (CI) B. P. Machaiah, requesting him to take over the operation because the Kollegala CI was busy investigating Veerappan-related cases in nearby Ramapura. The day's operation had not yielded any results, and for a very good reason: Veerappan and his gang were nowhere near the Karnataka side of the forest.

ONE EVENING IN 1989, ten days before the Sankranti festival in January, Veerappan proved yet again that he was not to be trifled with. He and his men, including Sethukuli Govindan, Swaminathan,

Athur Kolandai, Andiyappan, Mariappan, Perumal, Athur Gopala, Gurunathan, and Sunda, shot dead five men suspected to be police informers. Koteyur Ayyanna, Gunashekara, Muthukumara, Dhanapala, and Aiyyan Dorai were killed in the Thengaigombupallam forests in Tamil Nadu. Their bodies were hacked to pieces and thrown into the nearby Cauvery River under the cover of darkness. Fearing police action, Veerappan and his men decided to hide in the Tamil Nadu forests until the heat died down a little. While they were in hiding, away from the searching eyes of the police, they began a systematic assault on the sandalwood trees growing in abundance in the Baragur and Makampalyam areas of Tamil Nadu.

By December 1989, Veerappan and his gang had cut down huge quantities of sandalwood and had stored precious billets weighing over thirty tons and worth nearly ten million rupees in the Silvekkal forest area in Karnataka. The local police got wind of the booty hidden in their jungles, and along with the forest department, they carried out what was to become one of the biggest sandalwood seizures of all time. After this unexpected setback, Veerappan restricted himself largely to the Tamil Nadu forests. For three and a half months, he and his men roamed the area, perhaps waiting to avenge the huge loss that had been inflicted on them.


ON APRIL 9, 1990, at 1:45 p.m., a team of police officers, including Dinesh, Chandrappa, Ramalingu, Jagannath, and Krishne Urs, drove into the village of Gopinatham in a jeep. They had journeyed over rough roads strewn with stones, through dense jungle. Constables Mallanna and Srinivasa Murthy, the range forest officer (RFO) of MM Hills, accompanied them. None of them wore uniforms, for, although ostensibly on a mission to gather more information on Veerappan, they were actually heading for a picnic to Hogenekal Falls. The tension of policing Veerappan's territory had obviously gotten to them, and the picnic was intended to be relaxing. Chandrappa carried a revolver with him and Krishne Urs a pistol.

Reserve Subinspector (RSI) Parameshwarappa, who had been camping in Gopinatham with a team for a few days, met the police team from

MM Hills. Dinesh explained to him the reason for their arrival. "We've come to gather more information on the movements of the Veerappan gang. We conducted a combing operation yesterday under Bipin Gopalkrishna sahebru, though it didn't yield any results. But we are not giving up. If you could give us two armed constables, we could go around the jungles in this area seeking information."

Parameshwarappa obliged instantly. Constables Shankar Rao and Shivakumar were chosen to accompany the team. They were armed with .303 rifles and had fifty bullets between them. The team then left for Hogenekal, nine miles from the Tamil Nadu border.

It was around this time that Veerappan's efficient intelligence network swung into action. No sooner had the police team left in the direction of Hogenekal than a whisper wafted across the valleys in the forest to where the gang had been holed up for a long time. This was the opportunity Veerappan had been patiently waiting for for the past three months. Immediately, he along with Sethukuli Govindan, Gurunathan, Andiyappan, "Meesekara" Madiah, Mariappan, Armugam, Marimuthu, Swaminathan, Athur Gopala, Perumal, and fourteen others started to move toward the Cauvery River, which flowed silently through the thick forests bifurcating the states of Karnataka and Tamil Nadu. On the way, they met Karupanna, a local herdsman. He looked puzzled by the urgency in the gang's movement but didn't say a word. Not one to take chances while on a mission, Veerappan warned the man, "Do not utter a word to anyone about having seen us. I don't need to tell you of the consequences if you do. Now get out of my sight." Karupanna nodded and hurried away, terrified.

When they reached the riverbank, Veerappan and his men got onto rafts made of bamboo poles tied together with vines and crossed over to Karnataka, to the Chammedu forest. Once there, they wasted no time in searching for a suitable spot where an ambush could be set up. They eventually settled on a rock-strewn hillock situated in a northerly direction, to the right of the narrow road from Alambadi. About sixty feet high, it sloped toward the road at an angle. To the left flowed the waters of the Cauvery.

The men settled down amid the huge black boulders that gave them ample protection from any possible retaliatory action. While they lay in wait for the jeep to return from the falls, they saw at a distance two men walking along the deserted stretch of road. Veerappan was annoyed by this unexpected impediment to his avenging mission. Looking at Gurunathan, he said, "Who are they? Go catch them. We'll ask them."

Gurunathan smiled, picked up his single-barreled gun, and slid down the hillock. "Who are you?" he demanded, pointing the gun at them.

The two men, taken aback at the sudden appearance of a menacing stranger holding a gun, began to stutter in fright. "My name is Cauvery, son of Athur Rachappa," said one. "I'm Veera, Karibanna's son," mumbled the other.

"Come with me and don't make any noise," ordered Gurunathan, gesturing with his gun. The two meekly followed him up the hillock.

There, amid the huge black rocks, they were stupefied to see Veerappan himself along with a battery of men, all of them armed for battle. While Veerappan carried a double-barreled gun, all the others were armed with single-barreled country-made guns. "Sssh, sit here and don't move an inch," said Veerappan, pointing to a small hollow between the rocks. The two villagers did as they were told. Veerappan then instructed a few of his men to place boulders across the road. The jeep had to be stopped at precisely that spot. In all, twelve boulders were placed randomly from right to left, blocking the way. "Now get ready to fire all at once. I don't want even a single police bastard to escape with his life. Shoot and kill every one of them."

Time ticked by slowly. It was 3:30 p.m., and the forest was still but for the rustling of dry teak leaves as they drifted to the ground. The summer heat was stifling. Beads of perspiration showed on the men's faces. A little later, they saw a small boy walking toward them on the road from Hogenekal. He happened to be going home to Gopinatham. Veerappan's men caught hold of him. "Who are you? What work do you have here? Get out of this place at once." Terrified, the little boy ran as fast as he could in the direction from which he had come.

Another hour passed. The sun was beginning to set and it was slowly getting dark, the trees on either side casting lengthy shadows on the road. Then, in the distance, they heard the jeep approaching on the Hogenekal–Alambadi road on its way back to MM Hills via Gopinatham. The men readied themselves for action. Exactly as planned, the jeep screeched to a halt a little before the pile of boulders placed across the road, which was not more than twelve feet wide. At once, Veerappan and his men began to fire in the direction of the jeep. The hail of bullets caught the policemen totally by surprise, but they refused to go down without a fight. Krishne Urs and Chandrappa leaped out of the vehicle, took positions behind the rear wheel at the far end to the left, and returned fire. Veerappan's men, who had the benefit of a vantage point, kept up their fire. The battle raged for fifteen to twenty minutes.

Then all of a sudden Krishne Urs jumped into the driver's seat, started the jeep's engine, and slammed it into reverse gear. The vehicle bucked violently and began to hurtle backward. The engine groaned under the pressure. After juddering backward for a little distance, the jeep made a sudden U-turn at a small clearing and sped away toward Hogenekal. Veerappan climbed down the hillock and surveyed the spot. His right palm was bleeding a little where rock splinters had hit him during the firing and ricocheting bullets had lodged small rock pieces in Armugam's hand, but nobody in the gang was seriously injured.

When they inspected the spot for damages, they found bloodstains, splintered glass, small pools of diesel, and a black pistol. Veerappan picked up the weapon and put it in his shirt pocket. The two villagers, Cauvery and Veera, who had been forcibly held back by the gang, had remained silent witnesses to the bloodbath. They were shivering uncontrollably in fright. Veerappan let them go, then led his men across to Tamil Nadu. Just as they were entering the forest, they bumped into Karupanna, the villager whom Veerappan had spoken to in the afternoon. Stopping him, Veerappan boasted, "Hey, I just shot and killed the policemen from MM Hills. Here, see this pistol that I took away from them." Karupanna, as before, did not utter a word. Veerappan and his gang then melted into the depths of the Kongarapatti forests.

They left behind the marks of battle and destruction. At a distance of about twenty feet to the left of where the jeep had stood, there was a huge basari tree with bullet holes in its trunk. The boulders across the road also had bullet marks on them. To the left of the road lay eight empty pistol and revolver shells and ten live rounds of .303 ammunition. The gang had fired from the western edge of the hillock. Red-colored cartridges bearing the legend "Shakthiman Express" were found behind the rock where Andiyappan had crouched. Veerappan had taken position at a distance of ten feet from this spot where empty cartridges with the inscription KYNOOH 470 NITRO were found. Near a rock on a higher plane were found two more empty Shakthiman Express cartridges. This was the spot where Mariappan had fired from. Gurunathan had placed himself about six feet away, between two boulders. The spent ammunition was proof of how well armed the gang was. About thirty feet away stood a large karadi tree whose trunk was nearly two feet in diameter. Near the tree was a black boulder on which were found bloodstains, presumably from the wounds that a few of the gangsters had received in the gunfight. More bloodstains could be seen all along the forest track leading up to the river.

Meanwhile, the jeep carrying the ten policemen swayed precariously as it made its way in the direction of Hogenekal. Krishne Urs, although injured in the right arm, kept his composure, controlling the vehicle without looking back. The moans of the injured rose above the drone of the engine. At 8:30 p.m., Krishne Urs reached the bank of the Cauvery River. It was a miracle that he had managed to drive the jeep, which had a ruptured fuel tank. The hood and the rest of the body had more than twenty holes. The seats were torn and stained with blood. The windshield had been shattered, and so had the taillight. Jumping out of the vehicle, Urs rushed toward the river and started shouting for help. "Is there anybody here? I'm a policeman. Veerappan attacked us and some people have been badly injured. Can anyone take us to the other side of the river? If there is anyone here, please come out and rescue us. Please help us." It was dark and nobody seemed to be around. Even if there was someone in the vicinity, it was doubtful whether he would come forward. Such was the fear evoked by the name of Veerappan.

But finally someone did come to their rescue. Nanjappa, a coracle operator in the area, heard the cries for help. Rushing out of his hut on the other bank, he pulled his coracle into the waters and began to paddle furiously to reach the Karnataka side. To his horror, he found two men dead in a pool of blood near a thatched arrack-vending outlet. They were Jagannath and Dinesh. Farther away lay the body of Constable Shankar Rao. He could see six other men visibly in pain.

Hurriedly he dragged the injured men into his coracle with the help of Krishne Urs and began to paddle toward the opposite bank. On the way, one more man, Ramalingu, succumbed to his injuries. The raft finally reached Hogenekal. Nanjappa helped Krishne Urs reach the police station, where Head Constable (HC) Sabhapathi was on duty. He looked up in shock as a bloodstained and hysterical Krishne Urs rushed into the station. "I'm an SI from Karnataka. Veerappan and his gang ambushed us at about four-thirty in the evening. Many of our men have been injured seriously. I need your help to shift them to hospital immediately," he said, weariness making him nearly incoherent.

Sabhapathi immediately organized a private jeep and sent the five injured men to the Dharmapuri hospital. Krishne Urs booked a call to Mysore to inform his boss of the tragedy. "Sir, there is bad news. Veerappan ambushed us near Hogenekal a few hours ago. Jagannath is dead and so are Dinesh and Ramalingu. Shankar Rao is probably dead too by now. He was hurt very seriously in the gunfight. Sir, please do something to help us. We are in deep trouble."

Bipin Gopalkrishna went cold at the other end. Even before he could tell Urs that he would try and retrieve the situation, Urs had hung up. Bipin went on the line to Deputy Inspector General (DIG) V. V. Bhaskar immediately.

That night at about 11:45 p.m., Chamarajanagar CI Machaiah and his staff rushed to Gopinatham from MM Hills, where they had been camping. They picked up SI Parameshwarappa in Gopinatham and drove toward Hogenekal in a van. SP Bipin Gopalkrishna and DIG Bhaskar also left Mysore in the early hours of April 10 and started toward MM Hills en route to Hogenekal.

The injured policemen had been transferred to the Dharmapuri government hospital. Both SI Chandrappa and RFO Srinivasa Murthy had been grievously injured in the arm and had painful lacerations in the neck and waist. Both of them were referred to the National Institute of Mental Health and Neuro Sciences (NIMHANS) in Bangalore. Later, Chandrappa was shifted to the better-equipped St. John's Hospital, where emergency surgery was performed and two metal pieces were removed from his right forearm. Constable Mallanna had been wounded in the left arm and had abrasions on his nose and right cheek. There was a contusion on his lower lip as well. The other constable, Shivakumar, was hurt in the right elbow and shoulder. He had multiple wounds on his body. The driver, Seshappa, was injured in the face. Emergency X-rays were taken of all the injured men. The bodies of the dead officers and the constable were taken to Krishna Raja Hospital in Mysore for postmortem. The whole of Mysore city was hushed by the tragedy, as it mourned the death of the policemen. The city observed a *bandh* and all was still and quiet.

The murderous ambush turned out to be every bit the demoralizing blow Veerappan had obviously wanted it to be. Somewhere in the dense forest cover, he must have been laughing at the police department's helplessness against him. The police and the government had to act quickly. The incident had shaken up not just Mysore district but the entire state. On April 16, 1990, CM Veerendra Patil announced the constitution of a Special Task Force (STF). K. U. Shetty, IG, Karnataka State Reserve Police (KSRP), was appointed as its chief. Thus began the first sustained effort to capture Veerappan.

Within three months of its formation, the STF was successful in arresting Athur Gopala, a fringe member of the gang, On July 9, he was taken into custody in the Sendramalai forests bordering Tamil Nadu. It didn't take long in the interrogation chamber for Athur to break down and admit that he knew Veerappan and had been a member of his gang. He confessed to having taken part in the ambush of the policemen in April, and took the cops to a spot called Pongombu Halla, two and a half miles south of Gopinatham, where he showed them the place where his single-barreled gun lay hidden in the crevice of a rock. Another gang member, Marimuthu, was arrested on the same day in the Yekalmedu forests. His weapon was also seized after he led the police to a rocky place a mile and a quarter off the Alambadi road near Gopinatham, about one hundred yards southeast of a Kali temple. A month later, on August 2, "Meesekara" Madiah and his brother Swaminathan were caught in the Appagampatti forests by a team of forest and police officers. Their guns too were seized at a place called Yerke Halla. None of these guns had any markings, and they were rusty from long exposure to the elements. In December 1990, another gangster, Mariappa, fell into the hands of the Pennagaram police. Subsequently, the single-barreled gun he had stolen in 1989 from the house of Devalingachari, a forest guard at Meenyam, was recovered.

As the STF tightened its grip on the region, Commander Shetty quickly realized that the backbone of Veerappan's gang was the vast network of informants in the villages around the forests who played the most vital role of replenishing the gang's food stocks and also keeping it abreast of police movements. This support system had to be broken for the gang to collapse. Accordingly, the STF set about arresting a large number of people suspected of supporting Veerappan.

Although a semblance of order was restored in the forests of MM Hills through these arrests, Veerappan himself continued to elude the police dragnet. Even when the police systematically cut off ration supplies to the gang in an attempt to weaken it, he seemed undeterred. On the night of June 17, 1990, he again announced his presence in his usual dramatic fashion. He reached Gopinatham along with five of his gang members at about 3 a.m., when the whole village, including the resident police force, was asleep. Locating the house of Kote Naika, one of the villagers, he knocked on the door. Kote Naika opened the door sleepily. "Who is it?" he asked irritably. Even before he could make out who had disturbed him at such an unearthly hour, he was dead. Veerappan shot him at point-blank range. He had learned that Naika had become a police informer.

The gang disappeared into the darkness even as Kote's wife's anguished cries began to rend the air: "They've killed my husband. Isn't there anybody here? Oh, please come, please come."

The police were unable to lay their hands on Veerappan, but they arrested one of his associates, Shanmugam, near Bheemakalligudda and confiscated his single-barreled muzzle-loading gun. The cat-and-mouse game continued relentlessly, and the villagers remained stuck in the crossfire.

# 3

## Messiah of Gopinatham

As the battle against Veerappan intensified, a new player entered the field: P. Srinivas, deputy commandant (DCF) of the Special Task Force (STF). Srinivas was a forest officer posted in Chickmagalur. In November 1990, driven by the desire to participate in the action against Veerappan, he volunteered to work full-time for the STF.

Srinivas clearly stood out from his colleagues. A slight man with a beard, he was known to be methodical, committed, and selfless, and was particularly obsessed with putting an end to Veerappan's reign. In recognition of his bravery and tenacity, he was immediately taken on board. In fact, Srinivas was the only forest officer to be given the full status of a top-level functionary of the STF, even though the forest and police departments had totally different jurisdictions.

Srinivas already had a reputation as a conscientious and refreshingly imaginative forest officer. As the ACF and then DCF of Chamarajanagar, he had transformed the administration of his division. To him every single man in the hierarchy mattered; a guard was as important as a top-ranking officer. In 1985, Srinivas had started a dossier on forest offenders in the region, in which he recorded each one's modus operandi, contacts, network, and area of operation. He was determined to seriously and scientifically address the issue of poaching and smuggling of timber in the rich Chamarajanagar forests of which he was boss, and it was around this time that he had had his first run-in with the biggest offender of them all—Veerappan.

It happened in 1986, the year in which the second SAARC (South Asian Association for Regional Cooperation) summit was held in Bangalore. The Sri Lankan president, Junius Jayawardene, was one of the important participating dignitaries of the occasion, slated for November 16–17. A few days before the summit, the Bangalore police began to round up "antisocial elements" in the city as a precautionary measure. It was in the course of such routine activity that they chanced upon their most wanted criminal, Veerappan.

A police officer noticed a stranger at the Lords bar near the well-known Sangam cinema close to the Bangalore bus station, and not having seen him in the neighborhood before, began to question him—"What is your name? Where are you from? What are you doing in Bangalore? Where are you staying in Bangalore? Don't you know Kannada?" The questions took Veerappan by surprise. Also, he was not too conversant with the local language. When he fumbled in his replies, he was promptly arrested and taken to the Jayanagar police station. He was retained in the lockup for almost a week and was interrogated by SI Kauri. One of the things the officer discovered was that Veerappan was a regular visitor to Bangalore, either in search of arms and ammunition, or to sell contraband, and usually stayed at a lodge in the bustling Kalasipalyam area of the city.

Once Veerappan's identity was established, he was handed over by DSP Mahadevaswamy to M. V. Murthy, an SP of the forest cell. Srinivas, whose intelligence-gathering had meanwhile resulted in a growing body of comprehensive documentation, promptly appeared on the scene to help in the interrogation. The curious thing about Veerappan's arrest was that it was not regularized. In other words, there was nothing on record to show that he was in police custody. This was done ostensibly to avoid sending him to judicial custody, from where it would have been difficult to seek him out for interrogation.

Veerappan was in Srinivas's "custody" for nearly a month. During this time Srinivas took him to places like Salem and Satyamangalam in Tamil Nadu to find out more about his conduits there. Hours of interrogation, particularly about Veerappan's methods of poaching and sandalwood smuggling, allowed Srinivas to build up a hefty dossier on his criminal history. As the days went by, Veerappan revealed more and more information. One day, Srinivas took him, in handcuffs, to a forest guesthouse in the interior of the Boodipadaga forests, seventeen miles from Chamarajanagar. For some reason, perhaps because the police hadn't yet begun to view him as a dangerous bandit, only as a run-of-the-mill poacher and smuggler, or simply due to carelessness, security was lax. When Srinivas left the place for a while on personal work, the forest guards and constables on duty relaxed their vigil. It was then that Veerappan played his hand. "My head is aching very badly. I can't bear it. It's terrible. Could you rub some oil on my head to ease the pain?" he said to the unsuspecting guards, who obligingly massaged oil into his scalp. After the guards left the room where he was incarcerated, Veerappan began to rub both his wrists vigorously against his oiled head.

Lean as he was, Veerappan had become even thinner while in custody. Once the metal had been adequately lubricated, his thin wrists easily slipped through the handcuffs. He then squeezed himself through the small window of the room, which did not have grilles, and jumped out without making a noise. Making his way through the darkness, he cut through the Dimbam jungle and managed to reach the main highway. Once there he flagged down a lorry, which took him to Satyamangalam, thirty miles away. In the early hours of the morning, he boarded a bus for the thirty-five-mile journey to Kolathur in Salem district, where his sister-in-law Tangammal lived. He pleaded with her to give him shelter, and although she was afraid, she did not turn him away. Instead, she led him to a small granary in her backyard which was actually a large cemented pit dug in the ground, with a trapdoor for an entrance. When Veerappan had lowered himself into the pit, Tangammal covered it with haystacks.

He stayed concealed in the granary, with food and water being supplied to him at regular intervals by Tangammal, who did not reveal his presence even to her own family. He stayed inside for most of the day and emerged in the night for his ablutions. A month and a half later, after the police in the area had given up the search, he quietly slipped out of hiding and entered the forest, never to make the mistake of returning to a city again.

The IG (Corps of Detectives [COD]) S. N. S. Murthy, who conducted an official inquiry into the matter, was severe in his indictment of M. V. Murthy, the forest cell SP. There were whispers that the police had connived with Veerappan and facilitated his flight to freedom. It was rumored that more than 200,000 rupees had changed hands. It was also said that Somashekar Reddy, a CI serving in Kollegala during this time, who had allegedly abetted Veerappan in his criminal activities in the forests, was instrumental in his escape.

Whether the police were involved or not, there had always been dealings between some politicians in the area and Veerappan, especially during the early years of his criminal career. Most of his political contacts allegedly made use of him for financial benefit from the teak, rosewood, and sandalwood smuggling that went on unabated. There was also a widely circulated story of how Veerappan had canvassed for a Congress candidate from the Kollegala–Hanur–Ramapura belt during the 1989 Assembly elections.

The man who was most disturbed by Veerappan's escape was Srinivas. He felt responsible for it, as the poacher had been in his custody. He confided to a few close friends that he couldn't get over the feeling of guilt and had to do something to redeem himself.

In 1989, Srinivas was transferred to the coffee-rich district of Chickmagalur, almost a world away from the forests of the Chamarajanagar belt. Even after he took charge there, his heart and mind lay in his former area. Often, he would take the bus all the way from Chickmagalur to Chamarajanagar, a distance of nearly 150 miles one way, to try to pick up clues to Veerappan's whereabouts. He would ask the policemen on duty if there was any new information and satisfy himself that they were continuing with their efforts to track Veerappan. Occasionally he would borrow a jeep to drive around and survey the area himself. Such was his regret at having let the poacher slip away from the Boodipadaga area that as soon as the STF was formed in early 1990, he grabbed the opportunity to seek a special posting to the force.

On the morning of April 3, 1991, while at the STF base in MM Hills, Srinivas received a message from an informer that Veerappan and his gang were in the Sorakaimadu area, fifteen miles away. "Are you sure?" he asked the informer. "Take my word for it. The gang has been camping in the area for some time now. I waited for confirmation before informing you." Srinivas knew intuitively that the man was telling the truth. Immediately, he informed the STF commandant, Shetty. A long meeting took place in which strategy was discussed in detail. Finally, they decided to launch an operation the next day, as Srinivas had suggested.

On April 4, Srinivas rose at 3 a.m. for the assembly of the raiding team in Palar, thirteen miles down the winding forest road from MM Hills. An hour later, the group left Palar and proceeded in three jeeps toward the Sorakaimadu forests on the narrow Garkekandi road. It was pitch dark, and as the jeeps negotiated the mud track, their headlights lit up the surroundings momentarily. After a twenty-minute drive, the vehicles stopped near a crossing of the Perimalai quarry road, a mile and a quarter from Sorakaimadu. Noiselessly, the men slipped out of the jeeps and merged with the darkness.

The commandant divided them into three groups. The first group was headed by Shetty himself and included DCF Srinivas and six constables. The second group had M. D. Singh, DIG (Forest Cell); Shakeel Ahmed, SI, MM Hills; and Udaykumar, RFO on special duty. SP (Forest Cell) Wazir Ahmed and ACF Manjunath Thambakad were in the third group. They were armed with Sten guns, revolvers, pistols, and .303 rifles. Shetty explained the strategy: "Surround the hillock from all sides and close in on them. If we are vigilant they won't be able to get away."

The teams dispersed in three different directions to encircle the hillock. They worked their way through the undergrowth silently, their eyes trained on the hillock for any sign of movement. A dull haze of light was spreading slowly over the area, heralding the break of dawn. In the new light they could see the hillock looming large, ahead of them. It was covered with dense vegetation, and there were rocky crevices amid the trees. All along the way, Shetty whispered instructions and encouraging words into his walkie-talkie, monitoring the groups' movements and keeping their morale up. "Move slowly, carefully. Step lightly.

Do not fire indiscriminately if you sight the gang. Remember we have to get Veerappan alive at all costs."

By 5:30 a.m. the hillock was surrounded from all sides by the raiding party. Carefully they started to make their way up from the base. Suddenly the sound of gunshots split the morning air. The shots seemed to be coming from a cluster of rocks up on the summit. The outlaws had obviously sensed danger and started to fire. Shetty was unfazed and ordered his men to fire warning shots in the air. Immediately the firing from the top ceased. Shivamallu, a constable at MM Hills who was part of the team, raised his voice and shouted a warning in Kannada and then in Tamil: "You have been surrounded from all sides. Do not try to escape or you will all be shot dead. Lay down your arms and surrender before it is too late." RFO Udaykumar repeated the warning after a while. There was no response from the other side. The policemen waited, uncertain how to proceed. Was Veerappan one of those hidden on the summit? Would he actually lay down his arms and walk into the waiting arms of the police? Or would there be the usual violent backlash?

Just as the officers were bracing themselves for the unexpected, they heard a voice from amid the thick bushes. "We are willing to lay down our guns and surrender. Don't harm us. We are coming down. We shall do as we are told." The policemen stood poised for action. What if Veerappan and his men opened fire as they began to approach them? The gang was not known to lose opportunities to outgun law enforcers. But the chance had to be taken.

The three raiding groups began to approach the bushes cautiously, nerves on edge as they cradled their guns, fingers on triggers, ready to fire, their minds on full alert, their eyes trained to take in every minute movement. But the fugitives did exactly as they were told and, to everyone's surprise, surrendered quite meekly. The haul was much bigger than the cops had hoped for: twenty men and an impressive amount of arms and ammunition. The men were identified as Perumal, Kodaki Govindaraju, Ganesha, "Dadikara" Marimuthu, Kamarajapete Govinda, Vandi, Manickyam, Chinnakunji, Mani, Podur Madesha, Chinnaraju, Dhanapala, Kencha, Karumaran, Ootamalai Rama, Ponnimadiah, Peekari, Eshwara, Aiyyan Dorai, and Muniraju. Veerappan himself was not with them.

It turned out that the men had been camping in the safety of the bushes for the past two weeks. When their hideout was searched, the police found utensils, khaki clothes, and half a bag of rice, dal, tamarind paste, sambar powder, and a host of other provisions. Their weapons included eighteen single-barreled guns, a bag of gunpowder, gelatin sticks, detonators, bundles of fuse wire, ninety-one live twelve-gauge cartridges, and fifty-three empty ones. All these were seized. Then began the interrogation. It wasn't long before the prisoners revealed that there was sandalwood concealed in the bushes and rocky crevices on the hillock. A search party came up with a haul of nearly 1,750 pounds of the precious wood, worth a few hundred thousand rupees. The twenty men, along with the sandalwood, were taken to MM Hills under heavy security.

The Sorakaimadu arrests and sandalwood seizure lifted the morale of the STF and sent a clear warning to Veerappan that it meant business. Veerappan was obviously shaken by the sudden display of daring and efficiency on the part of the police. The surprise raid had cost him men and material and was a blow to his reign over the jungles. And he wasn't one to take things lying down. Exactly two weeks after the Sorakaimadu raid, Veerappan and a band of eight men pushed heavy boulders onto a deserted stretch of road between Nal Road and Hoogyam. Their intention was to waylay an *arrack* contractor's jeep that was expected to pass through the area.

At close to 11 a.m., the jeep turned in as anticipated and came to a halt in front of the boulders blocking the road. Veerappan and his men sprang out of their hiding place in the bushes and surrounded the vehicle. Veerappan snapped at the driver and the two passengers: "Get out of the jeep, all three of you, before I shoot you dead." They scrambled to obey. Veerappan grabbed a bag, containing nearly seven thousand rupees, that was lying in the jeep. And quickly he transferred the money to his pocket. Along with the cash, the gang made off with fifty to sixty *arrack* packets.

A month later, a similar holdup took place on the road between Vaddaradoddi and Bidaralli in the MM Hills range. The modus operandi was the same. Around 3:15 p.m., approximately fourteen members of Veerappan's gang stopped a jeep carrying *arrack* and snatched about eighteen thousand rupees and sixty sachets of the heady brew from the driver at gunpoint. Despite the recent successes by the police, Veerappan seemed to be constantly ahead of them.

A sense of hopelessness began to prevail in the ranks. DCF Srinivas alone refused to admit defeat. He decided to adopt a more hands-on approach, and toward the end of April 1991, he moved into a house in Veerappan's native village, Gopinatham. He hoped that by becoming a member of the local community he could gradually win the confidence of the villagers and through him they would learn to have faith in the STF. Practically the only hope of nabbing Veerappan rested in the local villagers; they knew and heard more about the outlaw and his movements than the police could ever hope to, and most of them knew every inch of the terrain, ignorance of which was the STF's chief handicap. Srinivas's gesture did to some extent allay the villagers' fear and their skepticism regarding the effectiveness of the police.


SRINIVAS BEGAN TO ENJOY his new calling. As the deputy commandant of the STF, he was an integral part of all the operations against Veerappan, and his decision to live in Gopinatham altered the scenario in Veerappan's stronghold. He initiated a few development projects in the village, which until then had been in a sad state of neglect. The roads became cleaner and the drains a little less clogged. The stench and squalor that had long been part of the village began to seem like things of the past. Srinivas participated in community events like helping in the construction of the Perumal temple in the village, and prevailed upon the MM Hills RFO to procure funds from the Zilla Parishad for the construction of houses for the poor. He knew he wasn't supposed to directly approach the Zilla Parishad, being more a member of the STF than of the forest department. But he was driven by the need to change the lives around him. Seeing the ramshackle conditions in which Srinivas himself lived—in a portion of the small house of the temple trustee Nataraj—and the amazing work he was doing, an IG once remarked that he wouldn't be able to perform such wonders even if he were offered a presidential medal.

Srinivas not only got the roads cleaned and the drains unclogged, he tried to improve the minds of the villagers and increase their faith in the police. Under his influence, most of them, perhaps for the first time in their lives, seemed to realize the futility of a criminal life. He urged them to change, and they listened to him, if not in agreement, at least without disdain. As the months went by, elderly villagers, most of whose children and grandchildren had joined Veerappan over the years, began to pressure the younger generations to give up their criminal ways. Slowly, the villagers began to realize that under Srinivas, the outlaws might receive a trial by law. Even the families of those who had taken part in the 1990 Hogenekal massacre were optimistic. For their relatives in hiding, a court trial was at least an alternative to instant death at the hands of the police.

Srinivas was also helpful when there was a medical emergency in the village. He would take pregnant women in his jeep to hospitals in Mettur, twenty-five miles away, or Kolathur, nineteen miles from Gopinatham, where medical facilities were available. With the little knowledge he had of Ayurvedic medicine, learned from his grandfather, who had been a well-known herbal specialist in his native Andhra Pradesh, he opened a small pharmacy, doling out basic medicines to villagers for common ailments like cold, cough, vomiting, and diarrhea. He invited Veerappan's sister, Mariamma, whom he had met in the early days after his move to Gopinatham, to join him in his work. Mariamma's husband, Perumal, was serving a term in jail as an abettor to her brother's crimes, and she was caring for her eight-year-old son and two little daughters. Srinivas's offer came as a relief to her, as she could keep herself occupied and also earn a little money. She began to help him by doing odd jobs like heating water for cleaning wounds and packing medicines for patients.

Finally, Srinivas's approach was beginning to show results. As the days went by, the generally hostile atmosphere in Gopinatham in the wake of Veerappan's depredations began to give way to an acceptance of the rule of law. Srinivas was increasingly regarded as a savior who could transform the villagers' lives at a time when most young people were attracted to the idea of joining Veerappan's gang—if they hadn't already done so. As many as twenty-two members of the Veerappan gang either surrendered willingly or allowed themselves to be arrested with the promise that they would stand trial in a court of law. Chief among the gangsters who laid down arms were Rangaswamy, Madesha, Krishna, Madiah, and, most surprisingly, Veerappan's own brother Arjunan. Muthulakshmi, Veerappan's wife, who also lived in Gopinatham, was made to stay indoors, under house arrest. In order to drive home the message that the police were sincere in their desire to rehabilitate them socially, news of the arrests was not allowed to spread. They were not even recorded in official files. Srinivas knew he had to erase their deep-rooted fear of the police before he could hope for active support from the villagers to bring Veerappan to book.

As a way to earn their trust, Srinivas allowed the reformed men to move about freely in the village. Even when someone went missing for a few days, he refused to be perturbed. When next he saw the person he would casually ask, "Where were you all these days? I haven't seen you in a while, have I?" He would never ask why the man had left the village. His goal was to make Veerappan see reason and give up his criminal ways. By making his associates feel comfortable with the prospect of facing the law, he hoped to persuade Veerappan to do the same.

But in May 1991, over a year after the force had been created, the STF came under scrutiny. Except for a handful of arrests and a few seizures of sandalwood, it had little to show for its efforts, despite Srinivas's progress in Gopinatham. Its combing operations so far had failed to capture Veerappan. The Congress government in Karnataka, led by CM Bangarappa, was faced with the prospect of answering uncomfortable questions from the opposition in the Assembly. The existence of the task force had to be justified and the efforts to capture Veerappan authenticated.

Under these circumstances, STF Commandant Shetty placed on record the arrest of the twenty-two gang members whose lives Srinivas had sworn to protect. Documents were readied to be sent to the Home Ministry, showing that the men had been arrested during a raid on one of Veerappan's hideouts. On the morning that the documents were to be sent to Bangalore, Shetty told Srinivas, "I'm sorry. I weighed the pros and cons for a long time last night. I have no option but to regularize the arrests and build a file for the government to study. Srinivas, you should understand that I'm under serious pressure to prove that my team has been performing." The arrested men who had been assured a fair trial were now faced with the prospect of being incarcerated in a police lockup before being sent to judicial custody. They were taken aback at this drastic alteration to the script. Not surprisingly, the sudden turnabout clouded the villagers' attitude toward Srinivas. Their savior had suddenly developed feet of clay. But Srinivas himself was helpless against the dictates of the government.

A month after the arrests had been formalized and the gang members sent to Mysore jail pending trial, Srinivas's tenure as the deputy commandant of the STF ended. His parent department was not anxious to have him back. Principal Chief Conservator of Forests (PCCF) Parameshwarappa, who was the head of the state forest department, seemed to feel that Srinivas was recalcitrant, stubborn, and difficult to handle. To compound matters, Parameshwarappa received word that there was a perceptible threat from members of the Jaffna-based extremist organization Liberation Tigers of Tamil Eelam (LTTE) to dams in Karnataka. As a result of this new development, a number of STF officers on Veerappan's trail were being relocated to posts in different parts of Karnataka to thwart any possible attack by the LTTE. With the temporary dilution in the strength of the STF, there was no possibility of accommodating Srinivas.

The police department was reluctant to take Srinivas back primarily because a few senior officers were uncomfortable reporting to a forest conservator who did not technically have jurisdictional authority over them. There had been a lot of heartburn while Srinivas was in the STF. But Shetty, who was at the helm of affairs, had a soft spot for him because he was convinced that he meant business. There was a sincerity in his approach that was uncommon in most other officers in the STF. In one instance, Shetty had been openly sarcastic about a senior officer who had slept through an operation, saying that even if Srinivas was unable to have enough sleep, there were others to make up for it. Such pinpricks were enough to antagonize the senior ranks, unaccustomed as they were to criticism. Ultimately it was Srinivas who was left in the lurch.

Refusing to give vent to his frustration, Srinivas began to conduct combing operations in the forests of MM Hills with the help of the lower-level staff of the forest department such as watchers and guards. He went about his task with single-minded devotion, indifferent to the fact that he was being isolated. He had become so confident he could bring Veerappan to book that he once told an ACF in Hanur that with twenty-five men he could make Veerappan surrender without having to fire a single shot. Around this time. Srinivas managed to arrange bail for Veerappan's brother Arjunan, who was languishing in Mysore jail. Arjunan responded by staying close to Srinivas and trailing him every-where once he was back in Gopinatham. Srinivas would tell him. "Arjunan, as you have realized, there is absolutely no point in running away from the law. We all make mistakes in life. There is no greater act than repenting for one's sin. Go tell your brother that it serves no pur-pose in the long run to be a criminal. Convince him to surrender before the law. Tell him there is no other way out. Otherwise, bring him to me and I shall convince him." Arjunan would look suitably impressed by these words and promise to talk to his brother when the opportunity arose. Srinivas had such faith in Arjunan that he even allowed him to an-swer police wireless messages on his behalf.

In the meantime, the MM Hills police, headed by SI Shakeel Ahmed, picked up Mariamma, Veerappan's sister, from her house in Gopinatham and took her to the station for interrogation. She was sus-pected to have helped Muthulakshmi, Veerappan's wife, escape to her husband in the forests sometime in August that year. She was also thought to have supplied rations to the gang. Although they are not known to have used any third-degree methods to make her talk, the po-licemen did threaten to send her to a gruesome death if she did not speak up in a week's time; not even her brother, they said, could save her. "You'll be stripped naked and two men will rip you apart," one of the constables said for effect. According to the policemen themselves, even they were a little hesitant to mess around with a woman who hap-pened to be Veerappan's sister.

Mariamma returned to Gopinatham, completely shaken. When she met Srinivas, she burst into tears. "The police are after me. They said I would be stripped naked and killed if I did not give them information about my brother in a week's time. If you don't help me, I'll die. I'm frightened, I don't know what to do."

Srinivas looked at her coldly and said, "I tried helping you and your family. But you have done certain things you ought not to have done. You betrayed me by helping Muthulakshmi escape. What can I do now if the police are threatening you? You'll have to face the music." He walked away, not heeding her plea for help. A few days later, he left for Mettur to meet an informer who had promised to give him information on Veerappan. He returned two days later to learn that Mariamma had committed suicide by consuming pesticide.

The news of Mariamma's death spread like wildfire. Deep inside the forests, in his hideout, Veerappan was livid. He was convinced that Srinivas was responsible for his sister's death. "He should die for what he has done. He is the one who killed her."

Veerappan hatched a diabolical plan to kill Srinivas. He forced the wife of Mariappan, one of the gang members, to consume poison at Alambadi, two and a half miles from Gopinatham. "Even if you die, it will be for a good cause. Believe me, you'll go straight to heaven. So don't think twice before doing what I ask you to do," he told her. He held her down and emptied a pesticide bottle down her throat as she thrashed about helplessly. There had been a number of poisoning cases in the area recently, and Veerappan knew that every time he had been asked for help, Srinivas had rushed to the scene and shifted the victim to hospital.

The game plan was to lure Srinivas to a place where he would be an easy target for Veerappan. It was toward evening that day that Srinivas got the news that a woman had consumed poison in Alambadi. A villager came running to him. "Sir, Mariappan's wife has consumed poison. She is writhing in pain. If you don't rush to Alambadi, she cannot be saved. Please, sir, hurry." Getting into his jeep, Srinivas rushed to the village on the banks of the Cauvery River. Meanwhile, Veerappan had positioned Mariamma's body in a clearing, in full view of the surrounding huts so that he and his men could take perfect aim from inside without being spotted.

Srinivas was quick to reach the spot where the woman lay, but sadly, she was already dead—and as it turned out, she died in vain, even from Veerappan's point of view. For the village elders had by then got together to persuade Veerappan not to kill Srinivas. "He is a man who has shown so much affection and concern for people in the area ever since he came to live here. Please do not take out your anger on him in this ruthless manner." They realized, too, that if Veerappan killed Srinivas, the police would descend upon the village and in the course of their inquiry would send the woman's body for a postmortem. "Her soul will not find a place in heaven if her body is mutilated," they told Veerappan. Finally, though Veerappan and his men took position inside the huts as planned, they chose not to open fire on Srinivas.

Unaware of his narrow escape, Srinivas continued to live in Gopinatham. On November 9, Arjunan, who had not been seen in the village for nearly a fortnight, met Srinivas in the evening with news of Veerappan's desire to surrender. "My brother has decided to lay down arms. I told him that coming in contact with you had transformed my life. I explained to him that it was time he gave up his criminal ways and faced trial—just as you had asked me to do. He is tired of living in the forests as a fugitive and has promised that he will surrender—but only before you."

Srinivas was elated. This was the news he had been waiting for, for the past many years. "Really! Did your brother really say this? Where is he now? I'm convinced no harm will come to him if he surrenders. Of course, he will have to stand trial, but once he has served his sentence, he can come out a new man and lead a normal life, like all other law-abiding citizens. I shall make sure he does." He was so happy that he hugged Arjunan for having brought the news. Arjunan told Srinivas that Veerappan would surrender at 10 a.m. the following day, at a place called Namdali, eight or nine miles away.

Srinivas then asked Arjunan why it had taken him so long to return to Gopinatham if Veerappan's camp wasn't too far away. Arjunan had a ready answer: "Locating my brother's hideout is always very difficult. As you know, he doesn't stay in one place for long. Plus, we were forced to extort about half a million rupees from Obala Chetty, a quarry owner. That took us a while. We'll need money to fight our case in court, won't we, sir?"

Srinivas castigated him for having committed another crime. "Arjunan, you promised to give all this up. You never seem to learn from your mistakes. I'm very disappointed in you." But Veerappan's surrender was foremost in his mind, and he didn't pursue the subject of Arjunan's crimes.

Srinivas spent the night in the house of Ooru Gounder Muniswamy, the village headman. They talked late into the night. "Muniswamy, the day I've been waiting for seems to be finally here. Nothing will bring me more joy than seeing Veerappan give up his criminal ways and turn a new leaf." He was as happy that Veerappan would be giving up crime as he was relieved that he would at last be able to vindicate his stand in the eyes of his detractors, who had scoffed at the idea of persuading Veerappan to surrender. He lay in bed unable to sleep for a long time that night. Finally, in the early hours of the morning, he blew out the kerosene lamp in the small room to try to get some sleep before he embarked on the all-important mission of his life.

Srinivas was ready at 4 a.m., bathed and outfitted in new clothes that he had saved for just such an occasion. The trek to Namdali began. With Srinivas were Arjunan, Krishna, Ooru Gounder Muniswamy, Veerappan's uncle Kirya Ponnuswamy, and another man also called Ponnuswamy. The air was cold and the first hint of light was yet to appear. The village slumbered in darkness. A thin veil of mist hung over the men as they walked soundlessly along a meandering path through the forest. By the time the group had covered a short distance, Ooru Gounder Muniswamy, for one, was beginning to get the feeling that there was something unnatural about the idea of meeting Veerappan in this manner. The thought made him pause in his stride. He tugged at Srinivas's shirt to attract his attention. But the officer was too deeply immersed in thought to notice him.

Gounder couldn't handle the uneasiness building up inside him. He called out to Srinivas, who was walking in front of him, "Sir, I'm beginning to feel that all is not well with this idea of going to Namdali to meet Veerappan. Why don't we go back and give it another thought?"

But Srinivas was too sure of himself to be deterred by anyone at this stage. "Gounder, what has happened to you? Why are you imagining such things? Don't worry, everything will go according to plan."

Gounder, however, could not be convinced. He decided to turn back alone.

At about 9 a.m. the group, minus Gounder, reached a place called

Yerke Halla. A shallow stream flowed in front of them. Arjunan suggested that they rest awhile and refresh themselves. "Let's relax for a
while before we go any farther." The men got down on their knees to
drink the fresh sparkling water. Srinivas bent down and scooped up
some water to splash on his face. As he straightened, a gunshot rang out
from one of the bushes on the far side of the stream. Another followed.
Srinivas slumped into the water, dead. The attack had been sudden and
death was swift. The crystal-clear waters of the stream began to redden
with the blood of the one man who had genuinely desired to rehabilitate Veerappan.

Krishna, Kirya Ponnuswamy, and his namesake were too shocked to
react. Speechlessly they looked at Srinivas's body lying in the stream.
They were too petrified to make a sound or cry for help. Then, suddenly
galvanized into action, Krishna dashed like a madman in the direction of
Gopinatham, unmindful of the thorny lantana bushes that lashed his
face and tore at his clothes. The other two began to run as well. Only
Arjunan stayed behind. Slowly he crossed the stream and joined his
older brother. His deception was complete.

The two brothers began to walk deeper into the forest, toward
Veerappan's camp. After having gone a short distance, Veerappan suddenly stopped. "Let's go back to Yerke Halla. I've left the job half done."
Arjunan was puzzled, but followed his brother back to the spot where
Srinivas's body lay. Veerappan knelt near it. He took the head by the hair
and lifted it slightly. Removing a sickle from his bag, he smote the head
off in one stroke. Why he went to such an extent is unclear. Perhaps it
had as much to do with his deep hatred for Srinivas as the superstitious
belief in those parts, especially among the Padiacchi Gounders, that
the body of a murdered man comes back to life in the form of a ghost,
if left intact.

He doused the torso with gasoline from a small bottle and set it on
fire. Then he rose, holding Srinivas's head by the hair. Blood dripped
from it and dyed the grass a deep red. He looked at Arjunan. "Come on,
let's go. I've completed my task." He walked away in the direction of his
hideout. Once there, he called out to his wife, Muthulakshmi, "Look
what I've brought. I've achieved today what I've been wanting to do for
a long time." Veerappan placed the head on the ground and told his wife

to kick it. "Aren't you the bastard who's been troubling us all this while? I'm happy you're gone." She kicked the head, which rolled to one side, the eyes bulging out and looking skyward in death. Much later, Veerappan went public on the murder of Srinivas, but it was Muthulakshmi herself who told a policeman during interrogation about her role in it.

SRINIVAS'S DEATH OUTRAGED EVERYONE in the government. Morale slumped, and there was a general feeling of hopelessness and even fear in the minds of those who were still part of the STF. The forest officers in the MM Hills area were shaken so badly that living there became a nightmare for them. They spent nights fearing a possible attack by Veerappan, who had proved beyond all doubt that he was in no mood to give up arms and that his vitriolic hatred of law enforcers was still intact. The fight against him had become frighteningly one-sided; Veerappan seemed to be winning at every step.

Three months passed. The STF did not seem capable of arriving at a concrete strategy to finish Veerappan. With Srinivas gone, the STF, although not keen to acknowledge how vital his services had been, was now missing him. There wasn't another man like him anywhere in government service, anyone whom they could think of as a replacement.

In February 1992, Veerappan struck again. This time it was a kidnapping for ransom. Sampangiramaiah was a quarry owner with a substantial stake in the granite business in the area. Originally from Hosur in Tamil Nadu's Dharmapuri district, he had shown considerable grit and enterprise in taking over and successfully running quarries around Yeriyur in Yelandur taluk and also at a place called Chengadi, about thirty miles from the small town of Hanur, in Veerappan's territory. In ten years, he had become a multimillionaire. Of all the people in the area, there was one man who had closely followed Sampangiramaiah's career graph, and that was Veerappan. He was plotting to extract some money from Sampangiramaiah, while he stayed in hiding in the Nallur forests after Srinivas's murder.

On February 16, Ramamurthy, Sampangiramaiah's thirty-year-old son, was driving down a forest road in his Gypsy after visiting the

Chengadi quarry along with their manager, Gunaskehar, and a few friends. He was on his way back to Hanur, where he lived. At about 3 p.m., in the huge expanse of forest where not a soul was to be seen, he came face to face with Veerappan.

"Get out of your vehicle. Listen to me, otherwise I'll kill you." The bandit forced Ramamurthy out of the jeep at gunpoint, blindfolded him, and led him into the forest. Before leaving he ordered Gunashekar, "Go and tell your boss that his son is with me. Ask him not to play any tricks like going to the police. All I want is twenty million rupees, which he can easily afford. If he doesn't pay up, he'll never see his son again. I shall send a note to him later about where he should bring the money. Now get out of my sight."

The trembling manager along with Ramamurthy's friends drove off in the jeep. Veerappan kept Ramamurthy hostage in the forests of the MM Hills range for nearly a month. Although the exact ransom amount paid to Veerappan was never made public, it was rumored that Sampangiramaiah finally had to fork out a million and a half rupees to buy his son's freedom.

# 4

## The Grand Plan

With the MM Hills area as his base, Veerappan moved fearlessly in the forested stretch around Baragur, Pudur, Kadambur, Satyamangalam, Bhavanisagar, Hasanur, Punajanur, Andiyur, and Dimbam, where his writ had become all-pervasive. The STF could do little to dislodge him. But there were two officers in the force who refused to give up hope. They were Harikrishna, SP (Intelligence) and Shakeel Ahmed, SI, MM Hills. Unknown to Veerappan, these two men were to come very close to putting him behind bars.

The story begins with three young men entirely unconnected to the police. Nataraj, a cashier in one of the local wine stores of Ramapura village, lived alone in a small rented room. Every night at 11 p.m., after the last sale had been made in the wine store and the accounts were closed, he would walk down to his friend Muthuram's small hotel. There the two men would settle down for a drink or two after Muthuram had sent his last customer out and half downed the shutters of his hotel. Occasionally, Nagaraj, a *coolie* who worked for a daily wage in the fields surrounding their small village, would join them. Gradually the acquaintance turned into friendship, helped in no small measure by the warmth of alcohol.

As the days went by, Muthuram noticed a significant change in Nagaraj's lifestyle. Money, which had always been in short supply, was now conspicuous by its presence. The *coolie* had begun to host parties for his friends and was buying food worth five to six thousand rupees from the local shops. For someone who earned fifty rupees for an entire day's hard labor, this was mystifying behavior. To compound the mystery, Nagaraj placed an order with a local tailor, Govindu, for seven pairs of khaki outfits, shirts and trousers, of varying sizes.

Muthuram and Nataraj couldn't help discussing these strange developments, but neither could resolve the mystery of Nagaraj's newfound wealth. Then suddenly, one day, Nagaraj disappeared. Days passed without any trace of him. Finally, on a rainy night in late October 1991, a man rushed into Muthuram's hotel, shielding himself from the sheets of pouring water with a plastic sheet held over his head. It was Nagaraj. "I had to go out of town for a while. How are you? I missed you and Nataraj. Will he be coming tonight for dinner?" To Muthuram's astonishment, Nagaraj was wearing flashy, well-tailored clothes, certainly not the kind one could buy in the village.

Just as he was about to ask Nagaraj where he had been for so long, in walked Nataraj on his customary visit to the hotel. "Where the hell were you all these days?" he asked Nagaraj. The *coolie* only smiled.

Before long, all three sat down to their pegs of whisky. After a while, Muthuram broached the subject with Nagaraj. "Tell me, where do you get so much money from these days? You seem to be spending lavishly on food and clothes. Don't tell me you unearthed a big treasure while working in the field!"

Nagaraj poured another measure of whisky into his glass, lit a *beedi*, and began to smoke it, as if lost in serious thought. He was testing their patience. "Tell us if you want to, we don't really give a damn," said Muthuram abruptly.

Nagaraj by then had polished off four stiff drinks. Looking up at the ceiling, he said, "Veerappan."

The name was enough to sober Muthu and Nataraj instantly.

"What?" they asked in unison, taken aback by the ease and familiarity with which Nagaraj had said the dreaded outlaw's name.

But Nagaraj seemed quite unaffected by his friends' reaction. "Yes, I'm earning well. Veerappan pays me up to one thousand rupees for my services. It's big money and I'm happy." Nagaraj had become a ration supplier to Veerappan and his gang. Since their life inside the jungle depended on the constant supply of essentials from the outside world, Veerappan always paid a hefty packet to the courier.

When Muthuram had recovered from the shock, he gave Nagaraj a piece of his mind. "Listen, you'll be in deep trouble if the police get wind of this. Why do you want to ruin your life for the sake of a few rupees? Don't you realize that you have a wife and children to look after? What will happen to them if you are sent to jail? For heaven's sake, stop doing this and lead a normal, decent life with whatever God has given you." Nagaraj had had too much to drink that night. He couldn't be bothered to either understand or react to Muthuram's well-intentioned speech. He got up, looked at Muthuram vacantly, and staggered into the darkness, on his way home.

Nataraj, who had been silent all this while, stood up and said, "Muthu, we'll talk tomorrow. I have to tell you something important." Later in the night, as Muthuram got into bed, his mind was filled with thoughts of Veerappan, and Nagaraj's recklessness in getting involved with him.

The following day, Nataraj came to Muthuram's hotel, not for dinner but for lunch. "Muthu, let's drive up the MM Hills road in the evening. I'll find someone to keep accounts in the wine store for an hour or two. I need to discuss something with you." Nataraj sounded serious. There was purpose in his tone, as if he had reached a decision and wanted Muthuram to be a part of it.

"What is it?" Muthuram asked. But Nataraj was cryptic in his reply. "You'll know in the evening." Nataraj quickly ate his lunch and hurried back to the wine store.

In many ways Nataraj and Muthuram were alike. Nataraj was a man in whom ambition had made a home for itself. It would prod him often, telling him to do something that would earn him fame and, of course, a little extra money. Muthuram too was a man who believed in living life on his terms. He was a bachelor and could afford to take risks. The two friends often tested their courage by driving into the nearby Meenyam jungles in the dead of night on Nataraj's scooter, after a drink or two, in the hope of encountering elephants. On several occasions they had been chased by irritated elephants that had charged straight at the scooter. Each time they had managed to give the angry animals the slip and returned to Ramapura to laugh about their adventure. It was their only act of rebellion in an otherwise dull existence.

That evening Nataraj stopped his scooter in front of Muthuram's hotel and revved the engine a few times. Muthuram climbed onto the pillion and the two set off. Their destination was a culvert near a banyan tree on the forest road going toward Kowdalli, nine miles away. When they reached the spot, Nataraj settled down on the culvert and began to speak. "Muthu, last night when Nagaraj revealed that he was in constant touch with the Veerappan gang, I was as shocked as you were. I was silent only because I was wondering what to do next. Now I think I know—why don't we use Nagaraj to try to get to Veerappan?"

Nataraj had worked it out already. "Muthu, we'll become famous and make a lot of money. After all, there's a huge reward out for anyone who gives information on Veerappan, and it will be all ours. Don't forget the interviews in the press. Newspapers and magazines will splash our photographs all over India. There will be journalists chasing us for interviews. Just imagine our status in the village then."

Muthuram stared blankly at his friend. He had not expected Nataraj to come up with such an idea, fraught as it was with danger. He tried reasoning with Nataraj. "I agree it is a thrilling prospect to think of nabbing Veerappan. I also know if we succeed we'll be heroes in everybody's eyes. The whole country will hail us for achieving the impossible. But have you thought of what will happen if this news leaks to Veerappan and he gets to know of our plan? For God's sake, let's not get entangled. We've always led simple lives, and let's continue to do so. Please keep me out of this." Nataraj tried convincing him, but Muthuram was firm in his decision.

Nataraj was disappointed by his friend's attitude but undaunted. "You're a fool," he told him. "There is no point chickening out in life when you have such a wonderful opportunity to make it big. How can

I convince you that it is a once-in-a-lifetime chance to realize our goal of living a good life?"

On the ride back to Ramapura, the two did not exchange a word. Nataraj was sure that he was on to a wonderful thing. Muthuram was skeptical but not completely closed on the issue, but by the time they reached the hotel, he had made a decision. Muthuram thought after all that it would be a great thing to try to capture Veerappan. It was a chance worth taking. Nataraj was ecstatic. He hugged his friend warmly, shook hands and left saying he would meet him at night, toward dinnertime.

That evening the two friends invited Nagaraj for a drink, an invitation the *coolie* never refused. While sipping whisky, they asked him how he had got in touch with Veerappan's gang. Nagaraj was candid. "It was Kamala Naika who introduced me to him. He told me Veerappan was desperately scouting for a reliable courier to supply rations to the gang. Naika asked me if I could do the job. When I realized how much money was involved, I agreed. He took me to the Nallur forests one night. Even before I could think, I was talking to Veerappan about the deal. I've been on the job for the past three months."

Kamala Naika was from a village called Andekurubara Doddi, five miles across the forest track from Ramapura. His entire family, including his father, Mitu Naika, and brothers, Shivarama Naika and Dauzi Naika, had been involved for a long time in forest-related crimes such as poaching and timber smuggling. So it wasn't surprising that Kamala Naika had links with Veerappan. He had once helped Veerappan sell a pair of tusks to Tibetan buyers at Wodeyarapalya, about two miles from his village. Nagaraj's wife came from the same village as Kamala Naika, and that was how they had become acquainted.

Muthuram and Nataraj began to work on Nagaraj. "Look, Nagaraj, you're our best friend and we're concerned about you. If the police find out that you are supplying rations to Veerappan, they'll arrest you and send you to jail forever. Your life will be finished, your entire family will be ruined. But if you are willing to do as we tell you, you'll not only extricate yourself from the mess you're in, but also end up making a lot of money."

Nagaraj stared back at them uncomprehendingly. "I don't understand," he said.

"Let me put this simply," said Muthuram. "If you help the police capture Veerappan, you can make as much as five hundred thousand rupees and also get the job of your choice in the department. But if you are caught entering the forests carrying rations for Veerappan, you are finished."

Nagaraj was beginning to look rattled. Muthuram and Nataraj looked at each other victoriously, and Muthuram continued, "Listen to us very carefully. Keep supplying rations to Veerappan. We will devise a plan soon to nab him. But you have to be extremely careful. You know the sort of man he is. If he ever gets even a hint of your intentions, he'll chop you into bits."

Nagaraj was beginning to be afraid. He had taken the job for the money it brought him, not stopping to think of the ramifications of dealing with a wanted criminal. Now, as if seeing for the first time the danger he was in, he swore that he would do as he was told.

The next day, Muthuram called the Ramapura police station. "May I speak to the subinspector, please? I have something important to tell him," he told the constable who answered the phone.

Soon, he was talking to SI Rachiah about the possibility of catching Veerappan using Nagaraj as the conduit. The officer was immediately interested. "Come over to the station immediately. We'll talk. Also bring this Nagaraj with you," he told Muthuram. But Muthuram insisted on first speaking to the seniormost officer in charge. Although Rachiah was a little taken aback by his presumptuousness, he agreed and promptly rang up the STF headquarters at MM Hills.

At 9 a.m. the following morning, the three friends jumped onto Nataraj's scooter and rode to the Kowdalli inspection bungalow, not too far from Ramapura. Just as they were sinking into the plush sofa in the veranda, a green jeep drew up in front of the bungalow and screeched to a halt under the canopy. The three men got to their feet, expecting to meet someone important. They were not disappointed. The two policemen who jumped out of the jeep were two of the most daring and high-profile officers in the STF on Veerappan's trail: Shakeel Ahmed, SI, STF, and Harikrishna, SP, STF.

SHAKEEL AND HARIKRISHNA HAD EARNED a reputation in the area for doing their job sincerely and without fear. The same could not be said of most of their colleagues in the STF, who resorted to excuses ranging from feigned illness to domestic emergencies to stay clear of Veerappan's line of fire as often as possible. On innumerable occasions, the two officers, together and separately, had ventured into the dense jungles in their operational area for days on end, looking for Veerappan, with rucksacks containing basic supplies, cans of drinking water, and loaded Sten guns. Shakeel slept with a loaded 9mm pistol by his head in his room in MM Hills in case of a surprise attack.

The two officers approached the veranda and introduced themselves. Pointing toward Nagaraj, who was standing quietly in a corner, Nataraj began to explain, "Sir, this is the man who has been supplying rations to Veerappan's gang for the past three months. We convinced him that he should be helping the police instead. He was confused and frightened to begin with, but has now agreed to do whatever he is told. We thought it best to discuss such a serious matter with someone senior in the police."

The STF officers were clearly surprised. This was obviously not what they would have expected of two ordinary-looking young men from a small village like Ramapura. They could barely conceal their growing excitement. "Tell us everything. We are your friends from this day on. You don't need to fear anything as long as we are with you. We promise." The police officers were always on the lookout for any clues they could get from the local villagers about Veerappan's whereabouts. It was rare for anyone to come forward offering help, and they never discounted anything they heard about Veerappan or his gang.

Enthused by the sudden possibility of success, they began to fire questions at Nagaraj. "Are you sure it was Veerappan you saw? What does he look like? Does he have a huge mustache? Does he carry a gun?"

Nagaraj was a little self-conscious to start with. But the two officers soon put him at ease, and slowly he began to open up. "I am sure it was Veerappan I met. I have been to his hideout in the Nallur forests four times in the past three months. I can't be wrong."

Muthuram and Nataraj looked on, rather amused at the persistent, repetitive, and obvious nature of the policemen's questioning. For them, it was a foregone conclusion that it was Veerappan whom Nagaraj had been meeting. They felt the two policemen's apprehensions were quite unnecessary. "The man Nagaraj is talking about is none other than

Veerappan. We want to help you catch him. All we want is recognition of our efforts and some money. We felt this was a great chance for us to have an adventure and also do our bit to help the government."

By now, Shakeel and Harikrishna were convinced. "All right, we'll make sure that your interests are taken care of. Just do whatever you can to help us get to Veerappan."

The five of them settled down then to formulate their plan of action. Considering Nagaraj's ready access to the gang and his familiarity with their location, the odds of a botched operation were about a million to one, and Shakeel and Harikrishna were seasoned police officers. But then, with Veerappan one could never tell, and they knew they must be cautious. They had to think of a plan that was both foolproof and realistic. Dealing with a criminal of Veerappan's cunning and barbarity was not easy, and they had to take care not let enthusiasm get the better of them. Reaching a consensus was difficult because each person had a different take on the issue. After four long hours of debate, Muthuram was struck with a plan that was as simple as it was feasible. He suggested that they pose as ivory buyers who could also organize arms and ammunition to be supplied to the gang. "Veerappan is bound to fall for it. Guns and bullets must always be in short supply, what with the STF hot on his trail. This is the best way to build a rapport with him and his gang. They would never doubt us if we gave them such a story."

Shakeel and Harikrishna decided to go along with the strategy. Before parting ways, Shakeel Ahmad thrust five hundred rupees into Nagaraj's hands—a "gift" to ensure his continued cooperation. He was instructed to keep in touch with them at the STF headquarters on MM Hills, and report at least once every four or five days with the latest news.

Muthuram and Nataraj, with Nagaraj squeezed in the middle, began the ride back to Ramapura on the ramshackle scooter. On the journey, they again warned Nagaraj to conduct himself normally every time he went to Veerappan's hideout carrying rations. "Behave with him the way you always have. Don't give him any indication of what just took place. You'll die a painful death at his hands if you do." These warnings were severe enough to make Nagaraj swear once again that he wouldn't let anyone else in on the secret.

Two months passed uneventfully. Veerappan's gang had settled down for the time being in the Nallur forests near Hoogyam. During this time, Muthuram and Nataraj would travel the twenty-five-mile stretch up the winding Ghat road often, to reach the STF headquarters on MM Hills. Shakeel and Harikrishna would be there to greet them with innumerable questions. "How is it going? Has Nagaraj met Veerappan recently? Does anybody else know of our plan? When can we expect some news we can act on? When did Nagaraj last supply rations?" Patiently, the two friends would report on Nagaraj's progress. During the two-month period after their discussion at the Kowdalli inspection bungalow, Nagaraj had gone to the bandit's hideout at least six times, lugging a sack full of soap, tea leaves, sambar powder, toothpaste, ragi, rice, dal, and salt for the gang. Each time the customary thousand rupees would be put into his pocket.

On one of his visits, Nagaraj spun his story to Veerappan about brokers from Bangalore who were looking to buy ivory from the gang and also supply guns and ammunition. Veerappan appeared interested and put his right-hand man, Gurunathan, on the job. Veerappan had no reason to doubt Nagaraj, who had been subservient to the point of touching his feet reverentially every time he met him, and Nagaraj had won the confidence of the entire gang. Gurunathan readily agreed to meet the "agents," who were supposed to drive down from Bangalore in a few days.

Nagaraj was in a state of high excitement. He rushed to Muthuram with the news. Muthuram was exultant. "Come, let's go tell Nataraj about this." Upon hearing the news, Nataraj decided to go straight to MM Hills to inform Shakeel and his boss.

At about 8:30 that night, with Muthu on the pillion, he started on the ride through the forest. "We have come with the news everyone's been waiting for. Veerappan has bought our story. He has deputed Gurunathan to meet the 'agents' and hold preliminary discussions before the actual deal is struck. Nagaraj just returned from Veerappan's hideout to inform us about it." The police officers asked the two to find out more and fix the details.

The next day Nagaraj was sent back to the forest to finalize a meeting with Gurunathan. Muthuram and Nataraj were beside themselves with excitement. It was 6 p.m. when Nagaraj returned to base. "We're going tomorrow," he said. "I've had it all fixed up. Gurunathan will meet the two of you at a spot about two or three miles inside the forest, to the left side of the road passing through Dinnalli Satyamangalam. So be prepared." There was a triumphant ring to his otherwise meek voice.

That night, neither Muthuram nor Nataraj could sleep. They fantasized about nabbing Veerappan, about the congratulatory handshakes from eminent police officers and ministers, the media coverage, interviews and press conferences, all the money that would be theirs.

At 3 p.m. the following day, the three left on their mission, with Nataraj riding the old Bajaj scooter. They traveled five miles before parking their vehicle in the middle of a clump of trees, surrounded by lantana bushes, where it couldn't be easily spotted. Then they slipped into the forest.

The trek began with Nagaraj leading the way. It must have been a little past 4 p.m. The forest echoed to the sound of birdcalls as the three men silently made their way through the bushes. The distant trumpeting of an elephant startled Muthuram for a moment, but Nagaraj gestured as if to say there was nothing to fear. When the group had covered two and a half miles through dense shrubbery amid the tall trees, Nagaraj started whistling what was obviously a signal, long and low. In reply, there was nothing but the eerie silence of the forest. At that moment, to Muthuram and Nataraj, the whole world seemed to be still, with not a soul stirring. Nagaraj looked at them and smiled faintly. He then waved his hand to say, let's move.

The three men walked another mile. Then suddenly, Nagaraj stopped. He began to look around him, as though studying the area minutely. Finally satisfied, he nodded his head and whispered, "This is it." He whistled again, the same tune as before. Minutes passed. There was no sign of anybody; only the peacocks strutted about, always keeping an eye on the three intruders. Suddenly, a similar whistle was heard from a point a few hundred yards ahead. Nagaraj's face lit up. He gestured to the others to follow him.

As they walked in single file, Muthuram suddenly spotted a human figure perched on the branch of a huge, gnarled tree. It was Gurunathan. The man jumped down to stand in front of Nagaraj. "So you have brought them, have you," he said in Tamil.

Nagaraj, unsure of what to do next, looked at Muthuram and Nataraj for guidance. Gurunathan was tall and burly, with a spiky mustache. "We are the brokers," Muthuram introduced himself and Nataraj.

Gurunathan shook hands and said, "Naga has told us all about you. We were eager to meet you." The two smiled and nodded, hiding their growing trepidation. Gurunathan was reputed to be Veerappan's closest confidant and an amazing sharpshooter, who could kill with just one shot from his rifle.

He sat down on the grass and stretched his long legs, then looked at the three men intently. "We want guns and bullets."

Muthuram nodded without uttering a word. Nataraj waved his hand and said, "That shouldn't be a problem. We can organize it for you. Just tell us the quantity and it shall be delivered to you whenever you want it. Our main agent is in Bombay. We shall give him a call tonight and inform him that there is a deal to be struck."

Gurunathan was taken in by his confident tone. He told them to come back with samples he could take to his boss, Veerappan. The three conspirators then bid goodbye to Gurunathan, who seemed pleased to have met them, and began to walk back to Dinnalli.

The sun had already taken refuge behind the heavy canopy of trees. In the twilight created by its absence the forest seemed to close in around them. The dying sun's rays could barely penetrate the thick foliage. It was 9:30 p.m. when they finally made it to the spot where the scooter was parked. The darkness enveloping the forest had made their trek difficult to start with, but once their eyes had got accustomed to the dull light of the stars, it had become easier to negotiate the forest track. Muthuram and Nataraj were happy that a good beginning had been made. Nagaraj was satisfied that he had played his part well by arranging the meeting. Hopping onto the scooter, the three men made their way back to Ramapura. They ate a hearty dinner and went back to their respective homes to catch up on their sleep. The long walk in the forest had taken its toll.

In the morning, they reported back to Harikrishna and Shakeel. The policemen were delighted and gave them a bullet to show Gurunathan. Before sending them on their way, Shakeel thoughtfully stuffed five hundred rupees into Muthuram's shirt pocket, saying, "Keep it for your travel expenses."

Two days later Muthuram, along with Nagaraj and Nataraj, met Gurunathan at the same spot in the Dinnalli forests. They showed him the bullet the police had given them. Gurunathan burst into loud laughter. "This won't kill even a deer, and we are talking of elephants!" He called Nataraj aside. "Get this type." Nataraj was given a bullet with the inscription "Shaktiman 12 bore" on it.

Three days passed before a box of bullets conforming to Gurunathan's specifications could be procured from Bangalore. On the third night, Muthuram, Nagaraj, and Nataraj sped on their way, this time on three mopeds borrowed from the constables at the Ramapura police station. With them was an "agent" from Bangalore: SI Shakeel Ahmed. He was dressed in a T-shirt and jeans and was wearing a pair of bathroom slippers.

They reached Dinnalli at 11:30 p.m. Muthuram noticed that Ahmed was carrying a loaded revolver. "Sir, there's no need for that. Please leave it in my house so we can go unarmed. Carrying a weapon may give rise to suspicion." Shakeel agreed. He seemed completely at ease in his new avatar.

It was a cold night and a stiff breeze was blowing from the direction of the forest. The group walked two or three miles into the forest before Nagaraj signaled their approach. Soon enough, the answering whistle was heard. The time was 2 a.m. Gurunathan peered from behind a big rock, flashing a torch, and there was a girl with him. Muthuram's jaw dropped when he saw her. It was Chandni, a Lambani girl from his own village. There was no hint of recognition in her eyes. When had this girl joined the Veerappan gang? What was she doing with Gurunathan at this hour? Muthuram set these distracting thoughts aside and tried to concentrate on the purpose of their meeting.

Muthu introduced Shakeel. "Meet Shivaraj, our contact from Bangalore. He landed this evening." Shakeel confidently shook hands with Gurunathan. There was no trace of tension in him. He then handed over the box containing the bullets.

Gurunathan opened the box and exclaimed, "This is it! This is it!" He looked at Shakeel and smiled. The two spoke for nearly an hour and a half. Muthu donned the role of official translator, since Shakeel couldn't speak a word of Tamil and Gurunathan didn't speak Kannada. The discussion centered on life in the forest as a fugitive, the number of elephants Gurunathan had shot, the shooting incidents involving the police and the gang, and Chandni, who Gurunathan said he would marry soon.

Gurunathan reiterated to Shakeel what he had already told Muthuram and the others during their last visit. "Give us guns and take the tusks." He opened a cloth bundle and took out a few tiger skins and claws, and deer and bear skins. "Take this," Gurunathan said, handing to Shakeel and the others a bunch of tiger claws. "Get pendants made of gold. They'll bring you good luck."

Muthu couldn't contain his curiosity any longer. He turned to Chandni and said, "Don't you remember me? I'm Muthuram of Dinnalli." He gestured to Gurunathan. "Are you going to marry him?"

The girl blushed. Gurunathan looked amused at the ribbing. It came out much later that the two had been introduced by Kamala Naika. Gurunathan had asked him if there was a girl in any of the villages around who was good enough for him to marry, whereupon Kamala Naika had lured Chandni, who was separated from her husband, into the forest.

Shakeel and the others returned to Dinnalli Satyamangalam soon after daybreak. They had promised Gurunathan they would return in a few days with more stuff. Riding straight to Ramapura, they stopped in front of the police station. The "agent" got into his jeep waiting there and went on to his headquarters, not in Bombay, but in MM Hills. He had to tell Harikrishna about his sojourn in the forest. The senior officer was delighted. "You must go again soon. That'll strengthen his belief in you. After that, we can close in for the kill."

Five days later, it was time to visit the forest again. It was the usual team, except for Nataraj, who had excused himself because of some domestic emergency. Nagaraj had achieved the impossible this time. He had set up a meeting with Veerappan himself in his hideout in the Nallur forests. It had been decided that Gurunathan was to come to a point near Dinnalli Satyamangalam early in the morning and escort the team to where Veerappan and the gang were holed up. The air was filled with expectancy. Gurunathan waited on the fringe of the village along with his fiancée, Chandni, for the "agent" and the others to turn up.

When they arrived, it was decided that Chandni should be left behind, for the journey would be arduous. But a safe place had to be found for her. After a little discussion, Nagaraj's house was chosen and Chandni was made to climb into the dilapidated attic in the house. She was to stay there until the team returned. Nagaraj instructed his wife to give her food and water in the attic itself. "Make sure nobody sees her," he warned before leaving. Gurunathan then led the team into the forest from a point close to the village bus stop, where he had been waiting, hidden behind a tree.

The tedium of the trek through the forest was broken by Gurunathan's bragging. He described in theatrical detail how he had recently shot an elephant. They trekked for four hours before Gurunathan halted the team by the side of a stream. "Refresh yourselves while I go and inform the boss about your arrival." Half an hour elapsed before he returned, making his way through a thicket. "Come, he's waiting." They walked nearly another mile before they reached the camp.

And there he was, Veerappan himself, seated on a small rock, exactly as they had pictured him. He looked slightly disheveled, and his strangely unblinking eyes were frightening in their intensity. There were thirty to thirty-five other men, and about six women. Some of the men lounged on the grass, smoking *beedis*. A few others were engrossed in skinning a deer, which had been shot just a while ago. The women were stirring huge pots with stout wooden sticks. Shakeel smelled ragi porridge.

Veerappan rose and raised his right hand by way of a greeting. Then, turning to Gurunathan, he said, "So, these are the men you were talking about." Pointing to a clearing, he invited them to make themselves comfortable on the grass. The meeting started. Shakeel began by saying that he could supply anything the gang wanted. Veerappan raised an eyebrow and after a pause said, "Take as much ivory as you want, even a couple hundred pounds," and he proceeded to show them a pair of glistening tusks wrapped in old newspaper.

Veerappan was clear about what he wanted. "Get us thirty-two Sten guns, each capable of firing twenty-four rounds per minute. We need them as soon as possible. Tell us when you can supply them to us." He pronounced the word "Sten" as "dhun." It was "dhun guns" he wanted.

Although shocked at the requirement, Shakeel said easily, "No problem. We can easily organize it for you through our Bombay contact." The talk then veered around to the buying of ivory.

Veerappan set his price at twelve hundred and fifty rupees per pound. Shakeel replied that he would be able to pay seven hundred and fifty rupees. But Veerappan stayed firm. He knew very well that the stuff fetched as much as twenty-five hundred rupees per pound in the market. Since he didn't have men to carry it, he offered it at a low price. There was no point in challenging Veerappan's knowledge of the ivory market. Finally, after a great deal of haggling, a price tag of one thousand rupees per pound was fixed. The negotiations had taken a full two hours.

Then, sounding as businesslike as a CEO after a long, tiring boardroom meeting, Veerappan said, "Let's have lunch." Their food was served on large leaves, freshly cut from a tree. Only Shakeel politely refused to eat. It wasn't that he had any misgivings about the quality of the food. It was just that the menu offered only one dish: langur meat, which he had no intention of trying. He was more than happy with the loaf of bread he had carried. The others were too hungry for such scruples and ate what was served to them. After lunch, Veerappan mentioned that Gurunathan's wedding had been set for February 25 at a place called Kariyyana Betta, deep inside the forest. Nagaraj was to have an important role in making the arrangements, but now Muthuram and Nataraj would be involved, too. "We will require a lot of supplies for the occasion. Make sure it's organized. As usual, this fellow can bring it to us," he said, pointing toward Nagaraj.

When it was time for the "agent" and his party to take leave of the gang, Shakeel pumped Veerappan's hand vigorously to seal the deal. He had played his part to the hilt.

It was dark by the time they reached the outskirts of Dinnalli Satyamangalam. Gurunathan accompanied them to pick up Chandni from Nagaraj's house. Shakeel and Muthuram went on to Ramapura, where they had biscuits and bananas, after waking up a roadside vendor who had curled up to sleep in his wooden box of a shop. Up on the hill, at the police camp, Harikrishna and SP Gopal Hosur were eagerly awaiting the outcome of the "negotiations." They came out as soon as they heard the drone of the jeep laboring up the steep, winding road. Shakeel jumped out of the vehicle and walked up to his superiors with unconcealed glee. "Veerappan has fallen for our bait. This is the best chance we've got to put a bullet in his head." They asked Muthuram to stay the night in a room in the adjoining guesthouse. So tired was he after the long day in the forest that he fell asleep instantly.

There was a buzz at the STF headquarters the next morning with the arrival of DIG Thimmappa Madiyal, who held concurrent charge of the STF from his base in Mysore. Shakeel introduced Muthuram to the senior officer as the most vital player in their bid to nab Veerappan. Madiyal patted Muthu warmly on the back. "Great work, my boy. Keep it up. Tell me what you want from the police department and it shall be done. We need your help to put an end to Veerappan. I hope we'll be able to do that soon, with you on our side." Muthuram had waited so long for an occasion like this, for a senior officer like Madiyal to praise him in the presence of a dozen others.

Later in the afternoon, Nataraj joined them, having driven up from Ramapura on his scooter. The day was spent discussing how to get to Veerappan and his gang. The policemen asked Muthuram and Nataraj for their suggestions. "We could mix poison in the food we'll be supplying for Gurunathan's marriage. That should do the job for us."

The officers looked unconvinced. Harikrishna shook his head in disapproval. "What if they asked all of you to join them for lunch? That would be like committing suicide!"

Nataraj was convinced that the only way out was to mix into the tea powder some poisonous substance that would take effect slowly. An SI suggested, "How about lacing their drinks with poison? They'll be too intoxicated to notice!" Veerappan had asked for two cases of whisky to be supplied along with the rations, and the liquor could be used as a base for the poison—except for one thing: Veerappan never drank. Strangely, there was no discussion of how Veerappan and his men could be arrested. The consensus was clear: to kill Veerappan and everyone in his gang, with as little risk to the police as possible.

Madiyal assured Muthuram and Nataraj that he would consult doctors and scientists to find out if there was any powder that could kill without altering the taste of the food. "I'll let you guys know as soon as I work out a method." By the time the discussion came to an end, it was already evening and time for Muthuram and Nataraj to go home. Before they left, they were reminded again that they should continue to keep a close watch on the gang and its movements.

Soon, preparations for Gurunathan's wedding began. Nagaraj got jewels made for Chandni from a jeweler in Kollegala. Muthuram and Nataraj met Gurunathan regularly at a forest hideout he had used to meet Chandni, not very far from Dinnalli Satyamangalam.

One day, Muthuram, on one of his regular excursions into the forest, saw three young men belonging to his village. He cautioned Gurunathan, "Don't get involved with those guys. They could turn out to be police informers. You don't want to get caught, do you?" The bandit had so much faith in Muthuram that he promptly dismissed the three. In an unforeseen way, Muthuram had begun to influence Gurunathan's actions.

On February 17, 1992, toward late evening, Muthuram was chatting with friends near the Mahadeshwara cinema tent when he was approached by SI Rachiah, who told him that he and Nataraj were wanted immediately at the Ramapura police station. Nataraj was away in Hanur. When Muthu arrived at the station, he was surprised to see Harikrishna and Shakeel Ahmed, who had driven down a while ago from MM Hills.

The moment Harikrishna saw Muthuram, he told him, "Muthu, take us to Gurunathan. It has to be done today at any cost."

The informer was perplexed at the sudden change in plans. "Sir, please don't be hasty. If we wait a little longer, we can catch Veerappan himself. What is the hurry?"

Harikrishna was visibly agitated. "Don't dictate terms to me. I know what I'm doing. Are you the SP here?" Muthuram felt slighted. He sat quietly for a while and then walked out of the room, saying he wouldn't be able to do a thing without Nataraj.

Shakeel followed him and persuaded him to go to Hanur to meet Nataraj. On the short journey, Muthuram sat without saying a word. It was Shakeel who did all the talking. "Look, Muthu, I want to get Veerappan as much as you do, but I'm helpless. The SP seems to have made up his mind to nab Gurunathan first. He's my boss and there's nothing I can do. Moreover, if by chance Gurunathan becomes suspicious and escapes, you and Nataraj could be in serious trouble. So let's do as the SP says."

Muthuram could not imagine how he or Nataraj could be accused of conniving with the gangsters. Veerappan's extermination had become an obsession for them by now, but he knew that the police department was capable of anything and he had no desire to test their patience.

Nataraj was woken up by the midnight knock on his door. Rubbing the sleep from his eyes, he tried to make sense of what was being said to him. "What's wrong with the SP? Why can't he be a little patient?" he said. "All the good work will be undone if we end up catching only Gurunathan. What a wonderful chance we have to get to Veerappan himself. Sir, surely you can convince your boss." But Shakeel merely repeated what he had told Muthuram, and Nataraj was left with no option either.

It was close to 1 a.m. when the police party left for Dinnalli Satyamangalam. The group consisted of Shakeel, Harikrishna, Muthuram, Nataraj, and thirty constables. The two officers and the informers traveled in a white Ambassador, while the constables followed in a lorry. Shakeel and Harikrishna, dressed in T-shirts and jeans, were armed to the teeth. They had loaded revolvers in their hip pockets and tucked inside their socks as backup.

The narrow road was surrounded by undulating forest on all sides. Even in the darkness, the jutting hillocks could be seen in silhouette. A little past 1:20 a.m., they reached the village. Harikrishna sent Muthuram to get Nagaraj from his house. The *coolie* was quickly produced before him. The officer looked at Nagaraj closely. "Naga, we have decided to nab Gurunathan. Go to the place where he is staying and bring him to us. Tell him that the man from Bombay has arrived with the goods. Make sure nothing goes wrong."

Nagaraj looked at the SP blankly. He dared not say a word. Slowly, he set off down the forest path and disappeared from view.

The car was parked on one side of the road. The lorry waited about half a mile behind. Shakeel and Harikrishna sat at the back while Muthu and Nataraj were squeezed into the front beside the driver. After

Nagaraj left, everyone in the car became quiet. The chirping of crickets in the grass and the occasional hooting of an owl were the only sounds to be heard.

The two officers leaned back in their seats, eyes closed. If they were tense, they didn't show it. An hour and a half later, a dark lean figure emerged from the bushes. It was Nagaraj. He walked up to the car slowly and began to speak in a whisper. "Gurunathan is hesitant to come to the main road. He wants you to enter the forest and meet him there."

Harikrishna listened silently. "Go and tell him that the man from Bombay is not used to forests and is too scared to step inside."

Ten minutes later, Gurunathan emerged with Nagaraj onto the main road. He was carrying a double-barreled gun. Walking close to him was a woman. She too carried a gun. It was Chandni. Gurunathan surveyed the area around him. Muthuram got down from the car. Gurunathan smiled nervously. "Ask your man to come over here." He pointed to a stone bench beside the road.

Muthuram gestured toward the car. "Oh no, not on the road. What if somebody comes along? Let's sit in the car comfortably and talk." Shakeel got down from the car to make way for Gurunathan to sit in the middle, in the backseat.

As soon as Gurunathan had pushed his heavy frame into the car's rear and settled down, he was introduced to Harikrishna. "This is our man from Bombay. He has taken a lot of risk and trouble to come all this way to deliver the guns." The SP nodded. Muthuram, sitting in the front, turned his body sideways to be able to see those at the back. Nataraj, in the meantime, engaged Chandni in conversation, standing near the car.

Shakeel chatted casually with the gangster. "How many elephants have you killed so far with this gun?" he asked, gently taking Gurunathan's gun in his hand.

"As many as the hairs on my head," said Gurunathan, smoothing down his thick mop of hair.

Harikrishna spoke for the first time. "What is life in the forest like? Isn't it tough to live like this, always changing places to evade the police?"

"Yes, sometimes it is. But we've been living like this for such a long time that we've gotten used to it. The police bastards can be really irritating, though."

As the two spoke, Shakeel, who was pretending to admire Gurunathan's weapon from different angles, casually passed it to Muthuram. Gurunathan didn't seem to notice. As Gurunathan continued to talk to Harikrishna, Muthu made bold to carefully uncock the gun and open the breech. He noticed two cartridges in the chambers, loaded and ready to fire.

Harikrishna continued, "Where do you sell the ivory? I hear there is a lucrative market in Bangalore because of the handicrafts business there. Do you get regular buyers?"

"Supplying tusks is not a major issue. But of late, it has become a problem to transport them out of the forest. There aren't too many people willing to take the risk of carting them to Bangalore." As Gurunathan continued to speak, Harikrishna removed the magazine from his Sten gun. He then handed the gun over to him. The gangster looked very pleased with the weapon. "Tell me, how much do you want for this?"

Shakeel replied, "We are expecting one hundred seventy-five thousand rupees. It is an excellent weapon. But since you want to buy in bulk, we'll settle for one point three hundred thousand per gun."

"We would be able to offer you one hundred thousand rupees apiece," said Gurunathan. Then Shakeel took up the negotiation and the discussion went back and forth.

As Gurunathan picked up the Sten gun to have another look at it before finalizing the price, Shakeel leaned back out of view of the gangster and winked at Muthuram. This was the signal for Muthuram to act. Gurunathan was still busy examining the gun, which was empty of cartridges. Shakeel and Harikrishna leaned sideways to get at the revolvers they carried in their hip pockets. Inside the cramped car, they had to move very slowly so as not to alarm Gurunathan, and it took them a while to lay their hands on the triggers. But the lack of space also carried an advantage. Gurunathan couldn't see what was happening in his immediate vicinity on either side.

Simultaneously, the two policemen whipped out their revolvers and held them to the gangster's head. At the same time, Muthuram jabbed the barrel of Gurunathan's own gun to his chest, ready to fire. Gurunathan was incapacitated almost instantaneously. The impossible suddenness of it all made him whimper in panic. Meanwhile, Nataraj, who had been talking to Chandni outside the car, snatched her gun and held her tightly by the hair. She began to sob. Shakeel grabbed Gurunathan's right hand and twisted it behind his back, then snapped on handcuffs.

# 5

# The Death of Gurunathan

The night of Gurunathan's capture had been one of the most dramatic since the STF began operations against Veerappan in April 1990. Minutes after the arrest of Gurunathan and Chandni, they were taken in the car, handcuffed, to the spot where the lorry with the constables was parked. There was a moment of stupefied silence as the police officers took in the scene before them—almost all the men were snoring peacefully, oblivious to the world around them. Harikrishna's shout of rage startled them out of sleep. "You guys are a disgrace to the force. It's better to die than live like this. Why don't you just get off of my team? What if something had happened to us? You idiots wouldn't have even known. And to think I was depending on you to come to our rescue in an emergency, you disgusting louts!" The policemen scampered to their feet, straightening their caps and grabbing their guns, as if they had been ambushed by Veerappan himself.

The two officers decided to send Chandni to MM Hills with Nataraj in the car, so that they could start a combing operation in the forests using Gurunathan to show them the way. Harikrishna didn't want to take any chances with a man of Gurunathan's criminal capabilities. So, hand-cuffed as he was, a thick rope was tightly tied to his waist. Another rope was fastened to his left ankle. Two gun-toting constables held the long ends of the ropes as if holding a dog on a leash. He was then ordered to lead the way to Veerappan's hideout in the forest.

Gurunathan looked dazed, his face a study of shock, fear, and help-lessness. He kept mumbling in Tamil, "Sir, please leave me. Don't do anything to me. I'll show you everything. I'll tell you everything." Pathetically, he appealed to Muthuram, "Please tell them, sir. Don't do anything to me." Just a few hours ago, he had been the master of all he surveyed, a man with an awesome reputation as a hunter, feared for his merciless acts of death and destruction. But now he was whimpering, afraid and begging for mercy.

"Take us to the place where the bastard is hiding. If you try any tricks, you know what will happen. If you want to save your life, just do as I say. Now move." Harikrishna was in control of the situation.

The gangster, shaken and cowering, nodded and assured him in a weak voice, "I'll show you everything." And so the group, led by Harikrishna, entered the forest in the hope that the man in their custody would lead them to Veerappan's hideout.

It looked like the police party was headed for war. The air crackled with the bristling presence of guns and ammunition. There were twenty policemen, along with Muthuram and Nagaraj, led from the front by the two determined officers, hell-bent on netting their prey.

The night air was cold. Drops of dew had settled on the leaves and the grass. As the team made its way through the maze of shrubbery, their faces and their clothes were brushed with moisture. But nothing seemed to daunt Harikrishna and Shakeel as they trekked silently through the night, Sten guns on the ready.

The forest was silent, its denizens totally unaware of the drama that was unfolding in their midst. The dull thudding of police boots on the grass was the only sound as the party wound its way through the forest, jumping over a small fallen log here and avoiding a little pit in the ground there. Gurunathan was walking almost in a stupor, but was aware that he couldn't afford to mislead the police. He kept looking in the direction of the two officers every now and then as if to say, "I'm tak-ing you to the right place, just as you ordered me to." Shakeel and

Harikrishna watched for any sign of human life in the dark forest. Their best chance was to take Veerappan and his gang by surprise as they slept. No one in the raiding party spoke a word.

Several miles down the thorny path, it became clear that there was little hope of stumbling upon Veerappan's gang before dawn. The first stirrings of daylight were visible inside the deep recesses of the forest where they found themselves. A jungle cock began to crow, and other birds took up the call. Soon it would be dawn.

Muthuram looked at his watch. It was 5 a.m. They were at least three miles inside the forest, at a place called Holeyan Bare. This was where Veerappan had camped, not too many days ago. Gurunathan, looking pale and tired, pointed to a spot near a huge tree where they had cooked and slept. He asked to be taken there. Suddenly he knelt down and started scraping the earth with his fingers. It came to light that the gang, as a precautionary measure, always dug a small pit and buried the ash collected after the day's cooking, to avoid leaving any clues to their location. Gurunathan said they had been instructed by Veerappan to do the same even after their daily ablutions.

Harikrishna was in no mood to waste time. "Hey, are you taking us on the right route or are you trying to play one of your stupid games? I'm warning you, if I find out that you are wasting our time, you'll die a dog's death right here."

"No sir, I'll take you to the exact place."

By now, the sun's first rays were filtering through the tree cover. Shakeel and Harikrishna had not slept at all. Neither had Muthuram and Nagaraj. The tiredness and the strain of the previous evening showed on their faces, and their eyes were red and weary. Shakeel and Harikrishna decided to rest briefly. They stretched themselves on the luxurious grass, and the others followed suit. Gurunathan sat down too, looking numb, fearful of what would happen to him in the days to come. They opened the water cans and drank as if they hadn't seen water in a week. One of the constables pushed a can in Gurunathan's direction. But he was too immersed in his thoughts to notice. A little later, they were up on their feet once again. They would now head toward the interior precincts of the Nallur forests, where, according to Gurunathan, the gang could be located.

The forest had woken up completely by then. An elephant herd, unnerved by the sight of so many intruders, moved away into the safety of a bamboo thicket nearby. Veils of swirling mist were rising, but neither Shakeel nor Harikrishna was in the mood to appreciate the beauty of the forest. Instead, they kept goading Gurunathan to move faster.

A little beyond the Nallur area, there is a place called Balambatti. It was here that Veerappan had been camping since the last three days, said Gurunathan. "How long before we can reach that place?" asked Shakeel.

Gurunathan replied that it would take two hours. Harikrishna addressed his team. "Look, men, this is a highly sensitive operation. All of you have to be on guard, eyes wide open. You must keep your wits about you. Follow my instructions at all times. Do not shoot indiscriminately. We have to get the bastard at all costs. You shall all be hailed as heroes then." The men responded enthusiastically, and Muthuram and Nagaraj found themselves swept up in the momentum as well. After an hour's walk, they caught a glimpse of a thickly wooded hillock in the distance. It was across the knoll, in a small valley below, that Veerappan and his men were supposed to be holed up. Climbing the hillock would not be easy with Sten guns in their hands and cans of water strapped to their backs. But there was no choice. The job had to be done.

Harikrishna gestured to the team to start climbing. Gurunathan, held by two constables, was in the middle of the advancing party. The hillock was steep, and low-hanging tree branches made progress difficult. As they neared the top, Harikrishna halted abruptly. He could hear noises in the valley below, as though someone was breaking branches off a tree. Could it be Veerappan and his men? Had they reached their destination?

Harikrishna waved his hand at the team as if to say "Stay down." Muthuram and Nagaraj were by now quite frightened. "Oh God, what if there is a volley of fire in our direction," Nagaraj whispered.

"Shut up. Don't imagine such things," Muthuram whispered back fiercely.

Harikrishna by then had inched his way up to the top of the hillock and was peering down cautiously. It was not Veerappan but an elephant standing below, feeding. The sounds he had heard were of falling tree branches pulled down by the animal's trunk.

When the rest of the team had caught up with Harikrishna at the top of the hillock, Gurunathan pointed to Balambatti down in the valley. But there was no trace of human habitation. The gang had obviously moved on. Disappointment and frustration combined with hunger made Harikrishna and Shakeel lose their cool. They banged their Sten guns against the trunk of a tree and slumped to the ground in exhaustion. It was finally decided that the team would return to Dinnalli Satyamangalam.

So the return journey started. It was nearing midday. The blazing heat wasn't exactly conducive to a long walk. They tramped on slowly, and two hours passed without incident. The forest was quiet, except for the usual birdcalls.

Suddenly Harikrishna stopped in his stride and ordered his men to remove the magazines of their Sten guns. The order was most unusual. But it was an order all the same, and had to be obeyed. The SP told them to stack their guns on the ground. Everyone looked at him quizzically. He then asked one of the constables to bundle the guns together and tie them firmly with a rope. He told another constable to untie Gurunathan, but to leave the handcuffs on.

While everyone else looked on baffled, Harikrishna hefted the bundle of guns onto Gurunathan's back and screamed, "March!" Silently, Gurunathan began to walk, bent under the crippling weight of twenty-two guns. "You bastard, this is what you wanted, isn't it? Sten guns! Now carry them all!" A few members of the team burst into laughter. Shakeel had a smile on his face.

When they reached the village it was nearly 4 p.m. They walked on, to a place called Kempayyana Gudde, about two miles away. Most of them were so tired that they collapsed on a patch of grass and lay there till a simple lunch of rice and sambar could be cooked under the trees by the roadside. The two officers, Shakeel and Harikrishna, got busy with their wireless sets, passing on the information of Gurunathan's arrest to their superiors.

They ate that day with the ravenousness of a pack of hungry hounds. Gurunathan, who was sitting silently a little away from the group, also ate. The SP, looking at him eat, said, "Eat well, this is your last meal anyway."

The cornered gangster begged him, "Please don't do anything to me.

I'll show him to you within the next two days. Please let me go." Harikrishna didn't bother to listen to what Gurunathan was saying. Soon after lunch, the two officers along with Muthuram and ten constables bundled Gurunathan into the lorry and started driving to Kothguli, three miles away, toward Ramapura. Gurunathan's last journey had begun.

The following account of Gurunathan's death was given later by one of the eyewitnesses. On reaching Kothguli, the policemen dragged their captive a little inside the woods off the main road. He kept mumbling, "Please don't do anything to me." He was made to stand in the middle of a dried-up stream.

Then Harikrishna turned to George, a constable. "Finish him." Gurunathan stood handcuffed and defenseless. His face was ashen. As he stared blankly into space, cold and numb, Muthuram saw tears forming in his eyes. Was Gurunathan showing remorse for the life of crime he had led, or was he crying out of fear? No one could say. But now there was no second chance for him. Harikrishna had made up his mind. He looked at George and simply said, "Come on."

George, too, seemed moved by Gurunathan's plight. As he took aim from a distance of only a few feet, his hands shook infinitesimally. The shot grazed Gurunathan's hand. He screamed in pain and fell to the ground. Harikrishna was unfazed. Looking at Muthuram, who stood aloof under a tree, he asked him if he wanted to take the next shot. Muthuram simply shook his head. His heart was heavy and he felt weighed down by grief. It was he who had shown such great enthusiasm and commitment in the quest for Veerappan's gang. Why was he feeling such sadness now? Memories of Gurunathan in his forest hideout flooded unbidden into Muthu's mind. The swagger, the bombast, the arrogance were all gone. Now he was gasping for breath, struggling for life as he lay on the hard ground, with terror in his eyes. Muthuram turned away.

George took aim again. This time the bullet hit Gurunathan below the chest. His body jerked. Six constables then kicked him brutally all over his body and stamped on his face with their shoes. They seemed possessed in their assault. Moments later, Harikrishna picked up his Sten gun, held it to Gurunathan's abdomen, and pressed the trigger once.

Gurunathan shuddered violently and then went still. The SP put his foot under Gurunathan's head and raised it a little, as if to check whether he was alive. The head lolled to one side, limp and lifeless. Gurunathan was dead. Of all the men present, only Muthuram showed his discomfort.

Just before Gurunathan's body could be moved to Kollegala, a development took place that surprised Muthu by its suddenness. A young man named Bhilawendra was arrested and brought to the makeshift police camp at Kempayyana Gudde from Sandanpalya, where he lived. Muthu had seen him a few times before, but he now discovered that he too was a ration supplier to the Veerappan gang. It was Gurunathan who had told the cops about Bhilawendra, just before he died.

News of Gurunathan's death spread like wildfire. He had been second in rank to Veerappan. His death whipped up considerable curiosity and interest in the neighboring towns and villages like Ramapura, Hanur, Kowdalli, and Kollegala.

The official version of Gurunathan's death was that he had been killed in an encounter with the police in the Dinnalli forests. And nobody had reason to disbelieve it.

Meanwhile, Chandni had been beaten black and blue in the MM Hills police station. Muthuram, who knew both her and her mother, came to her aid. He begged Shakeel and Harikrishna not to arrest her or press legal charges. After much deliberation, they relented and let her go with a warning never to get involved with anyone with a criminal background again. But when Chandni reached the village, she was in for a shock: she had been completely ostracized. The villagers didn't want to have anything to do with a woman who had had a relationship with a gangster.

Again it was Muthuram who helped her out. He allowed her to stay in a room at the back of his hotel along with his mother, who was moved by her grief. Chandni began helping in Muthuram's business by cleaning dishes and chopping vegetables. However, in a month's time, rumors about her relationship with Muthuram began to circulate. Sensing Muthuram's discomfort, Nataraj decided to take her to his uncle's house in Sira, in Tumkur district. Chandni stayed with the family for a short while till Nataraj's uncle discovered her history and promptly sent her back to Ramapura. Neither Muthuram nor Nataraj knew what to do next. Their moral obligation toward her was too binding for them to abandon her. They decided to take her to the Ramapura police station and hand her over to SI Rachaiah. "Sir, please help her out in whatever manner possible," they begged. Finally, she married a Central Reserve Police Force (CRPF) constable, Putta Mallachar, and now lives in Bangalore.

# PART II

# 6

## In Cold Blood

Gurunathan's death came as a shock to Veerappan and his companions. He had been Veerappan's trusted aide in all matters, and an integral part of the gang's operations for a long time.

For a month after the incident, Veerappan walked around as if in a stupor. Then slowly he began to reconcile himself to the fact that life had to go on. But an uncontrollable anger against those who had done this smoldered within him. He would go into fits of rage, screaming profanities against the men in uniform. "Bastards, what do they think of themselves? Do they think they can take me on? If they were men enough, they would have confronted me and challenged me instead of taking Gurunathan so cunningly. They are all cowards. I will not spare a single one of them—just wait and watch. Do you think I can keep quiet after what they did to my Gurunathan?"

One evening in early April 1992, Veerappan called one of his men, Sethukuli Govindan, aside and said, "We have to do something soon to smash the confidence of the police. The dogs are starting to snap at our heels a little too much for our comfort. Think of a good plan. We should show them once more that they cannot act up with us, the bastards."

Sethukuli Govindan was another gang member in whose criminal acumen, daring, and loyalty Veerappan had great faith. A man of few words, he was consulted on all important matters by Veerappan. After Gurunathan, he was the man who could be Veerappan's lieutenant.

In the middle of April, when the gang was in the Nallur forest, Veerappan directed a ration supplier, Ramu, to find out what was happening in Ramapura. "Snoop around and try to get any information you can on what the police are up to now. Be very discreet in your inquiries and don't let anyone get a clue that you are our informer." Ramu complied.

So began Ramu's job to collect information on what was happening in Ramapura police circles. Did the police have a plan to nab Veerappan? What was the prevailing mood after Gurunathan's death? Had extra forces been brought into the area to scour the forests in search of the gang? Ramu began to hang around the station premises, indulging in idle talk with the constables on duty. He had a nodding acquaintance with one of the constables, Basavaraju. Accosting him one day, he began, "How are things with you? Looks like you are in a good mood today. These days you people are looking quite happy anyway, after Gurunathan's death."

The constable responded heatedly. "Do you think it's fun being a policeman, especially in these parts? We might have killed Gurunathan, but that doesn't mean we can afford to take things easy. That fellow might appear at any time, who knows?" He was referring to Veerappan. "Our bosses have been thinking of bringing a District Armed Reserve force to the area to strengthen us. They know we just cannot afford to be complacent. What if Veerappan retaliates?"

Soon after Gurunathan's death, Basavaraju said, the gang had tried abducting a police informer called Govinda, but fortunately he had escaped. The situation in the forest areas surrounding Hanur, Ramapura, and Kowdalli was so tense that policemen would move around only in convoys of five or six jeeps, fully armed.

Ramu had had his fill of information for the day. The possibility of a District Armed Reserve (DAR) group coming to Ramapura was news, and it had to be conveyed immediately to Veerappan. In the heat of the afternoon, while the town slumbered, Ramu made the long trek to Veerappan's hideout. "Sir, I have some news for you. They are planning to bring a DAR team and station it in Ramapura. I just spoke to a constable who told me all about it. He even told me they are apprehensive you might attack them at any time. It seems they don't want to take chances."

Veerappan laughed. "How can they take chances with me? I had a feeling they would call for reinforcements. Now it seems I was right. Anyway, keep watching them and let me know if there is anything really important."

Ramu returned to Ramapura and continued to act as Veerappan's spy. One day toward the end of April, he noticed a blue van drawing up at the police station. It had brought DAR personnel to Ramapura on special duty. Among them were Assistant Head Constable (AHC) Mahadeva, AHC Nagaraju, and Constables Prem Kumar, Elangovan, Govindaraju, Sundara, and Jayaram. The constabulary of the Mamballi police station was also present. The Chamarajanagar DSP had deputed Constables Rachappa, Mallikarjuna Prasad, Krishne Nayaka, Nagesh, and Siddaraju to work under the direction of SI Rachaiah. The police had multiplied their strength in the town many times over.

The next few weeks passed uneventfully. Veerappan and his gang continued to hide in the thick forests not too far from Ramapura, and the police, bolstered by the presence of the DAR men, began to grow complacent. Then on May 17, Veerappan made a decision. He told his men that they would attack the Ramapura station and "teach the bastards a lesson."

ON THE NIGHT OF MAY 19, 1992, Constable Rachappa was on sentry duty at the station. His shift was from 8 p.m. to 2 a.m. As Rachappa took up his position on the porch, a liquor contractor called Cheluvaraju walked in. "How are you, Rachappa? I hope you've had dinner?" Rachappa smiled and nodded his head.

Assistant Sub Inspector Subbanna, who was sitting inside the station, saw his friend walking in. "Where have you been all these days? I haven't seen you in a long time," he exclaimed.

"Oh, I was busy bidding for an *arrack* contract," Cheluvaraju replied. The two men chatted for a while, then sat down to play a round of cards. They were soon joined in the game by Constable Basavaraju and Head Constable (HC) Kappanna. The night wore on, and the three men became immersed as the card game began to heat up.

At about 12:30 a.m., the sound of an approaching bus broke the silence of the night. It stopped to take on board Najundaswamy, the "writer" of the station, who was on his way to Hanur, six miles away, to visit a relative. Out on the veranda, DAR constables Prem Kumar, Elangovan, and Govindaraju had settled down for the night. They were fast asleep on the floor, with sheets over them. So were Civil Constables (CC) Nagesh and Siddaraju. The sentry Rachappa, who had been sitting on a chair since 8 p.m., also decided to join them on the floor. The DAR van remained parked outside. AHCs Mahadeva and Nagaraju and Constables Sundara and Jayaram, along with driver Mahadevappa, slept inside it. The lights inside the station were on. Across the road in front, a streetlight glowed. All was calm. Right in front of the station, about sixty yards away, was SI Rachaiah's house. He slept inside with an AK-47 rifle by his bedside.

At a little distance from the station, where the cluster of shops and hotels was situated, Muthuram was getting ready to retire for the night on a wooden bench inside his small hotel. His cousin Kitta was with him. The time was nearly 1 a.m. and the two were chatting in low tones. All of a sudden, they heard what sounded like the crack of gunshots, from the direction of the police station.

"What the hell was that?" asked Muthuram.

"I don't know," said Kitta. "Let's go and find out."

The two men came out on to the road, looking in the direction of the station, which was about two hundred yards away. Harish, a radio mechanic, Puttaraju, another hotel owner, and Mahadevappa, a tent-cinema owner, also came out of their homes in the vicinity, awaked by the strange sounds. They clustered together, speculating on what could have made such a noise.

"Do you think they were gunshots? Or did someone switch on a motor to pump water in the fields?" asked Mahadevappa, looking at his watch.

"Why don't we go and check?" suggested Harish.

Not one of them realized what was actually going on just two hundred yards from where they stood. As planned, Veerappan had launched an attack on the police station along with his brother Arjunan, Sethukuli Govindan, Mariappan, Kolandai, Sunda, Kolanur Shekara, N. S. Mani, Vodkehalla Doreswamy, "Watchman" Kaliappa, Simon, and twenty-one others. The sleeping policemen were the first to be shot. They were easy targets for the gang, armed with single- and double-barreled guns. They pumped bullets into the policemen at point-blank range. Veerappan, wearing a khaki uniform like all the others and standing under a dhoopa tree inside the compound, shouted, "Don't spare anybody. Kill them all. Keep firing. Don't let anyone go."

Inside the station, ASI Subbanna screamed at Constable Basavaraju, "Shut the door!" They bolted the door and switched off all the lights. The bullets started thudding into the door as the men cowered in fear. After a while, bullets came smashing through the back door as well. The station was surrounded on all sides. Veerappan's men were firing as though crazed. Outside, AHC Nagaraju, who was inside the van, tried getting out through the back door to rush toward the SI's quarters. One of the gangsters noticed him and fired. He collapsed near the compound, injured and bleeding from the left thigh. Constable Rachaiah, who had been waked up by the commotion just a few yards in front of his house, was too terrified to shoot.

The firing stopped as suddenly as it had begun. Veerappan shouted to his men, "Let's go, let's go. Let's get out of here." The gangsters disappeared into the darkness behind the station, in the opposite direction from where they had come. But before fleeing, they entered the station from the rear and grabbed six single-barreled guns from the storeroom. The police had seized these guns on previous occasions from members of the gang.

Unaware that Veerappan had attacked the station, Muthuram told the others that he would go up the road to see what was happening. He sneaked up to the compound and peered across the wall. He saw five men sprawled on the ground, looking fast asleep. "What irresponsibility! There has been so much noise near the station and these guys haven't even bothered to get up and check," he thought. He drew closer and gazed down at the sleeping forms, puzzled. Suddenly he froze. There was blood everywhere. These men were dead.

Inside, Constable Basavaraju went on the wireless to the STF head-quarters. "This is an emergency. Veerappan has attacked the Ramapura police station. I don't know how many men have been killed, but it looks bad. Send forces to the area immediately. It's an emergency." A little later, Subbanna opened the station door and came out, his heart thudding. On the veranda he saw the lifeless bodies of Elangovan, Govindaraju, Prem Kumar, Siddaraju, and Rachappa. Their jaws had been smashed by rifle butts. Constable Nagesh lay near the SI's motor-cycle, which was parked in the compound. He was bleeding from the left arm.

Basavaraju's wireless message had been relayed to Hanur and Nal Road, in a radius of fifteen miles. Nearly an hour passed before KSRP vans drove into Ramapura. Twenty policemen jumped out of the vehi-cles. Nagesh and Nagaraju were sent to the Kollegala government hos-pital in one of the vans, moaning in pain. Pools of blood were now drying on the floor where the five policemen had died. There were bul-let marks on the van as well as on the walls of Rachaiah's quarters.

At about 5 a.m. the next day, Kollegala CI Mandappa reached the spot. A little later, STF commandant DIG Thimmappa Madiyal's car drew up. Soon after, SP Harikrishna and SI Shakeel Ahmed also reached the scene. Harikrishna was beside himself with fury. "Rachaiah, how could you not have opened fire? You were close enough to shoot and you had an AK-47. Why didn't you use it? With people like you in the ranks, no wonder Veerappan finds it easy to terrorize the force." De-spite his anger and notwithstanding the sincerity of a few good men, Veerappan had got away scot-free, once again. Clearly it would take more than anger and a few earnest policemen to prevent Veerappan from getting away with yet another attack.

# 7

## Veerappan's Revenge

Toward the middle of March 1992, a notorious smuggler, Mitu Naika, and his sons Kamala, Shivarama, and Dauzi were arrested by Venkataswami, CI of Hanur. They were taken to MM Hills and kept in the police lockup. As they languished in custody, Kamala Naika, an avowed Veerappan sympathizer who had found the ill-fated Gurunathan his bride, started talking to Shakeel Ahmed and Harikrishna about ways to capture Veerappan. A new chapter in his story was about to begin.

When Muthuram and Nataraj found out about Kamala Naika's designs, they rushed to MM Hills to meet Shakeel and Harikrishna. They pleaded with them not to trust Kamala Naika, but Harikrishna would not be dissuaded. Perhaps it was his obsessive desire to get to Veerappan that blinded him. The two friends finally gave up, and as the days went by they lost touch with the two officers.

But Muthuram and Nataraj did not forget their own ambition to put a bullet in Veerappan's head. They began to wander the forests surrounding Dinnalli Satyamangalam. They would hide near water holes for hours on end, in the hope that the bandit would come to the spot to camp. Muthuram later said, "The only creatures that came to the water holes regularly were peacocks! Thinking about it now, nearly eight years later, I feel like laughing. It was sheer madness."

In the meantime, Kamala Naika was released from the lockup along with his family, having convinced the two police officers that he would do his best to help them get to Veerappan. He now began to terrorize the *coolie* Nagaraj. Once he held a knife to his two little sons' throats, saying that he would kill them if Nagaraj did not leave Ramapura. The terror-stricken Nagaraj packed his belongings and left for Hassan, along with his family, to work on the farm of Malavalli SI Yellappa. For Muthuram and Nataraj too, the aftermath of Gurunathan's killing was not pleasant. Every time there was a knock on the door they feared it was Veerappan, and every sound in the night made them sit up in fear.

The tension was sometimes too much to bear. Nataraj began to drink almost daily. After getting drunk, he would start abusing the police. "Not only did they not give us any money for having helped them, they are cold-shouldering us now, the bastards. . . ." Muthuram's parents became afraid for their son's safety and asked him to leave Ramapura and live elsewhere. Nataraj, however, continued to live in the village, but his paranoia began to deepen by the day. To make matters worse, the other villagers were certain that Veerappan would seek vengeance against the two men.

So Nataraj decided to electrify the compound around his house. Every night, before he slept, he would run a long length of thick metal wire all around the house and connect it to the main 240-volt line overhead. Nataraj reasoned that if Veerappan turned up, he would die of electric shock. Meanwhile, he lost his job at the wine store. His employer was afraid to incur Veerappan's wrath by keeping on his staff one of the men responsible for Gurunathan's death. Nataraj was forced to leave Ramapura, broken mentally and financially. He is said to be living somewhere near Sira in Tumkur district.

In the meantime, Harikrishna had prevailed upon his superiors to begin strictly enforcing Section 144 of the Criminal Procedure Code, forbidding the assembly of more than five persons in the MM Hills area. This was done to stop work in the granite quarries on the patta lands, where, despite a ban on quarrying, granite continued to be extracted. It was public knowledge by now that one of the main sources of Veerappan's income was the regular payments from the quarry owners.

In the summer of 1992, Shakeel's elder brother, Mansoor, who worked as a civil engineer in Sharjah, was on holiday in India. He visited MM Hills along with a few of his friends to spend some time with his brother. While he was there, Mansoor happened to witness an ugly argument between his brother and Harikrishna on one side and a multimillionaire quarry owner, Veeran Mahadev, on the other. Veeran Mahadev blamed Section 144 for the quarry's losses, which ran into hundreds of thousands of rupees. He accused the police of wielding too much power and threatened to have the two officers removed from duty. But they refused to budge from their position.

Five months had passed since Gurunathan's death. Kamala Naika, ostensibly on a mission to find Veerappan, was moving around the MM Hills area in the guise of a police informer. But in reality, he was plotting the death of Shakeel and Harikrishna. Veerappan, who could not forgive the two officers for having taken the life of his right-hand man, had found in Kamala Naika an able ally to act out his script of revenge.

On August 13, Kamala Naika told Shakeel Ahmed that he had definite information that Veerappan's gang would be camping the next day in the forest between Yerrambadi and Sulekobe beyond Meenyam, about twenty-five miles from Ramapura. They were supposed to sell a huge quantity of ivory to a buyer. Shakeel instructed Kamala Naika to keep the news to himself, then rang up Harikrishna in Mysore, where the SP had gone on work. Shakeel was told to reach Kollegala the next day along with the informer.

At 7 a.m. the next day, Shakeel left MM Hills along with Kamala Naika and Constables Vrushabendrappa, Rangaswamy, and Ninje Gowda in his jeep. He drove straight to the Irrigation Department guesthouse in Kollegala, where DIG Thimmappa Madiyal was camping. Soon Harikrishna, who had driven down from Mysore in a white Ambassador, joined them. The officers debated for over one and a half hours about the pros and cons of raiding the place Kamala Naika was talking about. In the end, it was decided they should risk it.

The next day, the two officers drove into Ramapura at about 10 a.m. They spent some time in discussion with Rachaiah, the SI of the station.

Soon after, a bus belonging to the N. S. Transport Company was stopped by the SI as it passed in front of the station on its way to Meenyam from Kollegala. Harikrishna had ordered him to commandeer a bus to transport constables for the operation against Veerappan. The passengers were told that the bus wouldn't proceed farther on the route as it was required by the police.

The passengers got off the bus, grumbling about being so rudely inconvenienced. But after they had all disembarked, Harikrishna changed his mind and decided not to take the bus on the mission. The driver and the conductor were told that they could continue on their route. The passengers got into the bus again, wondering what the exercise had been all about. The bus left soon afterward on its way to Meenyam, eighteen or nineteen miles away. A few minutes later, Shakeel Ahmed waved down a lorry carrying a few rice bags. The driver stopped the vehicle and got down to find out what the officer wanted. He was taken inside the station, and the rice bags were unloaded from the lorry.

A twenty-two-member force composed of Kollegala CI B. D. Mandappa, RSI S. Hanumanthappa, RSI Devendrappa, ASI (Wireless Section) S. B. Benegonda, National Security Guards (NSG) commandos HCs Gangadhar and Lingaraju, Constables Kalappa, Appachu, Sundar, Mudalageri, Subramani, Venkateshappa, Munivenkataswamy, H. D. Kumar, and Belliappa Gowda, Mysore KSRP constables Shive Gowda, M. Seshanna, K. M. Subramani, Mahadeva, and Appanna, Ramapura station constable M. S. Lakshminarayana, and Siddaraju Naidu, posted at the Hanur police station, boarded the lorry.

Seated in the white Ambassador that Harikrishna had brought from Mysore were Shakeel Ahmed, Constables Shafiulla, Nagaraju, and Vrushabendrappa, and informer Kamala Naika, with Harikrishna at the wheel. Harikrishna had instructed the lorry driver to follow his car at a safe distance. The well-armed police party was ready to start from Ramapura for its rendezvous with the Veerappan gang.

Even as the police team was making last-minute preparations to leave, a man named Venkatachala was racing toward Meenyam on his Yezdi motorcycle. He was on the most important mission of his life: to inform Veerappan and his men about the impending departure of the police party.

The road to Meenyam is winding and narrow. It passes through dense forests with a deep valley on the right side and a steep embankment at the base of a succession of hills to the left. It was on this stretch, at a place called Boodhikere Halla, fifteen miles from Ramapura, that Veerappan had chosen an elevated spot to ambush the approaching convoy.

The gang had spent the previous two days digging three trenches, deep and wide enough to accommodate at least twenty men. Veerappan wanted to take advantage of the elevation as well as the dense tree cover. The planning was clinical, and foolproof. Veerappan and his men took up positions in the early hours of that fateful morning. The bandit waited patiently with his eyes firmly focused on the long stretch of road at least twenty feet below. He was determined to finish Shakeel and Harikrishna, who were becoming serious threats to him. With him were his trusted men: Sethukuli Govindan, Mariappan, Kolandai, Sunda, Kolanur Shekara, Arnaku Kumar, N. S. Mani, Simon, Vodkehalla Doreswamy, Aiyyan Dorai, Palaniswami, Armugam, "Betekara" Govinda, Ponnuswamy, Veeraswamy, Tangavelu, Gangadhara, Selvaraju, Ramuru, Mani, "Watchman" Kaliappa, Kunjappa, Paniswamy, and Savariappan. In their possession were .303 rifles, twelve-gauge Magnum Express shotguns, single- and double-barreled guns, and crude bombs. Veerappan himself preferred the Magnum Express, with its spraying effect, rather than the flat trajectory of the .303 rifle. They had enough ammunition to kill a hundred men.

As Veerappan and his men waited in hiding, they heard the drone of an engine in the distance. It was the bus that had been let off at the last minute by Harikrishna. The time was 11:50 a.m. There was no sign of the police convoy, and Veerappan was beginning to get irritable. Suddenly, he saw Venkatachala on his Yezdi, riding furiously down the winding road. He gestured to Veerappan that the police were on their way and sped away.

In a flash, a few of the gangsters jumped down to the road from their perch and started to place boulders across it. The time was 12:30 p.m. The final elements of the deadly trap were nearly in place. The men settled back in their positions. Around the same time, the police convoy headed by Harikrishna left the Ramapura police station.

Harikrishna was immersed in his thoughts as he drove. So was

Shakeel Ahmed. The constables didn't speak a word either to their superiors or among themselves. Kamala Naika sat smugly in the belief
that he had successfully lured the police team, including Veerappan's
chief enemies Shakeel and Harikrishna, to their doom. The lorry was
following the car at a distance of about half a mile. The journey from
Ramapura to Meenyam and beyond, to the actual spot somewhere
between Yerrambadi and Sulekobe, would take over an hour. But
Boodikere Halla, where Veerappan waited, was just a few minutes away.

From atop his perch, Veerappan could hear the roar of the car engine and also the lorry's, when they were more than three miles away.
When the white Ambassador came into view, he took position in one of
the trenches, hand on his Magnum Express, finger on the trigger. So did
all the others.

Harikrishna stopped the car when he saw the boulders blocking the
road. Grumbling and impatient, he called to Kamala Naika to get off the
car and remove the stones. Kamala Naika was waiting for just such a reaction from the officer. He hurriedly opened the door, as if wanting to
remove the obstacles. But instead of going toward the front of the car,
he ran to the back, jumped into the valley on the right, and disappeared
into the thicket.

Seconds later, a fusillade of bullets rained down on the car from
above. The trajectory was perfect, and from the distance of only about
twenty-five feet the bullets couldn't fail to find their victims. Even before
they could reach for their guns, Harikrishna and Shakeel slumped on the
front seat, cold and lifeless. Death was instantaneous. Constables
Shafiulla, Vrushabendrappa, and Nagaraj, who had ducked the direct
line of fire, were injured grievously.

Roughly eight minutes later, the lorry carrying CI Mandappa and the
others reached the spot. The gangsters trained their guns on the unsuspecting men inside the lorry. Valiantly, the policemen returned fire. But
crouching inside the covered lorry, their sight was hampered. Yet they
kept firing in the general direction from where the bullets were coming.

To make matters worse for the policemen, Veerappan's men began
to hurl their crude bombs at the lorry. The splinters and the shrapnel
struck those inside with such force that their bodies were severly lacerated. Still, they continued the gunfight. The hills echoed the sounds of

gunfire. They could be heard in Meenyam, nearly three miles away, to the astonishment of the villagers.

After about ten minutes, the guns fell silent. Veerappan and his men swooped down on the lorry like vultures in the wild. They started to gather quickly the "spoils of war": three .303 rifles, three hundred cartridges, a VL pistol, a pair of binoculars, two Manpac wireless sets, and two walkie-talkie batteries.

Sprawled dead on the spot were ASI Benegonda and Constables Appachu, Kalappa, and Sundar. CI Mandappa, SI Hanumanthappa, Constables Subramani, Belliappa Gowda, Shive Gowda, Lakshminarayana, and Siddaraju Naidu were seriously injured. The eight other policemen had escaped with minor abrasions. Benegonda's body carried evidence of the spray of bullets that had been directed at the lorry. Eight of them had smashed into his body. The constables had been hit fatally in their backs. On the left side of the road there were signs of an explosion. The stones on the ground had turned brownish black from the smoke. Half-burned pieces of cloth, shreds of fuse wire, and wooden pieces with green paint were strewn around. Investigating police later recovered from the scene a handmade bomb that had failed to explode. After it had been defused, it was found to contain a gelatin stick, a detonator, and fuse wire. The gelatin stick was connected to the detonator through the wire, and a polythene cover containing small stones as projectiles, mixed with chili and sambar powder, was tied around the stick with burlap threads. The windshield and windows of the Ambassador had been blown to smithereens, spraying a fine dust of minute glass pieces all around. The car bore multiple bulletholes, making it look like a grotesque sieve on four wheels. The car seats were splashed with bloodstains, broken glass, and even pieces of human teeth. So violent was Veerappan's assault that it had shattered the faces of both Shakeel and Harikrishna almost beyond recognition. There were six shotgun bullet wounds on Shakeel's body. Harikrishna's body too was riddled with bullets, with gaping holes in the neck, shoulder, and back. On the lorry, the left door of the driver's cabin bore multiple pellet marks. Lead pellets, bloodstains, half-burned cloth, and fragments of wood were strewn inside the cabin.

At the sound of a bus approaching from the opposite direction,

Veerappan and his men fled. It was the same bus Harikrishna had let go a few hours ago, on its return journey from Meenyam to Kollegala. As the driver drew close enough to see the destruction ahead of him, he stopped the bus, shouting in horror. All the men inside the bus rushed out. The women and children huddled together in fear. People shouted in confusion. Some of the injured were moaning in pain, and a few others were crying out aloud, begging for help.

A few of the passengers showed presence of mind and began shifting the dead and the injured into the bus. The cries of pain increased in volume as the villagers tried inexpertly to move the injured men. Amid the ensuing chaos, a policeman noticed a man trying surreptitiously to make his way onto the bus. It was Kamala Naika, the informer. In a fit of rage, the policeman pumped three bullets into him, killing him on the spot.

THE BODIES OF THE DEAD were taken to the general hospital in Kollegala and later shifted to Mysore for postmortem. The injured were rushed to Basappa Memorial Hospital in Mysore for immediate treatment. Hundreds of people began to gather in front of the mortuary in Mysore as news of the tragedy spread. Shakeel's death, especially, had touched a chord. A number of people who had not known him personally but had heard of his courageous deeds broke down in grief. His father, Abdul Kareem, slumped in his chair in his Yadavagiri house, unable to comprehend the fact that his valiant son was no more. Preetha, Harikrishna's wife, was inconsolable. Her two small children looked on, not knowing the reason for their mother's grief.

But Veerappan, who had again escaped into the depths of the forests, had made a vow in a Kali temple soon after the death of Gurunathan. These killings were the fulfilment of that vow.

# 8

## Explosion at Sorakaimadu

V eerappan's gang now included 150 members, twenty-five of whom were women. Police records estimated that they had 150 weapons, including four .303 rifles, five double- and six single-barreled guns, one Magnum Express rifle, and 134 country-made muzzle-loaders. Veerappan was also known to have over eight million rupees, extorted mostly from quarry owners in the area. He had an ingenious method of safeguarding the cash. Rubber tire tubes were filled with bundles of currency notes enclosed in plastic, sprinkled with insecticide, and buried at various places in the forest. The thick rubber tubes were both waterproof and insect-proof. Although he trusted his gang, Veerappan did not take chances where money was concerned. Even his own brother Arjunan was never taken into confidence on financial matters, because, it is said, he had once cheated Veerappan in an ivory deal. Except for two of his gang members, Vodkehalla Doreswamy and Mariappan, whom he trusted implicitly, nobody knew exactly where the cash was stashed away.

As Veerappan began to acquire an aura of invincibility, the odds against his capture continued to increase. The long stretch of dense forest he inhabited, interspersed by inaccessible mountainous terrain spread over an incredible array of seventy-seven hills, was almost impenetrable. These hills lie mostly inside Karnataka, but there are several hill ranges that stretch across the Tamil Nadu border as well. Veerappan moved freely on both sides of the border. Tracking him was like looking for a needle in a long line of giant haystacks, all linked together.

The STF was ill equipped to capture Veerappan. It was largely made up of officers of the rank of SI, CI, and SP, apart from the constables. They were selected on recommendations made to the Home Ministry by high-ranking officers, including the SPs and DIGs of various districts. But these supposedly handpicked policemen were adept at handling crimes and criminals only in an urban setting. To take on a man of Veerappan's cunning and criminality inside the forest a totally different orientation and training were required, and this the policemen lacked. They were not trained in guerrilla combat, and at no point were they given a detailed, practical understanding of the topography of the region.

To add to their difficulties, gathering intelligence on Veerappan's movements was proving extremely difficult, as the STF had antagonized many people in the villages in Veerappan's territory by dealing with them callously. Most of the villagers were too frightened to talk about Veerappan and refused to divulge details about him because of the manner in which they were questioned. There seemed little doubt, too, that of the two, incurring the policemen's wrath was safer than angering Veerappan. The men of the STF did not seem to realize that they had to win the confidence of the locals before they could expect any cooperation from them. The more they tried to force information out of the villagers, the more stubbornly they clamped up. The STF camps, the villagers claimed, were often converted into torture chambers. One of the detention rooms at the STF headquarters on MM Hills was crudely named "workshop." A high-security area, the camp was strictly off limits to the public, especially journalists. It was here, according to the local people, that anybody suspected of having information about Veerappan or his men was beaten and tortured, and women were brought and raped on the flimsiest evidence of conspiring with the gang.

By 1993, Chief Minister Veerappa Moily's government had reached the end of its tether. Finally, the government chose DIG Shankar Mahadev Bidri to take over the operations. On February 18, 1993, he was given overall charge of the Karnataka STF as its commandant.

In November 1992, three months before Bidri could take charge, about twenty to twenty-five men led by Veerappan had abducted a man called Chinna Gounder from Nallur. The gang swooped down on the house of Muthu, Gounder's uncle, where he was staying, at about 10 p.m. and took him away. Believing him to be a police informant, they dragged him into the forest and murdered him. After this they moved away to the forests of north Baragur. It was here, in Tamil Nadu, that Veerappan felt more secure. His fluency in Tamil allowed him to communicate and build a rapport with the local villagers more easily than in the Kannada-speaking areas. For the same reason, a majority of the ration suppliers to his gang were Tamilians. It also seems that he believed the Tamil Nadu police were less rigorous than their Karnataka counterparts in their operations against him. Their stand, as reflected in statements made by government spokespersons and police chiefs, was that since Veerappan had committed almost all his grave crimes in Karnataka, it was the responsibility of the Karnataka government to bring him under control.

Five months after the murder of Chinna Gounder, Veerappan killed again, this time in Tamil Nadu. In the small village of Govindapadi, about three and a half miles from Palar in Tamil Nadu, lived a man named Bhandari. He had become a police informant after he realized that there was more money to be made by helping the police than as a farm laborer. Unfortunately for Bhandari, it was not long before Veerappan found out about his source of income. On April 8, 1993, Veerappan shot him dead at point-blank range near his house. He then took his gang into the Valangolipatti forests not too far from Palar, in Karnataka.

Within minutes of the murder, the wireless in the office of SP "Rambo" Gopalkrishnan crackled to life. "Sir, there has been an attack by Veerappan and his men. One of our informers, Bhandari, has been killed. We are guarding his body. Please come to the spot as soon as possible."

"Rambo" was the chief of jungle patrol, Mettur division. A tough man, he had earned his sobriquet because of his daring as a police officer. He immediately called one of his officers, Inspector Ashok Kumar, to his chamber. Together they left for the village.

On reaching the spot, Gopalkrishnan began to make inquiries. One of the villagers, Raja, described the scene: "Sir, we were sitting near the tea shop when we heard a gunshot from behind a cluster of huts there." He pointed toward the outskirts of the village, something less than a mile away. "We ran toward the spot. When we reached there we saw Bhandari lying dead. There was no trace of Veerappan or any of his gang members. We found out later that they had moved to the Valangolipatti area in the Silvekkal forests beyond Sorakaimadu."

Gopalkrishnan decided to camp along with his men in the forest guesthouse and organize a search the following day. Sadayan, who was Bhandari's brother-in-law, also decided to stay the night in the guesthouse along with the policemen, fearing for his life. That evening at 6:30 p.m., Gopalkrishnan called a meeting of all the informers in the area. There were about fifteen of them. "Listen to me carefully," he began. "I have decided to launch an operation in the Valangolipatti area tomorrow at the break of dawn, where Veerappan is supposed to be hiding. I want all of you to accompany me on the mission. I need you to show me the way and also to help in securing the gangsters."

The next day, at about 6 a.m., Gopalkrishnan heard that a banner had been put up near a tea stall on the main road of Kolathur, an adjoining village, daring him to enter the forests in search of Veerappan. An informer, Ratinam, brought the news. "Sir, he has put it up to insult you. You should not allow such things to happen," Ratinam told him indignantly.

The language used in the banner was obscenely provocative. "SP," it proclaimed, "you shall die a dog's death if you enter the forests. Your brains as well as your balls shall be blown to bits. Come after me if you are man enough. . . ." It was obviously the handiwork of Veerappan himself.

When Gopalkrishnan reached Kolathur, he found to his surprise that the banner had been removed. But the locals confirmed that there had indeed been such a banner, tied between two poles near the main road. "Swami, we saw it fluttering here for the past two days. We don't know who removed it." Gopalkrishnan refused to be angry. He was too seasoned an officer to be provoked by such schoolboy pranks.

The police team returned to Govindapadi and after breakfast at about 10 a.m. set off in three vehicles: a minibus, a Gypsy, and a Trax utility van. Fifteen minutes into the journey, the bus broke down, and Gopalkrishnan was forced to stop at Palar for help. He sought out the policeman on duty, Karnataka RSI Kallappa, and introduced himself. Kallappa in turn got in touch with his superior, Commandant Shankar Bidri in MM Hills, over the wireless. Gopalkrishnan's request for vehicles and men to help him continue with the operation was granted at once.

BUT BHANDARI'S MURDER was only a part of another plot against the police force. Toward the end of March 1993, Veerappan had directed his gang members Madiah, Perumal, Basava, Rayan, Aiyyan Dorai, Muruga, Palaniswamy, Kolandai, and another man also called Muruga to dig pits, each four feet deep, on the Sorakaimadu mud road, about a mile inside the forest off the MM Hills–Palar road. The job was to be done in complete secrecy, so that even the local villagers did not get to know of it.

More than thirty-five men got down to work with shovels, crowbars, and spades. The chosen spot was hardly two miles from the STF post near the Palar bridge. The gangsters dug the pits mostly after sunset to avoid being seen and worked by starlight, without making any noise. They worked for close to a week.

After fourteen pits had been dug in a row, with six to ten feet separating each one, Veerappan ordered them to stop. The men still didn't know what the pits were for.

In the next two days, Veerappan's plan was revealed to the rest of the gang: the pits were to be filled with powerful explosives, so that any police convoy coming that way would be blown to bits.

"I want to kill them in such a way that no policemen will ever dare to come after me. I want to show them what it's like to die and have their bodies rot like the flesh of dead dogs on the road."

Accordingly, the gang members placed a huge quantity of explosives in each of the pits, connected them to one long stretch of fuse wire, which was drawn underground, inside a narrow strip of earth dug up for the purpose, between the pits. The pits as well as the narrow conduit for the wire were filled with stones and mud. To the casual eye, it looked as if nothing had been touched. The fuse wire connecting all the explosive-filled pits was drawn a distance of some two hundred feet up a rocky hillock.

The explosives had been stolen from two big granite quarry owners, Obalachetty of Obli Granites, based in Mettur, and S. Muthuraju, in Salem. It was Veerappan himself, along with his senior gang members—Sethukuli Govindan, Simon, Saraiveetu Govinda, and his brother Arjunan—who had arranged for the explosives to reach the hideout. Simon knew how to handle explosives and was put in charge of detonating them along with Manikya, Selvaraj, Tangavelu, and Muruga. Veerappan, with the rest of his gang, retreated into the Valangolipatti forests and waited there. He knew the police would come looking for him now that they knew he was in the vicinity.

Back at the Palar STF camp, two buses were put at the disposal of "Rambo" Gopalkrishnan, along with a posse of policemen, including ASI Vishwanath Belladh, eighteen constables, three forest watchers, sixteen informers, and Inspector Ashok Kumar of the Mettur jungle patrol unit. The police were armed with AK-47 rifles, light machine guns, Sten guns, autoloading rifles, and .303 rifles. They also carried hundreds of rounds of ammunition in wooden boxes. Gopalkrishnan was taking no chances.

It was 10:45 a.m. when the two buses started toward Valangolipatti, through the Sorakaimadu road inside the forest. "Drive carefully. Keep an eye out for any movement in the bushes or behind trees. If you see anything unusual, stop the vehicle and alert me," Gopalkrishna told Puttaswamy, the driver.

With Gopalkrishnan in the first bus were Constables Mahendran, Mohan Das, Rajashekaran, Selvan, Vijayakumar, Sukumaran, Dayalan, Swaminathan, Ramesh, Panchalingam, Laxman, Achutanandan, and

Cholan; the informers Shankaran, Ramanan, Suryakantan, Rangu, Ratinam, Chinnakolandai, Metturan, Rangan, Palaniappa, Gurunathan, Mani, Kolandaippan, Sedayan, Palani, Amasi, and Irasar; and forest watchers Shanmugam, Alagesan, and Srirangan. Inspector Ashok Kumar and the others, including HCs Krishnaswamy and Palaniswamy and Constables Marikan, Aburaj, Vijaykumar, Prabhakaran, and Govindaswamy, followed in the other bus.

At 11 a.m., the buses entered the thicker part of the forest. The road was so narrow that there was just about enough space for one bus to go through. There was dense vegetation on all sides. As the bus in front reached the Sorakaimadu area, the five gangsters hiding on the hillock braced themselves.

When the first bus was well and truly in the midst of the covered pits, an explosion was detonated that could be heard for miles. A massive cloud of dust rose up into the sky and then rained down, bathing everything around in mud. A few trees in the vicinity crumpled from the impact, and on the leaves and branches of those still standing could be seen mounds of red earth.

The bus was torn to shreds, its massive chassis dismembered and strewn all over. The tires were torn from their rims, and two of them lay completely misshapen among the trees at a distance of about twenty-five feet. The only proof of the vehicle's existence was a mangled mass of metal and thousands of pieces of rubble. The men in the bus had been blown to bits. Pieces of flesh stuck to the branches of trees all around.

All the informers except Irasar were dead. So were five constables from Tamil Nadu: Sukumaran, Dayalan, Swaminathan, Ramesh, and Panchalingam. Of the three forest watchers, only Alagesan was breathing. Miraculously, "Rambo" Gopalkrishnan survived the ordeal, though gravely injured. The others who managed to get away with their lives were the bus driver Puttaswamy, ASI Vishwanath Belladh, and Constables Laxman, Achutanandan, Cholan, Mahendran, Mohan Das, Rajashekaran, Selvan, and Vijaykumar.

Inspector Ashok Kumar, whose bus had stopped short of the pits sheerly by chance, jumped out of the vehicle and started firing his AK-47 blindly in all directions, undeterred by the death of most of the police team. "Don't stop firing, no matter what happens. Don't stop, keep firing," he screamed to the others. Krishnaswamy, Palaniswamy, Marikan, Aburaj, Vijaykumar, Prabhakaran, and Govindaswamy also opened fire.

Suddenly, Alagesan noticed some men running down a hillock, with guns in their hands. Among them he recognized Veerappan, Arjunan, and Aiyyan Dorai. There were about ten others with them, and they seemed to be going to get the guns from the dead men. The team, led by Ashok Kumar, fired at the men, and they retreated, vanishing into the undergrowth.

In the few minutes that had elapsed, Inspector Ashok Kumar had fired nearly ninety rounds. Head Constable Krishnaswamy had fired 135 rounds from his light machine gun. Constable Aburaj had had discharged thirty-eight rounds from his Sten gun. HC Palaniswamy had fired nine rounds from his autoloading rifle.

When Ashok Kumar realized that the gangsters had gotten away, he and his men began carrying the injured into the second bus, which was intact, and had them taken to Mettur hospital. As "Rambo" was lowered onto the hospital bed, in terrible pain from the wounds on his shoulder, head, and arms, he could only close his eyes in a silent prayer to God for saving his life.

After the bus had left with the injured, Ashok Kumar examined the spot. He noticed that a pair of night-vision binoculars had been shattered in the blast. A wireless set, an AK-47 rifle, a Sten gun, and two self-loading rifles (SLR) had been damaged beyond repair. Ammunition boxes had been blown up, making it impossible to ascertain how much ammunition had actually been lost. A putrid smell of mutilated human bodies and burned metal pervaded the area. Burned shoes and torn slippers lay scattered all around. The pits that had been blown up were now huge craters, forty-five to sixty feet in diameter.

Up on the hillock, there was enough evidence to show that the gang had actually lived there for several days before perpetrating the crime. Small aluminum vessels, half-burned wood, and remnants of ash indicated that food had been cooked. Packets of provisions were also found, along with fuse wires, plastic bottles containing gunpowder, a bedsheet, and a flashlight.

Later, the police traced the route the explosives had taken to reach Veerappan's gang. Documents relating to the supply of these substances by two firms, Balaji Explosives and Sri Ganapathi Explosive Contractors to Obli Granites, were seized. They proved that explosives had been supplied to the granite company in 1990 and 1991, obviously for blasting rocks. Unfortunately, some of the stuff had found its way into Veerappan's hands.

It turned out later that Veerappan's plan could easily have been foiled if a sentry named Ezhumalai at the Palar STF camp had been more diligent. He had been told by a woman who did odd jobs at the camp in exchange for some food that her husband had been getting up at the unearthly hour of 3 a.m. for the past four to five days and carrying tea to someone. "*Swami*, there has been something strange about his behavior of late. He has been leaving home long before sunrise and going into the forest. He carries flasks of tea and if I ask who he is taking them for, he doesn't answer. I have been eating at your camp. I do not want to betray anyone who has fed me. Tell your officers to call him and ask him what he is up to." The woman's intentions were good, but the sentry didn't take her seriously, and did not bother to investigate her statement.

Ironically, when the Opposition in the Tamil Nadu Assembly had raised the issue of Veerappan a few days before this incident, Jayalalitha's government had stated that Veerappan did not exist at all. Even if he did, they said, he was somewhere in Bombay.

In spite of everything the police did, Veerappan continued to elude them. But they did succeed in capturing a few of his gang members. On June 27, Karnataka STF inspector Madhukar Musale arrested Guna in the Nadumalai forests. He was carrying a single-barreled muzzle-loader, some gunpowder, and seven iron balls to be used as pellets.

On the same day, Muthu of Karangalur and Madiah belonging to Devaramalai were taken into custody by CI Kumaraswamy. Two weeks later, two more gangsters, Mani from Kolathur Tanda and Ganesha of Urugampatti, were arrested. On July 25, an important member of the Veerappan gang, "Meke" Madiah, surrendered when the STF surrounded him. His single-barreled gun was seized. Five days later, Madhukar Musale hauled in two more gang members, Chinnasalatta

Mani and Krishna Chetty of Nallur. A single- and a double-barreled gun were seized from them.

Before these arrests, however, a little over a month after the Sorakaimadu blasts, yet another unsuspecting police convoy was ambushed, at a place called Rangaswami Oddu near MM Hills. The war of attrition seemed to go on and on.

# 9

## Change of Command

T he bombs that exploded at Sorakaimadu took with them not only the lives of twenty-two men but also any semblance of confidence that remained in the police ranks. Chief Ministers Veerappa Moily and Jayalalitha, in mutual consultation, appointed Walter Dawaram, an additional director general (ADDL. DGP) of the Tamil Nadu unit, as the joint commandant of both the Karnataka and Tamil Nadu STFs. Shankar Bidri was to be his second in command.

Dawaram was a tough policeman who led from the front. He had once stormed the Vellore prison to quell riots sparked by incarcerated LTTE members and had the reputation for motivating his men. Upon taking charge, he asked for volunteers from among the 82,000-member Tamil Nadu police force to fight Veerappan. Five hundred policemen answered Dawaram's call, out of which 250 of the fittest men were selected. After a month's training, on May 12, 1993, Dawaram and his men entered Veerappan's territory in the first concerted effort by the Tamil Nadu STF.

Meanwhile, in a converted portion of a row of public works department (PWD) guesthouses not very far from the famous Mahadeshwara temple, an agitated Shankar Bidri, the commandant of the Karnataka STF, sat in his office. Although he was just three months in office as the STF's commander, Bidri, a hard-nosed, no-nonsense officer, was anxious to launch an operation against Veerappan. He drew out a cigarette from the Three Fives packet lying on his table and lit it. As the smoke from his cigarette curled into the air, he indulged in dark thoughts about the most wanted man in his territory. He was jolted out of his reverie by the ash that fell from his cigarette tip, and burned into his trouser leg. He looked around impatiently for an ashtray, then shouted to the sentry, "Mahadevappa, how many times have I told you to clean my ashtray and keep it in its place here? Idiot . . . you'll never learn." As the panic-stricken sentry brought the ashtray, Bidri stubbed out the cigarette, walked out of his office, and drove away in his bulletproof Gypsy in the direction of Talbetta, eleven miles down the winding Ghat road. It was 11 a.m. Talbetta was at the foot of MM Hills, with a cluster of small shops and eateries. It was home to approximately fifteen families.

As Bidri drove down, six men were closely watching his every move. Rangaswami Shettiar, Rangaswamy, Dhanapala, Chikkeranna, Puttiah, and Halaga were Veerappan's informers. Keeping an eye on all police movements in the MM Hills area was their only duty. Any unusual activity had to be reported at once.

"We must go and tell *Aiyya* about this," said Halaga.

"Let's wait a little longer and see if there is any more police movement toward that area," replied Puttiah. "These police fellows never tire of chasing our *Aiyya*, by the looks of it. Even after the bomb blasts, this Bidri hasn't given up."

"What do we have to lose, anyway? *Aiyya* pays us well and that's all we want. To hell with everything else." Dhanapala was beginning to get restless. "Let's go and inform *Aiyya* about the police, especially Bidri. He's been in a bad mood since the bomb blasts. Come on, we have a long way to cover."

They climbed into a bus going toward Baragur in Tamil Nadu, about eighteen miles away, where Veerappan and his men had taken refuge after the Sorakaimadu bomb blasts. Arriving in Baragur, the informers spent most of the evening smoking *beedis* and drinking cups of tea at a roadside tea shop. They spoke to each other in low tones as they waited for nightfall. When the sun had set, they began their trek through the forest to Veerappan's hideout. The starlight was bright enough for them to find their way by, so accustomed were they to the forest and its routes.

The six men reached the hideout without any difficulty. *"Vanakkam Aiyya,"* they said with folded hands as they stood in front of Veerappan.

"What brings you here? Is there anything you have to tell me?"

*"Aiyya,* the police are in an angry mood. Bidri and his men are moving around, mainly in MM Hills. We saw Bidri going toward the Talbetta side this morning."

Veerappan didn't say anything. But after the informants left, he began ranting bombastically about another plan to intimidate the police. "So the police think they can scare me, do they? There is no one in this world who can take me on. If I decide to do something, nothing will stop me. I shall soon show the world my true strength. Men, start making preparations. Those bastards need to be told from time to time that there is only one Veerappan in this world and he can never be taken lightly."

Around this time, a police informer was also on the job. Rushing to MM Hills, he went straight to SP Gopal Hosur. Speaking in a hushed tone he said, *"Namaskara Swami,* I have brought some news about Veerappan for you. Credible enough for you to take seriously."

"What is it?" asked the SP, leaning forward in his chair.

The informer, who was also an LTTE sympathizer, looked around him as if to ensure nobody else was listening. He began, *"Swami,* Baby Veerappan will be going to Palani between May 20 and May 24 to shear his locks in fulfillment of a vow made to Lord Muruga. I'm sure you'll be able to nab him there without any difficulty." Baby Veerappan was one of Veerappan's closest aides, known for his long hair and his habit of imitating his older namesake.

Gopal Hosur was delighted with the news. "Good, very good. As you say, it shouldn't be difficult for us to get him, once he's in Palani." Palani, a famous temple town in Tamil Nadu, was at a distance of approximately 125 miles from MM Hills. Veerappan's men were known to grow their hair religiously for a period of one year every time they committed a major crime, before going to a temple to offer the hair.

Gopal Hosur was a committed officer who had volunteered to be part of the STF in late 1991 soon after the force was created. He had been posted as SP (Intelligence) in Belgaum at that time. Soon after he became part of the STF, he began to familiarize himself with Veerappan's terrain and habits. Because he disagreed with SP Harikrishna's methods of interrogation and intelligence gathering, he had gone back to his former position after only a couple of months in the STF. But he returned on May 10, 1993, on assignment from the government. A product of the famous Sainik School in Bijapur, Hosur was known for his tenacity.

As soon as the informer left, Hosur called a meeting of his subordinate officers, Inspectors Ashok Kumar, Ahmed Bawa, and Saudagar. It was decided that all of them, headed by Gopal Hosur, would leave for Palani immediately. The team was confident. It was clear that the gangster would not carry any firearms into the bustling temple town in full view of the thousands of devotees there. At best he would have a knife or dagger or some other small weapon. A police team could disarm him with ease.

Commandant Shankar Bidri was away in Bangalore for a couple of days. Gopal Hosur telephoned him from the STF headquarters to update him. On the night of May 20, a police team composed of Gopal Hosur, Ashok Kumar, Bawa, Saudagar, and ten constables left MM Hills in three jeeps for Mettur, en route to Palani. At Mettur, they met their informant.

Reaching Palani the next day, they donned civilian clothes and walked around the town in the guise of devotees. They had with them photographs of Baby Veerappan, with long flowing hair. Going up to a barber near the temple, Ashok Kumar chatted casually for a while before pulling out the photograph. "Have you seen someone like this man here in the photograph? He's a friend of mine and I'm looking for him."

The barber looked closely at the picture, then shook his head. "So many men come to me every day. I don't normally take a close look at any of them. Anyway, they all look so similar with their long hair." Making the rounds of almost all the barbers in the vicinity of the temple, Kumar drew a blank.

While they were in Palani waiting for the gangster to arrive, news came that there had been a bloody encounter between a Tamil Nadu police team led by Walter Dawaram and Veerappan's gang on the banks of the Palar River in the MM Hills area. Gopal Hosur decided to rush back immediately to MM Hills, because it appeared to have been a major encounter and the Tamil Nadu STF might need their help combing the forest. On reaching MM Hills, he learned that Walter Dawaram and his team, while on a routine combing operation, had sighted a few men, including Veerappan, bathing in the Palar River four or five miles inside the Sorakaimadu forest area. There had been an exchange of fire in which one gangster had been killed, but Veerappan and the others had managed to escape. The police later found out that the gangsters had been taking a ritualistic bath before leaving on the pilgrimage to Palani to fulfill their vow.

GOPAL HOSUR'S TRIP to Palani had been wasted. But the failed attempt in no way altered his resolve. "If not this time, we shall succeed the next time," he told his men.

Around this time, Hosur was preparing to go on leave for a few weeks to celebrate his sister's wedding on June 10 in Hubli. Unknown to the police, Veerappan had slipped back into the MM Hills area. Along with him were his men Mariappan, Naga, Papa, "Mese" Madiah, Aiyyan Dorai, Andiyappan, Amasi, Arjuna Kundan, Perumal, Murugan, and Raja.

The winding road from MM Hills to Talbetta and beyond, to the towns of Kowdalli, Ramapura, Hanur, and Kollegala, had twenty-seven hairpin bends. It passed through a densely forested mountainous region whose continuity was broken only by deep valleys and chasms, mostly inaccessible to humans. Between the eleven-mile stretch from the top of MM Hills to Talbetta at the base was a place called Rangaswami Oddu. Close by was a small temple, said to be very old, which was dedicated to Lord Shaneshwara. A banyan tree, a few hundred years old, stood by the side of the road. It was here, about two and a half miles from the top, that the eighteenth hairpin bend curved down the road. And it was here that Veerappan and his men positioned themselves, at Anehola, near the milestone. They knew that this was the only road up to the STF headquarters, and was therefore used by the police frequently.

On the evening of May 23, 1993, Hosur returned to MM Hills, completely exhausted. He had spent the entire day conducting an outreach program. The purpose was to establish contact with as many villagers as possible in Veerappan's area of operation, listen to their problems, suggest remedies, educate them about the futility of siding with Veerappan, and, more important, make them understand that with the STF on their side, they were completely safe from him. Hosur went about this task methodically. He would contact influential people in the villages, including the *headmen*, schoolteachers, nurses, and others in whose credibility the villagers had faith. Then he would impress upon them the need to put an end to the gang's menace. Hosur was so tired that evening that he fell asleep instantly, having left instructions to be waked up early the next day for his journey to Hubli.

Next morning, at 7:15 a.m., three jeeps stood in front of the main office of the STF headquarters on the hill. Gopal Hosur had asked to be escorted down MM Hills on his way. In the first jeep, driven by Constable Narasappa, were RSI Uthappa and Constables Machiah, Pooviah, Prabhakar, and Swami. The second jeep carried Hosur along with the driver, Constable Ravi. The third jeep, with HCs Mahadevaiah and Sheshappa and Constables Bopiah, Ashoka, Sanjeeva, and Venkatesha, brought up the rear. Senior police officers no longer moved around the MM Hills area without proper escort, for fear of an ambush. The police teams escorting Hosur were armed with SLRs capable of firing twelve rounds at once.

The convoy set off at 7:30 a.m. Gopal Hosur's jeep was in the middle. As the policemen wound their way through the gut-churning twists and turns of the Ghat road down the hill, disaster was waiting to strike them. Near Anehola, by the side of the road, behind the stone embankments, Veerappan and his men waited. Their planning had been meticulous and their timing was absolutely perfect. The three jeeps were traveling at a distance of roughly fifteen yards from one another. As the driver of the first jeep, Narasappa, was getting ready to bank the curve at the hairpin bend, he heard the unmistakable crack of a gunshot. Before anyone could register the impact of the first shot, which had hit the side of the jeep, there was a flurry of gunfire from the right side of the road. More bullets thudded into the car, and the policemen slumped in their seats one after the other.

The attack lasted for only about a minute, but in that minute, everyone in the jeep was killed: Uthappa, Machiah, Pooviah, Prabhakar, Swami, and the driver, Narasappa. They had no chance to return fire. Swami had been hit at the base of the neck from behind. The bullet had torn through his skull, rendering the face so grotesque that it looked like a hideous mask.

Gopal Hosur had been reading a newspaper as the jeeps meandered their way down the hill. No one could have anticipated an attack so close to one of the busiest roads in the region. At the sound of gunfire he looked out in horror at the bullet-ridden jeep in front. "Oh my God, we have been attacked, we have been attacked," he gasped, his face turning a bleached white in distress.

Veerappan urged his men on from behind the stone wall that was concealed from view by bushes. "Hit them, hit them. Don't stop firing. We can get all of them, there is no need to fear. They cannot even see us. Go ahead and finish them off." It was impossible for the policemen to target their attackers properly. As Gopal Hosur's jeep jammed to a halt near the scene of carnage, the gangsters resumed their fire with blinding ferocity. A ricocheting bullet hit Hosur in the neck. One smashed into Ravi's right elbow, and his hand dangled like a broken branch, with absolutely no strength in it. Without losing his composure, Ravi reversed the vehicle with his left hand and struggled to drive it back, out of the range of fire. "Take the jeep as far back as possible before you take a U-turn. Come on, be quick," cried Hosur, unmindful that he had been severely wounded and was completely drenched in blood.

The last jeep had come to a grinding halt as soon as the sound of firing was heard. HCs Mahadeviah and Sheshappa along with Constables Bopiah, Ashoka, Sanjeeva, and Venkatesha dived from their seats and took position behind trees. Their guns came to life as they began to fire in the direction of the gangsters. The ricocheting bullets scraped the tree trunks. As the constables kept firing, Veerappan and a few of his men emerged from behind the stone wall, onto the road. Running to the first jeep, they snatched five self-loading rifles (SLRs) and a cache of bullets. One of the gangsters rushed toward the third jeep and grabbed a wireless set. "Let's go, let's go. We have done enough, let's get out of here," Veerappan shouted.

In the meantime, Hosur had contacted the STF base on his wireless. "There has been a disaster. Veerappan has attacked our party . . . near Rangaswami Oddu. Our men have been killed . . . there are injuries . . . come with staff . . . be quick . . . Veerappan has got . . ." He couldn't complete the sentence. As his jeep sped on the road back to MM Hills, his mind went blank. The hit to the base of his neck had ruptured his throat, and blood poured out every time he gasped. His time was running out.

Back at headquarters, there was pandemonium. "How did it happen? How many men have died? Is SP *sahebru* all right?" Shankar Bidri was shouting to his men, "Be quick, get to the scene. Get there as fast as possible. Pick up your arms. Go, go."

As Inspectors Ashok Kumar, Bawa, and Saudagar and DSP Mudaliah and their men drove down the road, they met Gopal Hosur in his jeep. He was on the verge of collapse. "Veerappan has done it again. We have been ambushed. They are all dead . . . a little distance from here. . . . Do something about it. . . . They are there." He managed to point weakly in the direction from which he had come.

Inspector Ashok Kumar didn't waste even a minute. "Sir, you reach MM Hills," he said to Hosur. "We'll go to the spot as fast as we can. You keep going."

As soon as the SP's jeep had escaped toward MM Hills, Mariappan, Naga, Papa, and "Mese" Madiah had set into motion the second part of their plan. They chopped furiously to fell a tree by the two-and-a-half-mile milestone. It came crashing to the ground, across the road, and completely blocked the way for reinforcements arriving from MM Hills. Veerappan's attack, as usual, was military in precision and planning.

When Ashok Kumar's jeep reached the scene, he was furious. He roused his men to push the tree to one side. It took several minutes to do the job.

When Ashok Kumar and the others finally reached the scene, it presented a horrific picture. Six men lay dead in pools of blood. Their jeep had been pumped full of bullets. The seats had been ripped by the intensity of gunfire. Shreds of flesh were spattered all over.

The six dead policemen were immediately taken to the Kollegala government hospital, as were the injured constables, Ashoka and Bopiah.

SP Gopal Hosur was rushed in Shankar Bidri's car to Mettur Hospital, about eighteen miles away. But the services of a cardiothoracic surgeon were available only in Salem, thirty miles from Mettur. By then, wireless messages had been flashed to almost all the police stations on the route about the emergency. The police, under the direct instructions of the chief minister, had cleared the entire thirty-mile stretch of road from Mettur to Salem of all human and vehicular traffic to facilitate the passage of the car carrying Hosur. At the Salem Hospital, a team of doctors was in attendance, waiting to perform emergency surgery. After a few weeks, he was moved to St. John's Hospital in Bangalore, where he spent six excruciating months hovering between life and death. His life was eventually saved by an operation that rebuilt the muscular wall between the food and wind pipes, using a portion of his chest muscles.

Later, it came to light that information about Gopal Hosur's movements was leaked by a servant who had worked in SI Shakeel Ahmed's quarters in MM Hills.

# 10

## The STF Strikes Back

The STF headquarters on MM Hills had the appearance of a mini army camp. In addition to the operational units of policemen whose sole focus was the capture of Veerappan and his gang, there were two support teams in charge of intelligence gathering and security. While members of the intelligence team worked the villages in the area, usually disguised as laborers, seeking information about the fugitives, those in charge of security kept a twenty-four-hour vigil on the arms depot, the vehicle lot, and the provisions store at the camp. There were nearly forty-five jeeps, ten buses, a huge cache of arms and ammunition, and hundreds of pounds of food that had to be guarded. Gasoline and diesel fuel were also stored in the camp, in thousands of gallons. A team headed by the motor transport officer (MTO) was responsible for the vehicles in the camp. The assistant MTO was in charge of allotting vehicles to the ten platoons that were in operation. Mechanics worked on the daily maintenance of the vehicles. The security unit in camp consisted of an ASI, two HCs, and three constables, who worked in shifts.

Every member of the STF, regardless of rank, worked continuously for twenty-eight days, then took a week's leave. The policemen, although paid an additional 50 percent of their basic pay, worked under such high pressure that their leave period was eagerly anticipated. And when they finally boarded the private bus that would take them to Kollegala or Mysore, en route to their final leave destination, the policemen took care to disguise themselves as pilgrims visiting MM Hills, with a liberal smear of sacred ash on their foreheads and a spot of vermilion. It was a standard precaution in case Veerappan waylaid the bus.

Life in the STF ranks was far from easy. Search operations in the jungles sometimes extended to days, and involved trekking for miles with heavy equipment and the bare minimum of rations. Each man carried a water can, day-night-vision binoculars, AK-47 rifle, pistol, and dozens of cartridges, a sheet or a blanket, and food packets consisting mainly of dry chapattis and vegetables. Heavy grenades were stuffed into dungaree pockets, and there was always the danger of the grenades rubbing against each other and exploding, unless the safety pins were kept carefully in place. The presence of poisonous snakes and scorpions made the jungle a dangerous place, especially in the night, in spite of the heavy boots the men wore. The flashlights they carried only lit up the area just in front of their feet so they wouldn't give away their location.

Water was a precious commodity and would often run out before an operation concluded. Every time they found themselves without water in the jungle, the policemen would use their *banians*, or any other piece of cloth available, to filter the muddy water in the jungle ponds and quench their thirst.

Traveling by road during the night in a convoy of jeeps was no less stressful, especially for members of the pilot party, which carried powerful searchlights that they switched on only while returning to base from a combing operation. Holding these heavy lights aloft and panning them continuously, sometimes for hours, left them with aching elbows and limp hands at the end of an operation. They also traveled without any cover and were likely to be shot first in the event of an attack.

VEERAPPAN AND HIS GANG MELTED into the MM Hills forests after the Rangaswami Oddu incident, leaving the STF angry, humiliated, and desperate to retaliate. Shankar Bidri was furious at the ease with which the bandit had murdered his men time and again. Their morale had taken such a beating that it was difficult to find a policeman, irrespective of rank, who would patrol Veerappan's territory with any courage or conviction. The regular bursts of violence against unsuspecting policemen made the majority of them wish for a speedy transfer out.

The Karnataka government, led by CM Veerappa Moily, was beginning to despair. The CM was clearly clueless on how to contain the violence in the forest areas along the Karnataka–Tamil Nadu border. In Tamil Nadu, Jayalalitha finally decided that it was time to act. The two governments jointly decided to requisition the services of the Border Security Force (BSF). Five companies, headed by Commander Bhinder, were pressed into service. The BSF, with its superior fighting capabilities, was expected to finish off Veerappan easily.

The BSF was so confident of completing its mission within a few days that the train compartments that brought them to Mysore remained parked in a corner of the station for a short while, in preparation for their return.

But the BSF was taking on an enemy of rare cunning and in a terrain it was unfamiliar with. The forests were too vast and complex for the BSF to even comprehend. Their lack of familiarity with the local languages, Kannada and Tamil, was also a major impediment to intelligence gathering. Further, the BSF was never given independent command of the operations. The STF chief Shankar Bidri continued to be the man in command.

It appears, too, that a majority of the BSF *jawans* were simply unwilling to take orders from the policemen. They felt that it was beneath their dignity to work under a civilian outfit. Arguments and ego clashes were common. Most of the policemen in both the Tamil Nadu and the Karnataka STF did not speak Hindi and found it difficult to build a rapport with the *jawans*. In February 1994, the two governments decided to send back three companies of the BSF because they felt that not much headway was being made. Another company was sent back in August the same year, and the final company left in April 1995.

JUST TWO DAYS AFTER the attack on Gopal Hosur and the others, on May 24, 1993, the Tamil Nadu STF, while on a routine combing operation in the Kallatti forests, discovered and defused forty-five land mines planted by the gang. A few weeks later, on June 16, there was another encounter between the gang and the Tamil Nadu STF in the Donimaduvu forests in which as many as fourteen gangsters were arrested. One of the key men to be taken into custody was Simon, the explosives expert.

On the Karnataka side, Bidri made a few arrests, which brought some cheer to the STF camp. Pankade Shekara, Chinnakanna, Naga, Papa, Chinappa, Kolandairaju, Puttamadiah, Mahadeva, and Veeranna were some of the gang members taken into custody. The police also began to investigate and erode the nexus between gunrunners and the gang. Three gun repairers in the area, Ramachari, Rangaswamichari, and Chikkuduga, were rounded up. Chikkuduga confessed that Veerappan and his men had given him eleven guns to repair. He told the police he had hidden them in bushes inside the forest. Rangaswamichari also revealed that Veerappan had come to his house along with fifteen other men one night in the first week of June and had given him five single-barreled guns for repair. He had been paid an advance of fifty rupees. "As policemen visit my village, Kadatti, often, I couldn't repair the guns. I took them to the forest one night and hid them in the bushes."

The task force tightened under the command of Dawaram and Bidri, and they managed to eliminate a number of wanted gangsters. Two months after the Rangaswami Oddu ambush, five gangsters were shot dead near Parangi Betta after the STF surrounded their hideout, acting on information about the camp from informers. Soon after this encounter, nine more gangsters fell to police bullets in the Sankarmalai forests. Three more were killed near the Karikallu Gudda forest. Shankar Bidri had decided to focus on reducing the strength of the gang, even if he could not get Veerappan himself. The bandit was proving as elusive as ever. So fierce was his determination that in July of that year, he is said to have strangled a newborn baby of one of the gang members to prevent its cries from giving away the gang's location.

On September 28, Kulla, a police informer, brought interesting news to the Dimbam camp. "Namaskara Swami," he began with folded hands, "I have information that Veerappan and his gang are camping in the Minchguli forests. They've built a row of huts and are staying there without any fear of the police. I also know that there are women living with the gang now." Minchguli was in the Punajanur area about fifteen miles from Chamarajanagar.

The Tamil Nadu STF was immediately informed, and it was decided they would launch a joint operation the next day.

Deep inside the forests, Veerappan's wife, Muthulakshmi, was relaxing with a few other women, wives of the other members of the gang. Her brother-in-law Arjunan was with them. As the gang lounged in the soft warmth of the early-morning sun, shots began to ring out and there was panic in the camp. The police had surrounded the area. Arjunan sprang to his feet. He realized he had to make a quick getaway if he wanted to save his life. "Come on, quick, make a run for it. And be silent, don't make any noise," he whispered urgently to Muthulakshmi. Holding her hand, he began to run deeper into the forest. The other members of the gang too were running in different directions. In the thick outgrowth, the police could barely distinguish the figures of the fleeing men and women.

Within minutes, the gang members had vanished. When the police eventually reached the camp they saw that a lone woman was left behind. She was in an advanced stage of pregnancy. Veerappan himself had not been in the camp that day. He had told his wife and the others that he would be going out to some other part of the forest on "work." He had left word that in case there was a police raid on the hideout while he was away, they should make their way to the Mamarathapalli forests.

As the police surveyed the campsite, they were taken aback to see the comfort in which the gang had lived. There was a row of huts with thatched roofing to ward off the rain. Inside each hut was a bedroom and even a place to bathe. There were toilets in the form of septic tanks, hidden on all four sides by coconut fronds. It was clear that they had been living in the area for months, unmindful of police movement in the vicinity. Strangely, the police had never noticed the elaborately constructed structures, not very far from the Dimbam STF base.

As the police took over the campsite, Muthulakshmi wandered the forests, lonely and terrified. She had been abandoned by Arjunan and was now all alone. Her bare feet were lacerated by thorns. Her clothes were torn and leeches clung to her body. Blood oozed from the cuts and left a trail as she dragged herself along a forest path, not knowing where she was headed. To add to her misery, it began to rain heavily. She continued to walk with great difficulty, summoning all her courage and will, till she reached a *doddi* (cattle pen) deep inside the forest. By then she was soaking wet, and cold. Shivering violently, she called out desperately for help.

An old man working in the cattle pen heard her cries and went over to her. "What has happened to you? Come over here. You don't need to fear anything. Sit down and rest for a while. No harm shall come to you."

As Muthulakshmi tried to compose herself, he brought her a cup of curds. She drank it in one gulp. "Thank you so much. You saved my life. Otherwise I would have collapsed out of fear and exhaustion. Thank you." Even as she was wiping her mouth on the corner of her tattered saree, she heard footsteps in the undergrowth. At once she knew it was the police searching for her. She dived into a thick bush and hid there without making the slightest noise.

Moments later, about twenty policemen holding guns burst into the clearing. Looking at the old man, they hollered, "Hey you, did you see anyone running in this direction? Come on, tell us. Did you see anybody running past here?"

The old man looked at the bush where Muthulakshmi was hidden. A minute ticked by, then another—for Muthulakshmi, an eternity. "No, sirs, I have not seen anyone around," he said emphatically. The policemen left the place after looking around halfheartedly, grumbling to one another.

MUTHULAKSHMI REMAINED HIDDEN in the bush until evening. When she emerged close to sunset, two cattle-grazing boys confronted her. "Look at that, what a beauty! Who ever imagined we would find someone like this inside the forest? Hey, what's your name? Come close to us, come on," they coaxed. Their intentions were far from noble.

Muthulakshmi, not to be daunted, shouted back, "You dogs, don't you dare do anything to me or even come close to me. Do you know who I am? I'm Veerappan's wife." The moment they heard the name Veerappan, the two boys vanished without a trace.

Suddenly, night having fallen, Muthulakshmi realized she had no idea what to do or where to go. She began to walk aimlessly toward a hillock close by. It began to rain again. She climbed the hillock and slumped under a tall tree. She was crying by now, the tears welling up in her eyes uncontrollably. Cold and hungry, she decided to spend the night under the tree. She tried to imagine what her husband might be doing at this moment. Would she ever be with him again? What had happened to the others in the gang? Where was Arjunan? She battled with the demons of darkness and her own fears, unable to sleep, till the first rays of sunlight began to streak through the forest between the hills in the distance.

As she looked around in the new light, trying to gauge where she was, Muthulakshmi saw five elderly men walking along a narrow path, talking to each other in what sounded like Kannada, a language she didn't speak. Nonetheless, she began to speak to them in Tamil, gesticulating wildly to make herself understood. She told them what had happened the previous day and how she had escaped. None of the men could speak Tamil, but they understood enough to make out that she was Veerappan's wife.

The men made her understand that she should stay where she was, and that they'd return to help her escape to Tamil Nadu. "We cannot take you anywhere now," they finally told her. "What if the police spot us? Stay here till the evening and we'll return and then take you to a safe place from where you can take a bus and escape to Tamil Nadu. Don't panic. We promise to come back. You will have some cattle grazers for company."

Muthulakshmi stayed behind and soon saw two cattle grazers with their herd coming her way. Seeing a disheveled woman so deep inside the forest intrigued them and they fell into conversation with her. Muthulakshmi spent hours sitting on top of a huge rock, talking nervously to the two men, who seemed to empathize with her plight. From her perch, she could clearly see the little village of Punajanur down below. She could even see the people walking about. "If only I could reach that place and get into a bus going toward Tamil Nadu, I would be safe," she told herself.

Muthulakshmi was convinced that the five men she had met in the morning would return. And they did, after a few hours, but with the police in tow. They surrounded the rock. Muthulakshmi was left with no option but to come down the rock and give herself up. She had gone without food and water for almost two days and was so weak that she could barely stand. The policemen handcuffed her. As she was about to be dragged away, two men carrying milk cans appeared on the scene. "Give her some milk to drink before she dies. We want her alive," said one of the policemen. Her hands trembled as she held the glass of milk. She gulped it down all at once, spilling half of it on her clothes.

The policemen took her to a camp inside the forest and then on to the Dimbam camp. It was nearing 8 p.m. when they got there. Muthulakshmi was pushed into a room where STF commandant Shankar Bidri, SPs Shailendra Babu, and Singaravelu were present along with a few members of the BSF. "So this is the woman who is Veerappan's wife. Let us see what praises she will sing in honor of her husband now," said Bidri sarcastically. The others simply stared at her. They made Muthulakshmi remove her gold bangles and chain. She had about three hundred rupees with her. Bidri took the money into his possession.

Muthulakshmi was blindfolded and taken to the Bannari camp, near Dimbam. There she was pushed into a dingy cell, which held three other women. The next day, a few men from the Karnataka STF came to the camp and moved her into another room. There began the torture and derision she was to endure for the next three years. "So you are Veerappan's wife, are you? Where is he? Tell us all that you know, otherwise you will die like a bitch at our hands. Don't think we will show any mercy just because you are a woman. If you don't speak up, we know how to get information out of you. Tell us where your husband is hiding. How many are you in the gang?" The questioning went on and on. Muthulakshmi was dazed and terrified. A policeman slapped her. Her clothes were ripped off her body. Words barely came out of her mouth. Then one of the policemen attached wires to her ears and nipples and administered electric shocks. She screamed in pain and fainted.

The surprise raid on the hideout in the Minchguli forests had separated the gang. The forest was so vast that the gang members found it tough to regroup. Veerappan didn't know where most of his men were.

He was particularly anxious about Mariappan, who had not left his side for over twenty years.

Mariappan had walked for days through the forest alone and reached a place between Nagamalai and Gopinatham. There were a few *doddis* here, taken care of by Tammadi tribals, found only in the MM Hills belt. They are a set of very religious-minded people who worship Lord Shiva. Basically cattle grazers, they live on a simple meal of gruel twice a day for weeks on end and return to civilization occasionally, mainly to refurbish their stock of millet flour.

Mariappan was starving and exhausted to the point of collapse when he managed to reach a *doddi*. He called out weakly for help. A man named John happened to be at the *doddi* that day because he had some business with one of the Tammadis. Mariappan offered him money to arrange for food and provisions, giving him five hundred rupees as a guarantee. John was puzzled. Who was this man who had come out of the blue to a desolate place like this, and was now offering such a large sum of money? Could he be one of Veerappan's men?

"Give me some more money and I shall get you whatever you want. You can stay here until I return from MM Hills tomorrow. Make yourself comfortable," he told the stranger.

"No, no. I can't stay here. I shall return tomorrow toward evening to collect the rations," Mariappan said, and vanished into the wilderness. John started the walk back to MM Hills.

As he walked down the meandering pathways in the forest, his mind was agitated. Why had the man offered him so much money for basic rations like rice, dal, salt, and tamarind? Unable to put his mind at rest, he went straight to the STF headquarters. Meeting Inspector Poonacha there, he told him about the stranger in the forest. Poonacha knew immediately that it was indeed one of Veerappan's men, but couldn't have guessed it was someone of such a high rank as Mariappan.

Turning to John, he said, "I'll tell you what you should do. It will probably be dark when the man comes to the *doddi* tomorrow to pick up the rations. We may not even be able to spot him in the dark. So, as soon as he makes an appearance, talk to him casually and tell him you have brought the rations. Just to put him at ease, offer him a *beedi*, then move aside. When he lights the *beedi*, we'll fire in the direction of the light. Is that clear?"

And so, toward noon on September 18, Poonacha and a team of three BSF men left for the spot, accompanied by John. Carrying AK-47 rifles and a few grenades, the group made steady progress through the shrubbery. Climbing up and down the forested hills was not easy. Poonacha and the others had to reach the spot well before the gangster arrived. "How long before we get there?" Poonacha asked John.

"It should take us another hour and a half, sir. There is no need to worry. We'll be there in time to handle him," John assured him.

It was nearly 4 p.m. and the sky was overcast. There was a hint of rain in the air. "Let's hurry before it gets dark. It looks like it's going to rain as well. Come on, everybody, speed up." Poonacha pushed the team on.

Soon they reached the spot close to Nagamalai where the anonymous gangster was expected to appear at sunset. "You go and stay in the *doddi*. Be as relaxed as you can. Do not show even a hint of nervousness. Make it look like you have returned from MM Hills with all the rations he wanted. And don't forget to offer him a *beedi*. Otherwise, as I told you, we'll never be able to spot him in the darkness."

John reassured the police team and started walking toward the *doddi*. Poonacha and the others took cover between bushes about fifty yards away, amid a cluster of trees. Evening had come. Not a leaf stirred.

As Poonacha and his team waited tensely, they heard voices. They gripped their guns and readied themselves for an assault. "Be careful not to hurt John. Just concentrate on the point where you see the flare of the matchstick as the man lights up. This is very important. Now take positions."

A few moments passed and the voices could still be heard. The conversation wasn't audible, but it was clear that the man had arrived as he had said. As precious time went by, Poonacha began to get a little restless. There was no sign of a match being struck. In the darkness, it was impossible to know who was where. "What is happening, sir?" whispered a BSF man, impatiently.

"Sssh, don't make any noise. We'll wait and watch a little longer."

They waited with bated breath for the gangster to light a *beedi* and give away his position. They had no idea why things were not going according to plan. Mariappan had indeed been offered a *beedi* by John as planned, but much to John's chagrin, the gangster lit it with his palms cupped around it, not revealing even a speck of light.

But John kept his wits about him. Displaying great presence of mind, he started walking casually toward the bushes where the policemen were hiding. Mariappan followed him. As the two men came closer, Dheeraj, one of the BSF men, hit Mariappan hard on the back of his head with a pinned grenade. He stopped, stunned. Poonacha and the other two men grappled him down to the ground. Before he realized what was happening, Mariappa found himself handcuffed. "We've got him, we've got him. Tie him up," screamed Poonacha as the BSF men flung a rope around his waist and bound him tightly. They discovered only later that their catch was one of Veerappan's closest associates.

Mariappan was brought to the STF headquarters in MM Hills the next day. But no matter how the police questioned him, he refused to utter a word, either about Veerappan or about any of the other members of the gang. With extraordinary strength of will, he stonewalled every attempt to make him speak. Ultimately the cops gave up, worn out by his determination. He remained in custody for a week and then, like hundreds of others, died at the hands of the police in an "encounter."

Although the STF was now making inroads into Veerappan's gang by eliminating men like Mariappan, Muthulakshmi was their biggest catch since operations began in 1990. Veerappan was still proving difficult to catch, but with his wife in custody, the officers felt that credible information on his movements could be gathered. They saw her capture as a crucial step forward in their fight against the bandit.

Meanwhile, the police had been tipped off about the whereabouts of another key member of the gang, N. S. Mani. The "N. S." had become a prefix to his name after a daring *dacoity* he had committed in the Kollegala region some years ago, on a bus belonging to the N. S. Transport Company. The thought of capturing him was too tempting for Bidri to resist. An informer had told him that the gangster was hiding in the Tengumarada forest near Bejalatti. "I'm not sure who else is with him. Maybe if you take a chance, you'll be able to nab him. He is definitely in that area now. Who knows, you might even be able to get Veerappan himself," the informer said.

Bidri left immediately for the Bejalatti area, accompanied by Inspectors Ashok Kumar and Saudagar, ASI Bandiwad, and ten constables, at about 7:30 a.m. in two Gypsys. The date was October 31. A few hours later, they saw a rocky formation in the distance. As the policemen made their way surreptitiously toward it, they noticed a thin wisp of smoke emanating from near the rocks. Bidri gestured to his men. "They must be there. The smoke is a sure sign. Get ready for the assault," he said.

Bidri was right. As the police neared the rocks, they saw two men engrossed in worshiping a stone around which were kept four guns. There was camphor burning, flowers, and vermilion smeared on the stone and also on the guns. As the policemen surrounded them, the gangsters instinctively clutched their guns. "Fire," shouted Bidri. As the policemen opened fire from their AK-47s, one man slumped dead on the spot. He was N. S. Mani. The other man was Kolandai, who jumped behind a rock the moment the firing began and escaped through the bushes. Although Kolandai got away, Bidri was pleased that he had been able to get Mani, one more of Veerappan's trusted men.

The Tamil Nadu STF was making progress against the gang. A large number of men supplying rations and also arms and ammunition to the gang were either arrested or shot dead during this period. Sandalwood billets were seized at various places in the Kolathur and Baragur forest areas. Periodic encounters took place as the STFs of both the states went about their search. But Veerappan stayed one step ahead.

WHILE THE BSF STRUGGLED to achieve a breakthrough, Shankar Bidri had periodic brainstorming sessions with his team in MM Hills. One such meeting resulted in the birth of what came to be known as the "ragi squad": groups drawn from the surrounding villages who were willing to work as police informers. Bidri would pay them five thousand rupees each at the time of recruitment, with a promise of twenty thousand, a sum that was perhaps a lifetime's earning for most people in the area, if they helped the police track down Veerappan. The ragi squads would be sent into the forests with instructions to remain there for weeks on end in the guise of honey collectors to spy on the gang. They were expected to report to the nearest STF post if they sighted either Veerappan or any of his gang members. Each member of the squad would be given a few pounds of millet flour (ragi), the gruel which would be their only source of sustenance inside the forest.

The formation of the ragi squads opened up another avenue for the police to gather information. But Shankar Bidri and his team had not prepared for one possibility. The BSF ended up arresting ragi squad members, mistaking them for Veerappan's informers. To avert such confusion, Shankar Bidri gave each sqaud member a laminated card with the STF commandant's seal on it. They were expected to keep this identity card inside their underwear and produce it in the event of a chance encounter with either the Tamil Nadu STF or the BSF inside the forest.

Meanwhile, Veerappan was desperate to bring the gang back to its former strength. The Minchguli police raid was a shattering blow to the gang, which had rapidly disintegrated. The gang members needed urgently to regroup now. Veerappan, along with Aiyyan Dorai, Koteyur Mani, and ten others, reached the Katrimalai forests near Palar in early November to find out whether any of their associates had been arrested or killed recently. Hiding on a hillock in Katrimalai, Veerappan instructed his aides Aiyyan Dorai and Koteyur Mani to somehow reach the nearby village of Govindapadi and make inquiries about any police action against the gang in the aftermath of the Minchguli raid. "Don't hang around in the village for too long and be very careful who you talk to. Be as discreet as possible and don't ever give anybody the impression that we are trying to get information about our men."

Mani and Aiyyan Dorai left immediately on their mission. They reached the other side of the Katrimalai hillock and hid amid the bushes. Toward nightfall, Aiyyan Dorai asked Mani to go alone and find out the necessary information. It was decided that Mani would mimic the call of a deer upon his return from the village to reestablish contact with Aiyyan Dorai. "Be on your guard all the time," Dorai warned his colleague before sending him off. As Mani began to hurry toward Govindapadi, Aiyyan Dorai settled down to smoke a *beedi*.

But Mani did not go to Govindapadi. He went straight to his native village of Koteyur nearby. He hadn't seen his family for a long time and was feeling homesick. Having reached his home under the cover of darkness, he decided to have a few glasses of *arrack*. Soon he was so drunk that he could hardly get up. While Mani huddled in his house drinking, one of the men in his neighborhood had been on the alert. A police informer, he hurried to the nearest STF post at Palar, five miles away, on his tractor because no other means of conveyance was available.

Rushing into the inspector's office, he began excitedly, "*Swami*, Koteyur Mani is in his house. I peeped through the window and saw him sprawled on the floor, completely drunk. You can arrest him immediately."

Kallappa was taken aback. "Is that so?" he asked the informer incredulously. "Let's go at once." Kallappa went with the informer in his tractor to Koteyur, and after only a moment had taken Mani into custody. The gangster whom the police had so desperately wanted to capture for so long and who had so consistently eluded them didn't seem even to realize what was happening to him.

Back at the Palar camp, Kallappa contacted Shankar Bidri at the STF base. "Sir, Kallappa on the line. One member of Veerappan gang secured, sir. Name Koteyur Mani. Rush to Palar, sir. Waiting for orders. Over."

"Tango One on the line. Will reach Palar immediately. Over."

Shankar Bidri, along with Ashok Kumar, Bawa, Saudagar, and Mudaliah, left at once for Palar, thirteen miles away, on the Tamil Nadu border. Seeing the extent of the gangster's inebriation, Bidri called a doctor to come from MM Hills. She reached Palar after an hour and administered an injection that made Mani vomit. After most of the alcohol had been drained out of his system, he began to regain his composure. Opening his eyes slowly, he began to scan the room where he was lying. He went into a state of shock when he realized at last that he had been captured. "Sir, sir, please don't kill me. Please spare my life. I shall tell you all that I know about Veerappan," he began to cry even before the police could ask him questions.

He went on to tell the police all that had happened after the Minchguli episode and how Veerappan was anxious to ensure that the gang regrouped. "*Aiyya*, Veerappan, Aiyyan Dorai, and some ten others are in the Katrimalai area now. In fact, I was sent to Govindapadi to find out whether there had been any arrests of our gang members by the police." Mani then offered to lead the police to the place where Veerappan was hiding.

It was 2 a.m. on November 2 when Shankar Bidri, Ashok Kumar, Bawa, Saudagar, and Mudaliah set out along with Mani for the Katrimalai forest. They stopped to conduct a special *pooja* at a small roadside temple next to the bridge at Palar before embarking on the mission. The river flowed quietly below, snaking its way through the forest. The team started its trek, armed with AK-47s. They had to cross the river at a particular point about two miles from the post. Holding their rifles above their heads, the team waded across the waist-deep waters of the Palar. The moon shone brightly, lighting up their path. Trekking silently through the night, the party reached a small hillock toward daybreak. The faint rays of the early-morning sun were a relief to the men, who had persevered through the night, half wet from the river crossing.

The physical ordeal was taking its toll on Shankar Bidri. He halted near a tree and said, "Let's rest for a while here before we go any farther." The policemen stretched out on the ground for some well-earned respite till Bidri ordered them up again.

As Bidri and the others made their way to Katrimalai, a ragi squad passed by. The ten men in the squad waved at the policemen as they descended a hillock. Mani alerted the policemen that they were now nearing the spot where Veerappan was hiding. Standing behind a tree, Mani called out like a deer. All was silent. There was no response. Looking around, he repeated the call and waited. Again there was no response. Bidri began to get agitated. "Shoot this bastard. He has duped us. He said that he would lead us to Veerappan and look what's happened now. Shoot him." He was shouting in anger. Shankar Bidri could rarely keep his cool in a tense situation, even when absolute silence was essential.

As Mani kept repeating his calls, completely unknown to the police Veerappan and his men were observing them silently, seated high up on a rock, with their guns ready to fire. But for once, the bandit decided not to challenge the policemen; he knew that their firepower was far greater than his own. He knew, too, that his strength lay in setting up an ambush and not confronting the policemen one to one.

Veerappan slowly slipped down from the rock and disappeared along with his men into the bushes, even as Bidri and his men scoured the area around the hillock.

MEANWHILE, THE MEMBERS of the ragi squad had reached a pool in the middle of a rocky formation, in whose cool and refreshing waters they had decided to bathe. They romped nude in the pool, but their joy was to be brutally short-lived. Veerappan and his men, hurrying through the forest, away from the commandant of the STF, chanced upon the ten men enjoying a relaxed bath.

Veerappan stopped abruptly. Turning to his men, he said, "Come, let's find out who those fellows are." When they reached the pool, they found a heap of clothes lying on the rocky bank. Catching hold of two men who were sitting on the bank, he asked sternly, "Who are you? What are you doing here? Tell me the truth and the two of you shall be spared. Otherwise, you know what will happen."

"*Aiyya, Aiyya*, we . . . we . . . came to the forest . . . to . . . to gather some . . ." Even before the man could finish, Veerappan, from the corner of his eye, noticed a piece of paper and a crisp hundred-rupee note peeping out of the pocket of one of the shirts in the heap. He picked up the shirt and pulled out the piece of plastic-covered paper. From the seal, he immediately realized that these men had something to do with the police, although he could not read what the seal said. The money was self-explanatory. They were police informers.

"Bastards, for how long have you been eating the excreta of the police? Were you not born to your fathers? I always knew there were fellows in the Govindapadi area who were licking police boots for money. How dare you do something like this to me? You bastards, have you grown so big that you think you can take on Veerappan?" The men were quaking in terror. Veerappan couldn't shoot them, because gunfire would have alerted Bidri and the others who were hardly a quarter of a mile away. Instead, he grabbed a hatchet and killed eight of them on the spot. The two men whom he had caught initially were, surprisingly, spared.

Despite the failure of this mission, Shankar Bidri's resolve to go after the gang was only strengthened. By 1994 he had built up a strong network of informants who were kept active by monetary inducements. Among them was Rangashetty, a small-time farmer from a small village called Munishetti Doddi, close to Kuratti Hosur, on the fringe of the forest near Kowdalli. Rangashetty had spent four years in Mysore jail on a charge of murder. While in jail, he happened to share a cell with Veerappan's brother Arjunan and Vodkehalla Doreswamy, another close confidant, who had been sentenced for the murder of Koteyur Madiah and his brother Thangavelu. The brothers were killed at Kallatti near Gopinatham on May 20, 1986, for giving information about the gang to the forest department officers. Although Veerappan and nineteen others were named in the first information report, the police succeeded in convicting only Arjunan and Vodkehalla Doreswamy.

In his conversations with the two men, Rangashetty learned how their minds worked and the extent of their hatred for the police. When the three men were released, Rangashetty returned to his small village of Munishetti Doddi and the other two men rejoined Veerappan. But the two gangsters kept in touch with their cellmate after returning to MM Hills.

On the afternoon of January 16, Rangashetty traveled to MM Hills with the intention of meeting Shankar Bidri. *"Namaskara swami,* I have come to tell you something important," he began. Looking around nervously to make sure that nobody could overhear, he continued, "Veerappan came to my house at about six a.m. today. Arjunan, 'Meke' Rangaswamy, Baby Veerappan, and Vodkehalla Doreswamy were with him. Veerappan told me that he had heard about me from Arjunan. He said he had faith in me and gave me two thousand rupees to procure rations for the gang. He will return with the others and collect the rations tomorrow after nightfall. *Swami,* here is an opportunity for you to get the whole gang."

Bidri smiled and said, "Rangashetty, you have brought me just the news that I wanted. Here, take this. It's all yours." Bidri pushed a wad of notes amounting to five thousand rupees into the informer's hands.

Shankar Bidri immediately went on the wireless to Inspector Ashok Kumar, who was relaxing on a hammock near the Hogenekal Falls after a strenuous combing operation. The moment he heard his commandant's voice on the wireless, he rolled out of the hammock.

Bidri told him, "Rush to base immediately. There is something urgent to be discussed."

Without wasting a moment, Ashok began to drive toward MM Hills along the treacherous boulder-strewn road through the forest toward Palar, from where he could reach the STF base.

Covering the distance of nearly twenty-eight miles in an hour and a half, he went straight to Bidri's office. "Ashok, this man Rangashetty has brought information about Veerappan. He says that the gangster is expected to come to his house tomorrow evening along with his gang members to collect rations for which he has paid two thousand rupees. I have had a long chat with this guy, and he is sure that we can nab the gang. I think we should give it a shot." Ashok turned to look at Rangashetty, who was standing beside Bidri's table. Rangshetty nodded his head as if in confirmation.

"Sir, I shall undertake the mission myself," Ashok volunteered. "Please give me four men who can aid me in the operation. We shall give it all that we have and hope for the best."

Bidri respected Ashok Kumar for his courage and ability to take up challenges. The inspector had proved himself time and again in his various postings, and had earned the nickname "Tiger" for having daringly chased and apprehended two notorious chain snatchers on a motorcycle after a shootout on the main roads of Bangalore, in 1986 in an operation code-named Operation Tiger. "Very well, Ashok. Take the men of your choice and start tomorrow. I shall monitor the exercise from here and offer any backup that you and the team might need."

ASI Bandiwad, HCs Ponnappa and Lingaraju, and Constable Kalappa were selected for the mission. Later that evening, as he relaxed on the veranda of the officers' quarters, Inspectors Ahmed Bawa, Kumaraswamy, and Prabhakar came up to Ashok Kumar. "Ashok, have you thought this over seriously? Do you realize how dangerous the mission is? What if the whole thing is a setup? What if it is a ploy on Veerappan's part to lure the police to their death like Harikrishna and Shakeel?"

But Ashok Kumar was undaunted by the warnings. A native of the hill district of Kodagu near Mysore, which is known for its martial tradition, he would never consider giving up.

On January 17, after lunch, Ashok Kumar got into a jeep along with his team. Inspector Bawa was at the wheel and looked a little nervous. Ashok and the four other policemen accompanying him were in disguise. Dressed in faded and dirty *lungis*, torn shirts, and rubber slippers, they looked like coolies after a hard day. Each of them carried a gunny bag in which was concealed an AK-47. Ashok had tucked inside his belt his favorite Sturm Ruger revolver, which was his prized possession.

When the jeep reached the Kowdalli junction at the base of MM Hills, Ashok and his team got out without saying a word. Bawa walked across to a stall by the roadside, bought a piece of Mysorepak, and handed it to Ashok by way of wishing him well on his mission. But before Ashok could take it into his mouth, the sweet fell to the ground. Bawa immediately construed this as a bad omen. Ashok simply smiled. "Don't be a sentimental fool, Bawa. You are a policeman. Come on, grow up." Ashok picked up the sweet and wiped the dust off it. "Now, take a bite," he prodded Bawa and ate a bit of the sweet himself. Then he took out a cassette and gave it to Bawa. "Give this to my wife just in case something happens to me. I have spoken to her at length on what she should do to bring up our two children, just in case . . ." he trailed off. The others looked on, surprised by the unexpected show of emotion. Moments later, Ashok and the others bid goodbye to Bawa and began to hurry down the narrow path leading toward Munishetti Doddi, off the main road.

The time was already 4 p.m. Ashok and his team had to hurry in order to reach Rangashetty's house and take position before Veerappan and his gang arrived. "Keep a steady pace. We have to cover more than five miles, and we must get there as early as possible," said Ashok. In their disguise, they looked exactly like a bunch of laborers returning home after working in the fields. The few villagers who saw them did not even bother to give them a second glance. Ashok Kumar's thick, unkempt beard added to his rustic look.

The group walked in single file with Rangashetty leading the way. Not a single word was exchanged. After an hour's walk, the terrain began to get difficult. Thorny bushes tugged at their clothes as they wound their way through. A hillock rose in front and the tall trees all around cut off visibility beyond ten yards. As they continued to walk, they neared a fork in the road where they were to turn right. Rangashetty stopped abruptly. Turning to Ashok he said, "*Swami*, let us not go any farther on the road toward the right. Veerappan is very cunning. If by some chance he's got to know about this operation, he'll be lying in wait to ambush us. Let us not take any chances. I shall take you through another route on the left."

Constable Kalappa was not happy with the sudden change in route.

He took Ashok Kumar aside and whispered, "Sir, this man has changed the route at the very last minute. He could have told us in the beginning. You know Harikrishna and Shakeel died because they trusted Kamala Naika completely. For all you know, this could also be a ploy to lead us straight to Veerappan, who could be hiding there to finish us." Kalappa's eyes mirrored his tension and his voice trembled a little as he spoke.

Ashok too was taken aback by the sudden change of plan. Standing exactly at the base of the fork in the road, with darkness slowly setting in on the woods all around, he knew he had to make a quick decision, a decision that could well turn out to be the difference between life and death. One wrong move and there was no turning back. Ashok stood silently for almost a minute and then called Rangashetty to his side. "Look, Rangashetty, let me tell you something very plainly. I consider you as my god, such is my faith in you. Tell me now if Veerappan has held any of your family members hostage and forced you to bring us to a place where he can ambush us. I'll think of a way to get them released. Don't try and do to us what Kamala Naika did to Harikrishna and Shakeel. And I'll tell you something more. Don't be under the impression that I'm going to die from a single bullet fired at me by Veerappan, like they show in the movies. If we are fired upon as we walk along the new route you suggest, I swear I'll completely ignore whoever fires at us and shoot you dead even before you can blink."

Rangashetty fell at Ashok's feet. "*Swami*, do you have to doubt me like this? I'd rather die than do anything like that to you. Please, I beg of you, do not have any doubts about my sincerity. I suggested this alternate route just to take you as safely as possible to my house."

Ashok was moved. He hugged his informer and apologized. "Come on, let's do as Rangashetty tells us," he said.

As they started to follow the new route, every member of the team was doubly alert. Rangashetty's assurances hadn't completely erased the fear of an attack. Suddenly, Ashok Kumar stepped on a huge thorn, which pierced the soft, thin rubber sole of his left slipper. The sudden jab of pain caused him to lose his balance, and he fell on a bush full of thorns. ASI Bandiwad and the others rushed to help Ashok and untangled him from the bush. "Don't worry, I'm fine. I just stepped on something sharp. I'm fine. I'm fine."

As the group resumed its journey, Ashok's slipper began to feel un-
comfortably squishy. When he bent down to check, he realized that
blood was oozing out and had completely drenched the slipper. He
stopped and removed his shirt, then took off his banian, which he tore
up and tied firmly across the gash, winding it several times around his
foot. "That should help," he muttered, visibly in pain. "Let's get going."
But somewhere at the back of his mind was the memory of the ill omen
that Bawa had spoken about. Quickly he banished the thought from
his mind.

It was not long before they reached a maize field in the midst of the
wooded area. A few yards in front of the field they could see the small
house belonging to Rangashetty. A little to its left was a thatched cattle
shed. Ashok and his team entered the field and hid amid the long
stalks of maize that grew there. Ashok whispered to his informer,
"Rangashetty, go to your house and see if the gangsters have already arrived. If they have, then come out on the pretext of wanting to relieve
yourself, drop your white towel once, pick it up, and go inside. That'll
be an indication for us to close in and attack. If you don't find anyone,
then switch off the light and switch it on again. Do you understand?"
Rangashetty nodded.

Rangashetty walked toward the house. Ashok and the others waited
with bated breath. Minutes passed and there was no signal of any kind
from the informer. Why was he taking so long to give them the signal?
Was something amiss? Suddenly the lights in the house went off and
came on again. Ashok and his men hurried toward the house. They had
to take up positions before the gang turned up. "Bandiwad, take
Ponnappa and Lingaraju along and hide in the cattle shed. Don't open
fire until I tell you. Is that clear?"

"Yes, sir."

Ashok Kumar and Kalappa entered Rangashetty's house and hid behind the main door. The house was composed of just one main area
with a portion of it converted into a small kitchen and another portion
serving as the bathing area. As the two policemen crouched behind the
door with their AK-47s ready to fire, they could see outside clearly
through the gap between the hinges and the frame of the door.
"Rangashetty, you sit outside the house in such a manner that we can

see you. The moment the gangsters arrive, talk to them as you normally do. After engaging them in conversation for a while, tell them that you'll get the rations from inside and come into the house. The moment you come into the house, we'll try to overpower them."

Rangashetty, as planned, settled down outside the house on the floor. He was humming a tune, a devotional song in praise of Lord Ayyappa. A good omen, thought Ashok Kumar. He and Kalappa kept watch through the small gap from behind the door. Ten minutes passed without any sign of anybody. Twenty. Then, just as Ashok was beginning to get restless, two figures stood outlined in the light from the doorway. One of them looked burly while the other one was thin. Ashok could sense the tension building up inside his body as he gripped his rifle firmly. He could clearly see Rangashetty engaging the two men in conversation. But he couldn't make out whether they were Rangashetty's friends who had come visiting or Veerappan's gang members.

A few moments later, Ashok realized Rangashetty was making his way into the house. But to his shock, the two men began to follow Rangashetty. His plan had gone haywire. Not knowing how to react, he stood absolutely still along with Kalappa, behind the door. Soon all three men entered the small house, which could barely accommodate so many people. Just then, Rangashetty, in a move that was as sudden as it was brilliant, casually put his arm around the shoulders of one of the men and said, "So, what else do you have to tell me, Doreswamy?" Ashok immediately knew that the man was Vodkehalla Doreswamy, one of the most dreaded members of the gang. Strangely, the police did not even have a photograph of Doreswamy, although he had spent nearly four years in Mysore jail, between 1986 and 1990.

Before Doreswamy could respond, Ashok was upon him. He wrestled him to the floor, but the gangster was too burly to be subdued so easily. He struggled out of Ashok's grasp, and the lighter man was thrown against the opposite wall. Doreswamy scrambled for the door, but Ashok was up by then and threw himself at the man. Doreswamy fell, kicked out at Ashok wildly, and was on his feet again. In the melee, Rangashetty rushed out of the house and disappeared into the darkness.

As Ashok wrestled with Doreswamy inside the tiny house, Kalappa lifted his rifle and hit the second man, who had accompanied Doreswamy, hard on the jaw. He collapsed instantly, unconscious. As Ashok and Doreswamy struggled for the upper hand, Doreswamy began to shout, "Veerappa, Veerappa . . . shoot . . . police, police. Sethukuli, shoot, shoot." Ashok Kumar knew that there was serious danger lurking in the shadows beyond the house. He held Doreswamy with all his might and pushed him with brute force toward the opposite wall, hardly ten feet away. As Doreswamy fell violently against the wall, Ashok took advantage of the slight distance, whipped out his revolver, and fired. He had hoped only to incapacitate him, but Doreswamy slumped to the ground, dead. His open eyes stared wildly at Ashok Kumar.

ASI Bandiwad and the two HCs Ponnappa and Lingaraju, who were stationed in the cattle shed a few yards away, had no idea what was going on inside and remained in hiding. They had been clearly instructed by Ashok not to open fire. Inside, Ashok Kumar tried contacting Shankar Bidri on his radio. "Bravo to Tango One, Bravo to Tango One . . ." he kept shouting into the instrument. But Rangashetty's house was built in a slight depression, with thick tree cover all around, and the radio failed to pick up signals.

"Kalappa, I shall go up the hillock there and try again," said Ashok. But Kalappa begged him not to venture out of the house, fearing that Veerappan might be lurking nearby. Ashok said, "Kalappa, how long do you expect us to stay inside the house without informing the others? We have to speak to the commandant."

Ashok Kumar crept up the small hillock, holding his revolver in one hand and the wireless in the other. "Bravo to Tango One, Bravo to Tango One," he began. But there was no response from the commandant.

Then suddenly a voice crackled on the wireless. "Bravo, this is Vijaya Giri. Go on." Vijaya Giri was the name of an elevated spot near Dimbam, in the middle of a coffee estate owned by the Birlas, over sixty miles away, where the STF had set up a wireless base.

"Operation successful. Inform commandant to get here as soon as possible with full force. Over," whispered Ashok urgently.

Within moments, Shankar Bidri was on the line. "Well done. Leaving immediately for spot. Hold fort until we come. Over."

Two hours later, Bidri arrived with a team that included Inspectors

Bawa, Kumaraswamy, and Saudagar. All of them congratulated Ashok on a job executed perfectly.

"Sir, it would have been better if I had managed to catch him alive. He would at least have shown us where the gang has hidden money. With his money confiscated, Veerappan would have had to emerge for a kidnapping or a robbery or something, and we would have had more chances of encountering him." Vodkehalla Doreswamy was the only gangster other than Mariappan whom Veerappan had trusted completely regarding money.

Still, Ashok Kumar had achieved a monumental breakthrough in the fight against Veerappan by eliminating one of the most dangerous men in the gang. His death was bound to weaken Veerappan. As for the other gangster who had fainted from the brutal blow from Kalappa's rifle butt, he was taken in handcuffs to the Kollegala government hospital, twenty-odd miles away. By 1:30 a.m., he had recovered enough to be able to answer questions. "My name is Kolathur Shekara. I've been with Veerappan for the past ten years," he said haltingly.

"Tell us where Veerappan and the others would have moved after this evening's incident," growled Bidri. He knew that the gang always fled in different directions after every encounter with the police, then re-grouped at a predesignated place.

"*Swami*, I'll tell you everything. Please don't kill me," begged Shekara, looking helplessly at the officers who surrounded him. "*Swami*, Veerappan had asked us to reach a hillock near Chengadi, three or four miles from Rangashetty's house inside the forest, in case of a police attack. The others are all bound to be there now. I can take you to that place right now if you so wish."

Shankar Bidri looked at his officers and said, "Let's go immediately before they leave. This man can lead us." Accompanying Bidri on the mission were Inspectors Ashok Kumar, Saudagar, Bawa, and Kumaraswamy, SI Srikantraje Urs, DSP Mudaliah, ASI Bandiwad, Constable Kalappa, and HC Lingaraju. Head Constable Ponnappa led the group, with a Doberman on a leash. The dog had proved to be a highly sensitive sniffer and was an integral part of the team. The policemen left Kollegala around 2:30 a.m. in two jeeps, with high hopes of encountering the gang near Chengadi. The stillness of the night was broken only by the drone of the jeeps. There was no movement except for the forest rats that caught the glare of the jeeps' headlights as they crisscrossed the road at regular intervals. After an hour's journey, the two jeeps stopped on the fringe of the forest. "*Swami*, we have to walk from here. I know the exact place and shall lead you to it," blurted Shekara nervously.

"Are you telling us the truth or . . ." threatened Bidri.

"Really *swami*, I know where to find Veerappan and the others. I'll take you to the spot."

Bidri looked at his watch. It was nearly 4 a.m. He gestured to his men to start walking. Shekara was made to walk in front. After a little while, the dog began to whine softly. The long leash tightened a bit as it began to pull its handler Ponnappa toward a bush a little distance away. Bidri and the others became alert at the sudden change in the dog's behavior. As Ponnappa tried to control the dog, which by then had become very agitated, a shot rang out from the direction of the bush. The policemen were stunned. They couldn't see a thing in the near total darkness. "Take cover and fire," screamed Shankar Bidri. But the darkness was like a blanket over the policemen's eyes. Unable to even place the gang's position, the policemen opened fire indiscriminately while retreating as quickly as they could. Ponnappa was the unluckiest of the lot. The first bullet, fired at close range, killed him instantly.

Subinspector Srikantraje Urs, who had dived to the ground after the first shot, found himself hit by a spray of pellets in the thigh and buttock. He lay helplessly on the ground, unable to move. As he lay there, he realized to his shock that the retreating party was firing so indiscriminately that there was every possibility of one of his own colleagues' bullets hitting and killing him. Urs clenched his teeth and tried to crawl to safety. But there was a stinging pain in his leg, and try as he might, he couldn't lift it. Blood soaked through his trousers. His lips were dry and he was gasping for breath. Mercifully the firing stopped after ten minutes, and Srikantraje Urs lived to see another day. For him, those were the longest ten minutes of his life.

He was taken from the spot by Ashok Kumar, Bandiwad, Kalappa, and Lingaraju on a makeshift stretcher fashioned out of bamboo poles, which were cut on the spot and tied together with vines. With a great deal of effort, they made it to the place where the jeeps had been parked.

Urs was going numb in the body and he kept mumbling in acute pain. He was given first aid in the Kollegala public health unit before being shifted to the Basappa Memorial Hospital in Mysore. He stayed in his hospital bed for nearly four months, then volunteered to return to the STF, ready to fight another battle.

As the hunt for Veerappan continued, Kolandai, the gang member who had escaped during the police raid near Bejallatti in which N. S. Mani had been killed, hid in his sister's house in Kolathur. He had been attacked by a gaur in the forest and had fractured his hand. Shankar Bidri got wind of this and set his men on him. When the police surrounded his sister's house on January 24, Kolandai committed suicide by consuming pesticide.

Veerappan moved his gang after this incident to the densely forested slopes near Pillur in the Nilgiris. Neither the Tamil Nadu STF nor the Karnataka force was able to trace the gang's movements for nearly four months. Toward the end of May, Shankar Bidri received information through some intermediaries that Veerappan was willing to surrender. This came as a surprise to Bidri. On June 2 he sent word that Veerappan could do so in the presence of respectable citizens in any court of law either in Karnataka or in Tamil Nadu. But there was no response from the bandit.

After a lull, there was talk again of Veerappan surrendering. Between July 27 and August 9, for the first time, audiocassettes were exchanged between SP Sanjay Arora, of the Tamil Nadu STF, and Veerappan. But the "negotiations" were stopped after a message from Veerappan which said, "The SP should meet me in the south Talamalai forests, alone and unarmed. I shall discuss the terms of my surrender with him." The bandit's record was too treacherous for Arora to take a chance.

As hopes of surrender died down, the police were spurred into action again. The STF was badly hampered by the absence of Dawaram, who had gone on leave for six months after a near-fatal road accident. But SP Sanjay Arora kept up the tempo. On September 17, a Tamil Nadu STF group along with a BSF platoon sighted the gang at a heavily fortified elevated point at Kailaspallam in the north Talamalai forests. There was an encounter in which a BSF jawan, Bhupinder Singh, died. A Karnataka STF group, which was engaged in a combing operation nearby, rushed to the spot and joined the gun battle. Veerappan and his men escaped from the scene, leaving behind more than 140 rounds of ammunition as well as a large quantity of food and other provisions.

Another two and a half months passed without a trace of the gang. Then suddenly the bandit struck again. On December 3, Veerappan, along with Arjunan, Aiyyan Dorai, and another gang member, Karangalur Rangaswamy, kidnapped Chidambaranath, a DSP in the Anticorruption Bureau, Coimbatore; his brother, an HC in Erode; and a high school teacher near Gadavayal village, in the Sirumugai forest area. The three men were returning from Chidambaranath's farm close by.

Holding the three men hostage, Veerappan initiated negotiations for his surrender with Shankar, the collector of Coimbatore. Again, audio-cassettes were exchanged on a regular basis. At one point, Veerappan even demanded that the Coimbatore station All India Radio (AIR) air Shankar's telephone number, so that he could talk to him directly. In the middle of all this, Arjunan was badly injured in the leg. How he injured himself is a matter of conjecture. While some said that it was a result of intragang rivalry, others said that it was an accident. Whatever the cause, Arjunan was in need of urgent medical treatment. He, along with Aiyyan Dorai and Karangalur Rangaswamy, boldly made his way to the government hospital in Coimbatore and in full view of everyone got himself admitted for treatment. He was sure that the police would not do anything to him and his mates as long as his brother Veerappan held Chidambaranath and the two others hostage. Two of the hostages belonged to the police department, and the government would not take chances with their lives, he thought.

But as fate would have it, Jayalalitha, at this very juncture, decided to halt all negotiations and launch a full-fledged operation headed by Walter Dawaram to rescue the hostages. Even as Arjunan lay in the hospital, a joint operation involving the STFs of both states was ordered out on December 28. The police attack was swift and sudden. For once they had taken Veerappan by surprise, and in escaping he left the hostages behind. Meanwhile at the hospital, Arjunan and the other two gangsters were promptly arrested and sent to judicial custody.

While Arjunan and his companions were in judicial custody, the Karnataka STF filed repeated applications before the district court in

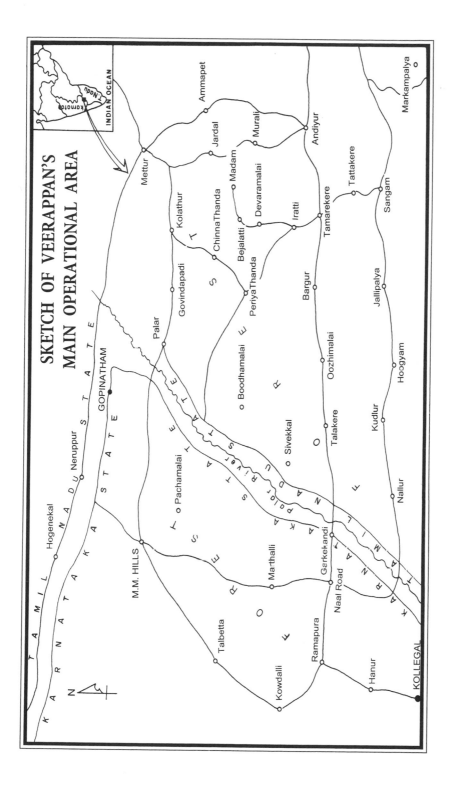

# SKETCH OF VEERAPPAN'S
## MAIN OPERATIONAL AREA

Veerappan in police custody, 1986.
(*Courtesy Ashok Kumar*)

An overview of Veerappan's operational area. (*Courtesy Netra Raju*)

Gopinatham, where Veerappan was born. (*Courtesy Lokesh*)

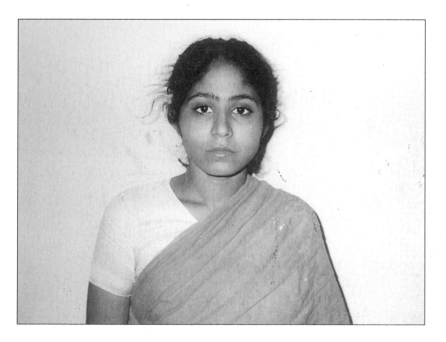

Veerappan's wife, Muthulakshmi. (*Courtesy Ashok Kumar*)

DCF Srinivas, who was killed by
Veerappan in November 1991.
(*Courtesy Ashok Kumar*)

Yerkehalla, where Srinivas was killed. (*Courtesy Ashok Kumar*)

Local villagers cook for an STF team on the banks of the Palar. (*Courtesy Ashok Kumar*)

The skeletal remains of two villagers killed by Veerappan near Nallur.
(*Courtesy Ashok Kumar*)

SI Shakeel Ahmed, at the STF camp. (*Courtesy Ashok Kumar*)

SP Harikrishna, in his office.
(*Courtesy Ashok Kumar*)

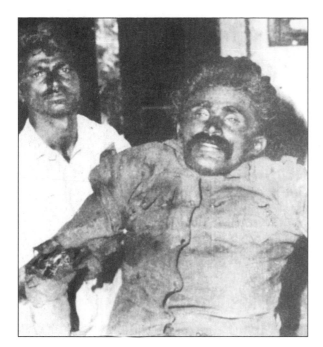

The body of Gurunathan, one of Veerappan's closest aides, who was killed by the police in 1992. (*Courtesy Ashok Kumar*)

The site of the Hogenekal ambush (April 9, 1990) on the bank of the Cauvery River. (*Courtesy Ashok Kumar*)

An STF team, led by DIG Thimmappa Madiyal, crossing the Palar.
(*Courtesy Ashok Kumar*)

The bullet-riddled car in which SP Harikrishna and SI Shakeel Ahmed were killed,
on August 14, 1992. (*Courtesy Ashok Kumar*)

The mangled remains of the police bus blasted by Veerappan and his gang near Sorakaimadu on April 9, 1993. (*Courtesy Netra Raju*)

"Rambo" Gopalkrishna (center), who miraculously survived the Sorakaimadu ambush.
(*Courtesy Ashok Kumar*)

An STF unit, ready for action. (*Courtesy Ashok Kumar*)

Commander Shankar Bidri (left), with Inspector Ashok Kumar.
(*Courtesy Ashok Kumar*)

NSG commandos disguised as local villagers. (*Courtesy Lokesh*)

STF chief Walter Dawaram.
(*Courtesy Netra Raju*)

The Perumal temple built by Veerappan on his land near Gopinatham.
(*Courtesy Lokesh*)

Material confiscated from Veerappan's gang, including two pairs of elephant tusks.
(*Courtesy Netra Raju*)

A rocky shrine in the forest where Veerappan prays regularly.
(*Courtesy Netra Raju*)

Negotiations between *Nakkeeran*'s R. R. Gopal and Veerappan.
(*Photo by Shivasubramaniyam / courtesy* Nakkeeran)

Rajkumar's ancestral home in Gajanur. (*Courtesy Lokesh*)

Rajkumar's newly built mansion, across the road from his ancestral home.
(*Courtesy Lokesh*)

Veerappan explains his point of view.
*(Photo by Shivasubramaniyam / courtesy* Nakkeeran)

Gopal and Veerappan sleep as a sentry keeps vigil.
*(Photo by Shivasubramaniyam / courtesy* Nakkeeran)

Veerappan, Rajkumar, and Gopal in the forest.
*(Photo by Shivasubramaniyam / courtesy* Nakkeeran)

Rajkumar returns to a tumultuous welcome from his fans and family,
November 16, 2000. *(Photo courtesy Kannada Prabha)*

Mysore, seeking permission for interrogation. The Tamil Nadu police were not keen to hand over the three men, but finally they were forced to send them to Mysore, where the Karnataka police took them into custody after a formal sanction from the court on June 26, 1995. The same day the police decided to shift Arjunan, Aiyyan Dorai, and Karangalur Rangaswamy to the STF base in MM Hills, eighty-five miles away.

As the police van carrying the three men moved toward the base, the inspector in charge, Madhukar Musale, heard a commotion in the cabin at the back. They were about twenty-eight miles from Mysore then, between T Narasipur and Mugur.

"Stop the van immediately. There's something wrong at the back," he shouted to the driver. The van stopped, and the inspector jumped out and flung the cabin door open. He found the three men writhing in pain. They had apparently consumed cyanide.

The bizarre death of three of the most important members of the Veerappan gang, in mysterious circumstances, raised questions that were debated furiously in the following days. How could these men in handcuffs, who had been in jail for months, procure something as rare as a vial of cyanide? Were they not searched before being brought to court and again before being taken into custody by the Karnataka police? Who could have supplied them the poison, considering the tight security around them? Why did they decide to consume cyanide suddenly, after being in custody for nearly six months? As such questions began to do the rounds in the press, there were whispers that the three had been brutally beaten to death by the police inside the van, out of sheer frustration and anger at not having been able to get even with the gang for so long. Whether their deaths were suicide or murder, the three gangsters took to their graves vital information on the activities of the gang.

Within a span of two years, Veerappan's gang had been reduced from 150 in 1993 to only about five members. As many as fifty-six gangsters had been killed and ninety arrested. Veerappan had also suffered two personally debilitating blows—the arrest of his wife, Muthulakshmi, and the death of his brother Arjunan. Although these incidents did not break his spirit, they increased his desperation.

Veerappan was convinced that a few villagers in Punajanur had played a role in his wife's arrest. On August 9, 1995, just after sunset, he showed up there and changed the lives of its inhabitants forever. Punajanur is a small village close to the Dimbam forests, composed of some four hundred houses. Walking straight to the house of the village headman, Muthe Gowda, Veerappan shouted, "So your son thought that he would become a hero by helping the police dogs capture my wife? Now you'll know the consequences." Muthe Gowda's son Doreswamy had spoken to the press soon after Muthulakshmi's arrest, telling them how his family had informed the police about her whereabouts in the Minchguli forests. He had obviously not considered the possibility of Veerappan hearing the news as well.

As Veerappan was shouting at Muthe Gowda, a small crowd began to collect in front of the house. They were mostly women and children. Looking at the women, Veerappan asked, "Couldn't you have shown her mercy? Wasn't my wife also a woman in your eyes? Did you not have the heart to help her while she was in distress? How could you let this man and his family do such a thing to her?" As his voice began to rise, the crowd melted away silently. Doreswamy, who had heard the commotion in front of his house, bolted through the back door into the darkness. Veerappan's gaze was firmly fixed on Muthe Gowda, who was standing silently with his head bent low. Along with him stood his family members Mahalinga, Nagaraja, Dundappa, and Bhadre Gowda.

Veerappan did not say another word. He lifted his rifle and shot all of them at point-blank range. As the shots rang out in the darkness of the night, the men in the village ran for their lives, abandoning their wives and children in their homes. Ghafoor, a *coolie* who had gone to Muthe Gowda's house to find out the cause of the commotion, was hit in the left arm by a bullet. Later, his hand had to be amputated, although he begged the doctors to save it. He was paid a compensation of twenty thousand rupees by the government, but it sufficed only for his medical expenses. He couldn't work as a *coolie* with only one hand.

After this episode, most of the villagers sold their fertile lands at throwaway prices to buyers—mostly from Kerala—and left the village forever. They later joined the K. K. Birla–owned Honnemeti coffee estate nearby as daily-wagers drawing salaries ranging from forty to sixty rupees a day. Muthe Gowda's son Doreswamy, whose one act of indiscretion had resulted in the elimination of his whole family, retreated into a permanent daze. The Karnataka government promised to pay 100,000 rupees as compensation to the kin of those killed, but has paid only half the promised amount to date.

# 11

# Face to Face

A rjunan's death shattered Veerappan. He was convinced that
the police had killed his brother while he was in their custody. The death had been sudden and completely unexpected. His sense of outrage was further compounded by a
surprise encounter on December 12, 1995, between him and his gang
members and a Karnataka STF party near a place called Kodangadipatti
in the south Baragur forests. The gang had little chance to retaliate.
Veerappan and his men were left with no option but to run for their
lives, abandoning their hideout.

They regrouped at Balapadagu, a tribal hamlet deep inside the north
Talamalai forests. But the police action had a lasting impact on two of the
gang members, Chinnan and Balan. For the first time they began to
seriously fear for their lives. They abandoned the gang, traveling to
Mettupalyam, where they surrendered before Rajan, the SP, on January
12, 1996. Undaunted, Veerappan and the others continued to move
around in the Balapadagu area. He still had immense support from the
villagers belonging to the hamlets of Kolipalya, Makanpalya, Ettidoddina
Koppalu, Tadasalatti, Bejalatti, Ittare, Mavanatta, Galidimba, and Iggalur,

all part of the vast Satyamangalam belt. They referred to him as "Velu Muruga," the son of Lord Shiva.

While they were holed up in the north Talamalai forests, Veerappan came in contact with a Soliga tribal named "Tupaki" Sidda. Sidda, along with his wife, Kumbhi, joined the gang. With "Tupaki" Sidda's entry into the gang, Veerappan's hands were strengthened. Sidda was deadly when it came to handling guns and was known to be completely fearless—two qualities Veerappan expected from his companions. Sidda talked to about twenty-five Soligas in the Kallabandipura and Balapadagu areas and brought them into the fold. Veerappan was beginning to regain confidence.

The gang had positioned itself directly on the Karnataka–Tamil Nadu border. It was thickly forested, with valleys and gorges so deep that as usual the task of locating the gang was a nightmare for the police. On the evening of February 16, Veerappan decided to move out of his hideout near Balapadagu and head for Arepalya, about fifteen miles away. He had learned that the police used the usually deserted Germalam–Dimbam road through the forest often. He set up camp in the area and lay in wait.

The next day, toward evening, he noticed a police jeep making its way through the forest. It belonged to the Tamil Nadu STF, and seated inside were SP Tamil Selvan, Inspector Mohan Navaz, and HC Selvaraj. As the jeep neared a bend on the impossibly treacherous road filled with gaping potholes, there was a hail of bullets. The gang fled when Karnataka STF Inspector Jayamaruthi arrived on the scene unexpectedly. Although the weapons were saved, Jayamaruthi could not save Selvaraj, who succumbed to his bullet wounds. Commandant Shankar Bidri, who was at the Dimbam camp twelve miles away, arrived with a team and took the injured SP and Mohan Nawaz, who was shaken but not injured, to the base.

Soon after this attack, Veerappan found his way to the dense forests of south Talamalai. Around this time, two intrepid young journalists based in Erode, Jeeva Tangavelu and Shiva Subramaniam, managed to establish contact with Veerappan. Thus far, meeting Veerappan had been unthinkable for anyone, including journalists, because of the bandit's murderous record. But these two Tamil men managed to get through to him. Veerappan, who never took chances with strangers no matter what their credentials, agreed to meet and speak to the two reporters in part because Shiva Subramaniam had supposedly been close to his brother Arjunan and had known him since childhood. Also, Veerappan himself was on the lookout for someone he could trust to take his story to the outside world and make him the icon he yearned to be.

In the third week of February, Veerappan sent word to Tangavelu and Subramaniam that they should reach Thignare in the south Talamalai forests, where a gang member would meet them and escort them to his hideout. At the appointed hour, toward late afternoon, they were met by "Tupaki" Sidda near Thignare. "Come with me," he said. Veerappan had ordered the two men to wear red shirts, which would serve as their identification.

Tangavelu and Subramaniam, armed with a still and a video camera, gingerly followed him. After a two-hour trek they realized that they were in such a dense part of the forest that it would be impossible for them to make their way back without the help of someone from the gang. The hideout was deep in the bowels of the Chikkiranakatte and Soolagittikadu forests. The same evening the two men were brought face to face with Veerappan.

The aura of mystery around Veerappan had been magnified by the absence of any photographs of him, except for one black-and-white shot taken in 1986 while he was in police custody. This one picture appeared regularly whenever there was a media report abbout him. In the three days that the two men spent with Veerappan, they recorded nearly nine hours of tape. Veerappan, for the first time in his life, spoke his mind to the outside world. What he said was revealing, even shocking in parts. He narrated in graphic detail all the killings and kidnappings that he had committed till then.

He said, "I began life as a cattle grazer in my village of Gopinatham. Ours was a very poor family with hardly any means for a regular livelihood. There were hungry mouths to feed and money was always a major problem. I know what hunger is because I have experienced it so many times in my life. Slowly I took to hunting, and mainly for food. The proceeds of the hunt would always be shared with everybody in the village. We believed in community living. The forest department officials in my area would take bribes from me regularly and allow me to hunt. I never kept any money I earned through hunting. I always made it a point to give it away to those in more need of it than me."

He then went on to narrate in great detail how his life had taken different turns. "Bribing the forest officers had become a way of life for me. I then slowly shifted to smuggling sandalwood. Anyway, the forests around my village were so rich in that wood. As the years went by, I began to be looked upon as a sort of a leader and was even invited to settle disputes in the village. If the poor villagers went to court, it would take ages for them to see their cases settled. Moreover, where would they get the money to pay the lawyers? I would even settle cases of murder by ordering compensation to be paid to the victim's family."

The two reporters by now realized they were sitting on a gold mine. As the camera kept rolling, Veerappan seemed to get more and more enthused to speak. He talked about corrupt forest officers who had given him a full rein of the forests for a fee. "I continued my illegal operations in the forest for years with the full knowledge of government officials. All they expected from me was money. That I would throw at their faces like you throw crumbs to a dog. They would stop barking then and wag their tails!"

He spoke of how the state had unleashed terror and violence on the hapless villagers the minute he stopped greasing palms. His voice rose and his fists clenched tightly as he recounted incidents that had happened years ago. "The corrupt dogs began to torture, rape, and abuse poor villagers after they realized that there was no more money coming their way," he said. "To rape innocent women, the policemen in my area are given a daily allowance of eighty rupees!"

Veerappan narrated the story of "Rambo" Gopalkrishnan, who was known as Aadu Thiruda ("Goat Stealer") among the local villagers. "He would come with some fifty policemen, claiming that he was looking for me. But in reality, the bastard's intention was to steal some fifteen to twenty goats from the village. He would ask his men to catch them, tie their legs, bundle them in his jeep, and take them away. He and his men would then make a good meal of them. He even made villagers toil on a farm he owned on some patta land, from morning till evening. An SP is expected to secure the law. But this fellow . . ." He trailed off. He then added, "The bastard escaped with his life miraculously in the Sorakaimadu bomb blast incident. It doesn't matter. At least the goats in the village are living freely now!"

Quite expectedly, Veerappan's greatest grudge was against policemen. He explained how his whole family had been targeted. "My dear brother Arjunan died at the hands of the police. My sister Mariamma consumed pesticide, unable to withstand the harassment at their hands. They completely ruined my family. Even my hunting dogs were not spared. Cinniah, Veetha, Chikka, Seena, and Cinnakutty—I had lovingly reared them for years. The policemen fed them poisoned idlis and killed them. I always reciprocated these acts by seeking revenge. The cycle of violence has continued."

Veerappan was a firm believer in the concept of destiny. The cosmic roll of the dice, he said, was what determined the fate of men. "Rama was destined to experience *vanavasa* (exile) of fourteen years. It was twelve years for the Pandavas. God has fixed twenty-five years for me," he said with a shrug of his shoulders.

He was scathing in his criticism of the manner in which the government was removed from the reality of life in little villages like Gopinatham. Hunting and timber smuggling, he said, had to be viewed in the context of the terrible poverty he and his family experienced. "Judges who decide the lives of thousands of men, sitting on a pedestal in a court hall, come to the forests to hunt. I've seen it with my own eyes. They carry guns. The forest ranger, the DFO, and all the others run around like peons and do their bidding. They bring crates of whisky, indulge in revelry and merrymaking. Nobody can question them. But if Veerappan does something out of sheer hunger, he is labeled a criminal. Is this fair? Four lorry loads of rosewood reach Anthiyur Member of the Legislative Assembly (MLA) Periyaswamy's house every day. Checkposts open automatically for his vehicle to pass. But nobody calls him 'Rosewood' Periyaswamy. But they have the nerve to attach the word 'sandalwood' to my name."

Shiva Subramaniam and Jeeva Tangavelu realized that they were about to pull off a major journalistic coup. Veerappan did not disappoint them. He continued to speak. He even had a word of advice for terrorists: "Don't plant bombs in buses, trains, and on the roads. Innocent people will be killed. Target politicians who cheat people of their vote, rape women, take bribes, and indulge in unjust acts. And also those ugly bureaucrats who misuse their powers and take people for granted. If you harass people already tormented in life, what will you gain?"

His criticism of the country's political leaders was harsh. "People like Jayalalitha, Deve Gowda, Karunanidhi, and Rajiv Gandhi have looted our country of its riches. They have played with innocent people's lives. Why did Rajiv Gandhi have to send the army to Jaffna? Did he not know that it was our own brothers and sisters who were fighting a war for their freedom there? Not for nothing did he die such a horrible death. He deserved it."

Veerappan had a ready justification for all his criminal acts. His ethical realm is clearly far removed from the rest of the world's interpretation of law. His logic of governance was his own. "Yes, I have killed hundreds of elephants. But haven't I helped the innumerable birds, animals, and insects that feed on the carcass? Also, the elephant dies without really experiencing any great pain. I always aim at its forehead, you see."

Having exhausted his ire, Veerappan made a plea to the government to consider his terms and conditions for surrender. He began pompously: "I shall surrender only before the president of India by laying down arms." But when he was informed by the reporters that it might not be possible for the president to personally oversee the surrender, the bandit modified his terms. "I shall surrender in public with an order for clemency signed by the president stating, 'Public clemency has been given to Veerappan and if any injury is caused to him, the government will take action against the culprits.'

"I must immediately be given police protection and an inquiry must be conducted into police atrocities. Hundreds of women were raped and several men killed by the police. I shall get all the raped women to testify before any commission of inquiry. The government should compensate the families of those killed by the police. A minimum of one hundred thousand rupees should be paid."

It was clear that Veerappan was trying to portray himself as a savior to the villagers in his area. But the next set of conditions was farcical. "I belong to a traditional hunting family. Since I conduct *pooja* of my weapons daily, I should be given three types of gun licenses—one for a revolver, a second for a .375 rifle, and a third one for a double-barreled gun. These licenses are only for my protection. I swear upon God that I shall never use these weapons against people. I also want gambling and hunting licenses. The hunting license is to keep forest officials wanting to harass me at bay when I visit the forests to worship family deities. I should also be given an annual quota of three hundred to four hundred bullets and cartridges.

"I should be given five billion rupees as compensation for the properties seized by the police from my family members." The properties included his old house, some four acres of agricultural land, a well, and a pump set.

"The police destroyed the Perumal temple that I built, and looted hundreds of thousands of rupees from the hundi"—the sacred receptacle into which devotees put monetary donations. "They also stole a silver spear and gold ornaments worth hundreds of thousands. I should be compensated for all this."

He then demanded clemency for all his associates lodged in various jails in Tamil Nadu and Karnataka. "All criminal cases against me should be quashed. Police forces stationed in my area should be withdrawn at once. Till the negotiations are complete, I promise that I shall not kill even a dog. Also, the police took away six sets of elephant tusks that I had kept for a religious purpose. They should be returned to me immediately."

He was firm on instigating a Central Bureau of Investigation (CBI) inquiry into the death of Arjunan, Aiyyan Dorai, and Karangalur Rangaswamy. "The police killed them and then said that they consumed cyanide. Two politicians, Jayalalitha and Deve Gowda, know all about the criminal conspiracy." Lastly, the bandit expected the government to allow his filmmaking skills to flower. "I want to produce a biographical film which should not be banned just because it would contain derogatory remarks on politicians, the bureaucracy, and the police."

The journalists returned with their extraordinary documentation of Veerappan's life, and soon afterward their coup was splashed on the pages of the Tamil biweekly *Nakkeeran*, headquartered in Chennai.

The editor of *Nakkeeran*, R. R. Gopal, was a native of Aruppukottai, a small village near Madurai. He had started his journalistic career as a layout artist. But it was as the editor of *Nakkeeran* that he came into his own. He created a buzz in Tamil journalism in the late 1980s and 1990s with his regular and exhaustive exposés of criminals. In fact, his magazine was named after a mythical sage who had questioned Lord Shiva himself about the veracity of a verse that he had written. It was during Jayalalitha's regime, between 1991 and 1996, that *Nakkeeran* became well known for its features on murky affairs in the corridors of power.

Gopal antagonized the ruling All India Dravida Munnetra Khazhagam (AIADMK) by publishing a hard-hitting article, accompanied by telling photographs, about a scuffle between its rival factions, one led by Jayalalitha herself and the other by Thirunavukkarasu, over the possession of the party headquarters. He also printed pictures of alleged AIADMK men savagely attacking Union minister P. Chidambaram's car at Tiruchi in August 1991.

The AIADMK government ordered raids on Gopal's office, and party cadres tore magazines from newsstands and burned them. On several occasions, *Nakkeeran*'s reporters, photographers, and even hawkers were roughed up in Chennai for the insinuating articles. The magazine's publisher, Ganesan, died after allegedly being tortured by the police. But the gritty Gopal carried on with his sensational exposés.

Gopal's serializing of the life and times of "Auto" Shankar, an auto driver turned maniacal serial killer, who had stalked the streets of Chennai in the late 1980s, contributed to the magazine's popularity. *Nakkeeran* soon became a best-selling periodical with a big fan following in Tamil Nadu.

A shrewd man, Gopal had now begun to write extensively and almost exclusively on the life of Veerappan, much to the frustration of his competitors. Copies of his magazine began to sell like hotcakes across Tamil Nadu and particularly in places like Salem, Erode, and Periyar, where the bandit had become a cult figure.

It was not long before Gopal began to accompany his correspondents to the smuggler's hideout. Within the next six months, Shiva Subramaniam met the bandit as many as six times, and Gopal twice.

Although it confounded everybody that Gopal and his men could enter the forests and meet Veerappan at will, while the police continued to grope in the dark, completely clueless, it was clear that the Tamil Nadu government under whose jurisdiction he carried on his "journalistic" missions had no desire either to question him seriously or think of a strategy to trail him and his men into the bandit's den. Gopal's alleged closeness to Karunanidhi, who had taken over from Jayalealitha in late 1995, was said to be the main reason for this reluctance. The Karnataka government, on the other hand, had very little to say in the matter, because Gopal, as a rule, confined himself to the boundaries of Tamil Nadu when he interacted with Veerappan. The Karnataka government then filed a criminal case against him on charges of willfully concealing information about a man wanted by the state. Gopal, however, pleaded the right to journalistic freedom, and the Karnataka high court found in his favor. There was nothing the police could do.

Veerappan repeatedly sent word through Gopal emphasizing his desire to surrender, but the governments, quite expectedly, did not respond to his terms and conditions. Despite reaching out through his newfound friends, Veerappan was destined to live in the jungle for many more years.

# PART III

# 12

## Muthulakshmi's Story

I was born in 1973, the last of three children to my parents, Aiyyan and Pappamma, in Neruppur village close to Hogenekal in Dharmapuri district. I'm twenty-seven years old now. My brother's name is Sengondan, and my sister is called Chinna Ponnu. Ours was a poor family which owned a small bit of land. As a young girl, I would go with my parents to work on the land.

During those days, there was a lot of sandalwood growing in the forests surrounding our area. I had heard of a man called Veerappan who was known to cut sandalwood and take it to far-off places to sell. My friend Bhanumathi would talk about him often. As days went by, I started to notice this man moving around in our area quite regularly.

Bhanumathi had a nodding acquaintance with Veerappan. One day I asked her to introduce me to him. She was surprised. But she didn't know that I had begun to like him. His mustache, the way he walked, the way he settled disputes in the village, everything. In fact, people in the area would queue up to get their disputes settled by him. There was a kind of authority in his tone and his gait, which I liked.

Bhanumathi finally introduced me to him. That day I was so happy,

I went home smiling all the way. Veerappan began to visit us. It looked like he also liked me. Every time he visited us, I would feel good. My parents, though, had no idea about my fascination for him. One morning when he came home to see us, he sat in the yard in front of our small hut and said to my father, "*Aiyya*, I want to marry your daughter. Please don't disappoint me. I promise you that I shall take care of her well."

My father was taken aback. He had never expected a marriage proposal from a man like Veerappan. "No, it is not possible. I'm sorry. We have already decided to get her married off to one of our relatives. Please don't force us to change our plans at this stage."

My parents had decided, even without my knowledge, to marry me off to one of my cousins. It was only when my father told Veerappan that I came to know of his plans. I had no say in all this. I was considered too young to be even consulted on such matters. Deep down, I was beginning to feel sad.

A few months passed. I did not see Veerappan after that. One afternoon I was relaxing alone in the hut when I saw a familiar figure entering. It was Veerappan. I saw that he had brought some betel nuts and leaves with him. In our part of the world, they are considered very auspicious. He said, "Muthu, you'll have to swear on this plate of betel leaves that you'll never marry anyone other than me. Here, I shall also do the same." Saying this he made me place my hand on the plate and did the same himself.

I was thrilled. I was willing to do anything that he asked me to. I told him, "My brother Sengondan and uncle Mattukaran can convince my parents, if you can talk to them."

Veerappan smiled and said, "Muthu, I shall not leave your side, no matter what happens. So don't worry. Everything will be fine. We shall get married, no matter what happens."

Ultimately, after all the discussions were over, my mother relented but my father was firm in his decision to marry me off to my cousin.

Soon after this, I ran away from home, with Veerappan. We got married at a forest temple with only *vanadevathe* [Mother Nature] for a witness. I was overjoyed at the very thought of being known as Veerappan's wife. Soon after our marriage, I went away to the forest and joined the other members of his gang. At that time, there were hundreds of men in the gang. My brother-in-law Arjunan was also there. I was the only woman in the entire gang. But it didn't matter. They all took good care of me.

Soon I found myself pregnant. We would change our location in the forest regularly, and being pregnant, I found it quite difficult to walk on the rough tracks in the forest. I somehow managed until I was eight months into my pregnancy. After that it became quite impossible to live in the forest. Veerappan was also concerned about my condition. One evening he told me, "Muthu, tomorrow morning you should start back for your village. There is no woman to take care of you or to deliver the baby. Also, I don't want the baby's cries to give away our position just in case the police come after us." I was not at all willing to go back to Neruppur, leaving my husband in the forest. But finally I had to relent, as there was no other way out.

Next morning Veerappan called his trusted aide Sethukuli Govindan aside and spoke to him. "Take Muthu safely to the outskirts of Neruppur. Leave her there and make sure she reaches her parents' house safely," he said. Sethukuli escorted me as instructed by Veerappan. My parents were dumbfounded to see me at their doorstep so unexpectedly. When they saw that I was pregnant, they took me inside.

"We missed you so much all these days. Did you have to do this to us? How have you been? Where were you and how is Veerappan?" asked my mother, her maternal affection overflowing. I was given food to eat and was made comfortable in the hut.

There were cases pending against my husband in the Dharmapuri police station at that time. My father was afraid that the police would somehow get wind of my arrival at Neruppur and arrest me. So he decided to take me to the home of a lawyer, Appun, in Dharmapuri, where he thought I would be safe. My father and I spent the night in the lawyer's house. He was a kind man who understood our plight. He said, "The police are bound to come after you sooner or later. For all you know, they might have found out about your arrival already. So I suggest that you go to Chennai and surrender before the police there. By doing that, you'll be saving yourself a lot of harassment."

The next morning, I took a bus to Chennai with my father. I surrendered before the police there. They sent me to Mary Hostel, a women's hostel somewhere in Chennai. There was a constable assigned to keep an eye on me all the time. Soon I gave birth to a baby girl. I was so happy to be a mother. How I wished my husband was also there to rejoice at the birth of our child. But I was fated not to have him around.

After a few days I was allowed to return to Dharmapuri, where I was given refuge by the kind lawyer. I stayed in a portion of his house for six months along with the baby. My mother also stayed with me. My baby was given a name. She was called Vidya Rani. The man who named her was none other than SP Shailendra Babu. After a while, he even allowed me to go my village, Neruppur. But there was a twenty-four-hour vigil of fifteen constables and one DSP around my house.

As days went by, I began to feel secure in the company of my family members, especially my little one. I was not allowed to go out anywhere, but it did not seem to matter. One day, one of my husband's men came to our hut, posing as our relative. The minute he entered the hut he whispered to me, "*Aiyya* wants you to join him immediately. He is missing you very much. He wants you to leave the baby behind with your parents and leave for the forest."

I could not even think of leaving my little one behind. How could I desert such a small baby who needed me at all times? Oh no, it was just not in me to think of doing anything like that. I decided not to go to my husband. I did miss him. On the other hand, there was this tiny little being who looked at me with such innocence and love. No, I did not want to be separated from her.

Two months passed. I began to think of my husband. How was he coping with life without me? When would I see him again? Was I destined to join him again? One day, finally, I decided to join him. I convinced myself that the baby had to be left behind so that it could grow up in total security, join school, study well, and come up in life. In 1992, I escaped under the cover of darkness with the help of my sister-in-law, Mariamma. I tricked the police by telling them that I wanted to attend nature's call. Soon I was reunited with my husband. Oh, it was such a wonderful feeling to be in his company again. Even he was beaming with joy to have me back.

For three years I roamed the forests with my husband. He would get me whatever I wanted—cosmetics, sarees, jewels. He always wanted me to be dressed well and look my best. Life in the forest was not a big problem, except that I had to walk for miles on end. We would stay in tents or sometimes in caves inside the forest. Food was no problem. We would eat good dried meat, dal, rice, sambar, and even instant dosas.

Every time my husband left the hideout to shoot an elephant or cut sandalwood, I would spend the day playing *ghattabara* (a game of dice) with those left to provide security for me. Never once did I ask my husband questions about his activities. I was his life partner, never a business partner! While in the forests, we'd change camps often to avoid being detected by the police. Our camping spots would always be near a water hole, a pond, or a stream. In fact, after I rejoined the gang, I was quite overjoyed to find that most of the gang members had gotten married and I would have the pleasure of their wives' company.

Moving from forest to forest, we reached the Punajanur area in 1993. We built huts and stayed there for months without any fear of a police attack. It was a safe area to stay in—until one day, when the police learned our whereabouts and raided the place. I was taken into custody. They took me blindfolded to the Bannari police camp. The worst part of my life was about to unfold in the dark confines of a cell there. I noticed that there were three other women inside. Two policemen walked up to me and kicked me, saying, "You bitch, if you don't tell us all that you know, you'll never be able to go out alive." They made me remove my blouse and even my brassiere, placed two clips on my nipples, and gave me electric shocks. The torture had just begun. My body convulsed every time they subjected me to the shock treatment. They had murder in their eyes. It was so scary that I fainted, unable to withstand the pain and humiliation.

I was finally left to lie in the cell, blindfolded. I was numb with pain and shivering uncontrollably. As I was blindfolded, I did not even see the break of dawn. Suddenly, I heard the sound of boots stamping the ground. I knew that my tormentors had returned. I was cowering in fright and my mind went blank. Inspector Kumaraswamy of the Karnataka STF came in and told one of the men to take me to another room.

The torture began all over again: electric shock treatment, which began at 8 a.m. and went on sporadically till 4 p.m. This went on for fifteen days. I had already told them all that I knew about my husband. But they were harping on only one point. They wanted me to reveal the exact location of his hideout. How could I tell them about the exact whereabouts of a man who changes his place of stay almost daily? They just did not seem to understand.

As days passed, it was becoming increasingly difficult to withstand the torture in the camp. But I gritted my teeth and bore everything. Then the most horrifying experience of my life took place. Inspector Kumaraswamy came to me one morning. There were two other constables with him. He ordered them, "Tear off all her clothes. She'll soon know what it is to be Veerappan's wife and move around the forests like a queen." He was full of sarcasm. I was so scared that I did not know how to react.

Although the two constables seemed hesitant to do their superior's bidding, they had no choice. I found myself stark naked. I was helpless and completely lost. Did I have a choice? They took out some chili powder from a packet. Pulling me toward them, they stuffed the powder into my eyes and tied a piece of cloth tightly around them. My eyes began to burn and I began to scream like a madwoman. But they were unmoved.

The policemen then tied both my hands behind my back. This was the beginning of another kind of torture. A long rope connecting my hands was then passed through a hook on the ceiling. Two policemen began to pull the rope hanging from the ceiling. My hands tightened behind my back and I was lifted and suspended in the air a few feet from the ground. The police, I found out later, call it "airplane." The bones in my entire body felt like they were being broken into pieces. A shooting pain ripped through my body and I was howling in uncontrollable pain. I thought I was going to die. My eyes were burning like hot coals, my joints were being mercilessly pounded, and my whole body ached so much that it is hard to even put it in words. The searing pain coursed madly through every single nerve inside me and made me scream like a woman possessed.

But the policemen were not satisfied. They placed a wire close to my private parts and applied electric current even as I was suspended in air. As my screams began to grow louder, so did their laughter. They were deriving some sort of a demonic thrill out of the whole thing. They looked so perverted that I did not have even the faintest hope that I would be alive for long. It would have been so much better if they had killed me at once.

This "airplane" torture went on till late afternoon. After that, they untied my hands and made me stand in front of them, facing the wall. Then they asked me to sit down. My body had been reduced to pulp inside. The pain and trauma was the worst any human being could experience. My eyes were blood-red and burning, and tears were flowing in torrents. Then they gave me some rice to eat. I tried eating a morsel but just couldn't. Like someone with a mental problem, I found that there was no coordination between my hand and my mouth.

After this, the policemen in the camp started to indulge in another kind of harassment. They would hold me by the hand and try and pull me toward them. I always knew what their intentions were. They would stare at me and wink. Some of them would even follow me to the toilet and make lewd remarks. One constable, belonging to the Tamil Nadu STF, was particularly vulgar and indecent.

While the Karnataka police tortured me like this, the policemen belonging to Tamil Nadu would stand and watch. One day, SP Sanjay Arora came to the camp. He wanted to see me. I mustered up my courage and spoke to him. I said, "Swami, the policemen here have not only tortured me but also make sexual advances. I cannot bear it any longer. Please advise them not to do such things to me."

My voice was so weak that he could barely hear me. He came across as a decent man. He listened to me patiently and asked me, "Can you tell me the names of those who have done such things to you?"

I said, "No, I would not know their names. But I can surely recognize them by face."

After listening to my tale of woe, the officer seemed quite moved. He gave an order that those on sentry duty should be changed. Soon he left. But after he was gone, the constable who had harassed me was very angry. He came into my cell and slapped me so hard that I almost fainted. An SI who was present intervened and saved me from undergoing more torture at that man's hands.

As I continued to languish in the camp, the Tamil Nadu police began to wonder what they should finally do with me. I had become a bit of a headache for them. I would hear them discuss among themselves whether they should file cases against me or even finish me off in one go. As these things went on, a photographer was summoned to the camp. They forced me to strip to my undergarments. The photographer took some photos of me in that state. It was so humiliating, but in the presence of such devils what could I do to safeguard my honor?

Food was given to me the way a stray dog is thrown leftovers. It would either be a small piece of dosa or some rice and rasam that they would give me for the day. I had to beg them even for a glass of water. I had not experienced such hardship even when I was in the forest.

The policemen were not capable of taking on my husband. They were a bunch of cowards. But they took out their frustration and anger on me because I happened to be Veerappan's wife. In the meantime, in December 1994, my husband kidnapped DSP Chidambaranathan and two others from the Sirumugai forests. A lot of things happened after that, and eventually my brother-in-law Arjunan and a couple of others began to negotiate with the collector of Coimbatore. During this time, my husband sent Baby Veerappan to Bhavani to look me up. He brought a small tape recorder with him.

He came to my cell and said, "*Aiyya* has sent me to find out how you are doing. Here, take this. Record whatever you want to say to him on this tape. I shall immediately take it to him." I spoke into the tape recorder and informed my husband about the kinds of torture that I had undergone at the hands of the police since my capture from the Minchguli forests. I even named men like Kumaraswamy, Venkataswamy, Rajendran, and Musale.

Baby Veerappan took the tape and handed it to my husband, who was furious. He gave a press statement that he would mercilessly chop to pieces all those men who had tortured me. When the press, in places like Erode, Satyamangalam, and Dharmapuri, carried the news of Veerappan's ire, it only angered the policemen further. Mohan Nawaz, an SI, came to me. He began to shout at the top of his voice, "So you have sent a cassette to your husband, have you? Let's see if he will come through the roof and save you. What do you think of yourself? We'll finish you now." He hit me with a baton and shouted profanities at me. I bore all this in silence.

Once a man named Nellur Madiah came to the camp. He was a police informer. He had been with my husband for a long time. He was also involved in sandalwood smuggling and elephant poaching. But now he had turned a police informer.

Looking at me he asked, "Do you know me?"

I said, "Of course I remember you. Are you not the same fellow who was with my husband as his follower?"

He tried being sarcastic and insulting. "So who is your husband? Is he a minister or some sort of a big shot? Who is he?"

"Of course my husband will one day become a minister. Just because you are now with the police, don't think the others don't know your past."

He went away in a huff.

I was unable to withstand the different sorts of mental and physical torture they were inflicting on me in the camp. One day I decided to end my life by starving myself to death. I started to refuse food and water. Even then the police said, "This woman has now started to please the gods with her vratha. She wants us to die and her husband to prosper." After a couple of days, my resolve to end my life became firmer. I noticed a bottle of phenol in a corner of the toilet. That was it. I decided to drink it and kill myself. I did not eat a morsel or drink even a drop of water that day. On an empty stomach, I knew the poison would take effect immediately.

That night I pretended to sleep. My cellmates, Selva Mary, Ratnamma, and Periya Thayi, who had been rounded up by the police soon after my arrest, were also deep in sleep. I noticed that the two policemen guarding me had already begun to snore outside my cell. I got up slowly and in the darkness, I reached the toilet. Taking hold of the phenol bottle, I opened the cap. The smell was so strong that it hit me in the nostrils. But I had made up my mind. Closing my eyes firmly and covering my nostrils tightly, I emptied the entire bottle into my mouth. I collapsed on the floor in sheer tension. After ten minutes, my head started to reel and my mind began to go blank.

Half an hour later, I began to get a vomiting sensation. Even before I could try to control it, I had begun to throw up. I lay in a pool of vomit. The noise of my retching woke up the other women, who rushed to my side and began to cry loudly. The policemen woke up with a start and peeped through the toilet window. Not knowing what had happened, they ran to Mohan Nawaz's quarters nearby and woke him.

I was taken to the government hospital in Satyamangalam. But the police made sure that no journalist came anywhere near the hospital. A few journalists who had heard of my tales of torture through a few nurses there ran stories in their papers that I had been admitted to the hospital after being inhumanly tortured.

The publicity in the press made the policemen panic a little. They decided to release me and the other three women. We were told that we were free to return to our homes. But I was scared of the Karnataka police. "Who will save us if the Karnataka police arrest and take us away after we reach our villages?" I asked.

"It is none of our concern," they replied.

I stayed in Bannari for about fifteen days and recouped my energies to some extent. I had become a physical wreck by then. Even my mental faculties seemed to be affected to a large extent.

After this, the police took me to the Mettur inspection bungalow. By this time, my husband, who had found out almost all the details of my torture through the press, had sent a letter to a Tamil organization requesting it to get me released from police custody. The officers of the organization approached the court and sent a legal notice to the police. Tamil Nadu deputy superintendent of police (DSP) Ashok Kumar told me the court had been moved. He said, "Now you'll have to tell the court what we tell you to. Otherwise, you'll be in trouble. If you go out without informing the court, chances are the Karnataka police will arrest you. Then we will not be responsible for you. So do as we say."

The other women who were with me were more terrified at the thought of being picked up by the Karnataka police than I was. They began to plead with me, "Let's do as the police say. Otherwise we'll all die at the hands of the Karnataka police. Please listen to us. We've been together all this while and undergone such terrible hardships. So even if we live it should be together. Please try and understand our feelings."

Two of the women were nursing mothers at that time. When I saw them suckling their babies, I was so moved by their plight that I gave the whole thing serious thought. I told myself that there was nothing left in the issue. The torture and harassment had gone on for nearly three years. Now there was an opportunity to put together the broken pieces of my life. I felt there was no point in fighting for justice in the courts. I would have to run behind lawyers and hang around in the court complex for years and years. I was mentally and physically so exhausted that I did not have the will to do that. I finally decided to go along with what the other women had told me. I said to the police, "We are willing to tell the court whatever you ask us to tell it." The policemen seemed relieved.

As I sat in my cell along with the other women, my thoughts went back to the days when my child was a tiny toddler. How I wanted to see her, take her in my arms and play with her. I was desperate to call out to her by her name and ask her to come close to me. But would she recognize me after all these years? Would she show the same love toward me now?

I begged the policemen to fetch my daughter. "*Aiyya*, I want to see my little one. I'm longing to hold her in my arms. It's been so many years since I saw her face. Please allow me this one desire in life. Please do not refuse this one humble request. I fold my hands in prayer to you. I shall fall at your feet if you want me to. But please do not refuse me."

Perhaps because I had told the police that I was willing to do their bidding in court, they relented easily. "All right, we shall bring your daughter from your house in Dharmapuri. We understand your feelings."

I could hardly sleep that night from sheer excitement. The next day, I rose early and bathed. I was so eager to see my little girl. Very soon she would be here, and I was full of joy. I just couldn't control myself. I shouted to my cellmates excitedly, "My little girl is coming to see me. She should be here any moment. Oh God, am I not lucky to be alive to see her again in life? I'm so grateful."

As I paced about in my cell, thrilled at the prospect of seeing my daughter after what seemed like ages, I heard the sound of a jeep drawing up to the portico of the building. From my cell, I could hear the jeep's engine being switched off. But I couldn't see anybody. Suddenly I heard footsteps. Was it the police bringing my daughter to me? My heart was beating excitedly in anticipation. My hands began to tremble. I was so eager to see her. How did she look after all these years, I wondered.

As the footsteps neared my cell, I saw my elder sister Chinna Ponnu. I was craning my neck to see if my little one was also there. I noticed a small figure following my sister. Yes, there she was, my little darling. I was seeing her for the first time in six long years. How much she had grown. I had last seen her when she was just six months old. I had left her in my parents' house to join my husband then. I couldn't control the tears rolling down my cheeks. There she was, looking so sweet, with her hair in a bob and wearing a lovely little clip. As she walked behind my sister, I called out to her. I stretched out both my hands through the cell door as she neared me.

The policemen opened the cell and let me out. I rushed out madly. But the little one was hesitant to come to me. She clung to my sister tightly. "Go to her. She is your mother," coaxed my sister, unable to hold back her tears. It was such an emotional moment.

"Come, my dearest one. Don't you remember me? I'm sure you do. I'm your mother. Oh, how much I missed you. Only my soul knows the kind of pain I bore just to be able to see you again. Come my little one, don't be scared. I'm your mother, my baby. Come, come."

After a while, my little daughter slowly began to walk toward me. I hugged her tightly, unaware that I was crying aloud in joy. I kept kissing and hugging her. It was the ultimate moment of my life. My heart had yearned for this moment and only I knew the intensity of it.

After a while, my little one began to realize that I was indeed her mother. She hugged me with her small arms. "When will you come home? Won't you send me to school? I want to be with you all the time," she said.

"Oh my little one, I shall come out of here soon. And I shall certainly send you to school. Don't you worry," I cried. Although I had decided to end my life on many previous occasions, now there was this great desire in me to live just for the sake of my daughter. I told my sister that I would return home soon after deposing before the court.

The next day, a few police officers came to meet us. They said, "Tell the court what you have been told to say. Do not change your version in the least when you're there." We were then taken to the Mettur general hospital, where a medical examination was conducted. Even there we told the doctors that we had not been beaten while in custody. Later we found ourselves in a police van, which took us to Chennai. We were housed for the night in a small room somewhere in the city. The next day a government lawyer who came to see us said we should tell the court that we had surrendered on our own and that no torture was administered to us while we were in custody. After tutoring us one last time, the police left us to spend the rest of the day in our room.

On the third day, we were taken to the Chennai High Court and made to stand in front of a judge. As soon as we started telling the judge what we had been told by the police, an independent lawyer who was present in the court hall rose and began to tell the judge that we were lying because of the fear of the police. "Please ask the policemen present here to leave the hall, your honor," he said. The judge asked the policemen to leave.

None of us wanted to take chances. We had decided to tell the court what the policemen had asked us to. I began, "We surrendered before the police. After they asked us a few questions, they asked us to leave the Bannari camp. But we stayed put because we were scared of Veerappan. We thought we would be killed by his men if we ventured out again. In fact, we were treated very well by the police all these days." The judge heard each one of us and passed a judgment that we should be released immediately from custody.

We were brought back to Mettur. SPs Sanjay Arora and Tamil Selvam were there along with their wives. They advised us, "Don't go back to a life of crime. Now you are free to return to your villages. We assure you that no policeman will ever harass you from now on. Go and lead a good life." In fact, Tamil Selvam was still under treatment for the injuries he had sustained when my husband had fired on him near Dimbam. Still, he was considerate to me. The wives of the officers even got the two little babies of my cellmates inoculated. Then we were finally allowed to leave.

DSP Ashok Kumar took us to Coimbatore, where he organized a room for the four of us to stay, free of cost. He even got us jobs at a weaving factory in nearby Annur. I spent three years working as a helper in that factory. I had no problems as I was earning some money. But my ill luck had not deserted me fully. One day a reporter belonging to *Junior Vikatan* spotted me. He took my photograph and published it in the newspaper. Everybody came to know that I was Veerappan's wife. The factory owner, who thought that he would become entangled in some kind of case, dismissed me from my job.

After this even my former cellmates quit their jobs and returned to their villages. I returned to my native village of Neruppur. I stayed with my parents for two months. After that I joined a banian-manufacturing factory in Tiruppur as a helper. My salary was one thousand and one hundred rupees per month. I joined a women's hostel. The hostel cost six hundred rupees per month. I managed to secure admission for my daughter at a fairly decent residential school that taught in English. Her expenses were about seven hundred rupees per month. Managing my finances was a fine balancing act every month. I was always tense because even if I fell short by a few rupees, there was nobody I could turn to. I somehow managed to go on like this for one year.

Since I knew a bit of tailoring, I thought of augmenting my income by buying a sewing machine and working as a ladies' tailor after factory hours. My brother-in-law Koose Madiah's wife's family lived somewhere near the Workshop Road in Mettur. In desperation, I decided to locate them and seek their help. I succeeded in finding Koose Madiah's sister-in-law, Ramayi. She was running a small tea stall there. She was happy to see me. When she heard my story she was not only sad for me but also quite upset with me.

"Did you think that we were all dead? Couldn't you have come to us earlier, instead of struggling the way you did? Quit the hostel and come and live with us. What are relatives for, if they don't help you in times of need?"

Ramayi helped me set up a tiny cigarette outlet in front of her tea stall. I moved in with her family and even put my little daughter, Vidya Rani, in a good convent school. I didn't want the media to hound her, so I decided to put her in a hostel attached to the school. My greatest desire in life is to ensure that she grows up to be a doctor who can save the lives of the poor and the oppressed.

# PART IV

# 13

# The Negotiator

In July 1997, the forest areas of Kollegala were hit with severe rains. There seemed to be no letup, as though the rain gods had decided to target the region for special treatment. It poured incessantly, sometimes almost throughout the day. RFO Jayendrappa was worried. He was afraid that the makeshift bridges, constructed of wooden logs bound closely together in a row, laid across small streams running through the deep gorges inside the forest, would be unable to withstand nature's fury. The upkeep of these bridges was vital to maintaining access routes for the staff on routine inspections inside the forest.

On July 11, 1997, the downpour was at last reduced to a trickle, and Jayendrappa decided to take advantage of the change in weather. The sky had cleared slightly and the sun was making desperate attempts to emerge from its weeklong incarceration behind the clouds. The RFO drove his jeep straight to the Gundal range, which nestles in the foothills of the Biligirirangana Betta, six miles from Hanur. As he drove through the forest, his heart, as always, lifted at the sight of the greenery all around. But not for long. When he reached the Marpala bridge, an important link to the other forest ranges in the area, he found it had given way.

Returning to Kollegala, he called a meeting of his staff. Forester Velayudhan, guards Andani and Vishakanta, and daily wagers Dasa, Jadiya, Kumbha, Raju, Mahadeva, and Nanjanayaka were made responsible for carrying out repairs on the bridge. "Start the work tomorrow. I want it to be ready by evening." Jayendrappa was anxious to plant teak saplings and develop a nursery in the area near where the bridge had collapsed.

The repair team left the next day at 7 a.m. in a van driven by Basavaraju, who belonged to the Chamarajanagar wildlife division. Marpala was thirteen miles from Kollegala, but it took them nearly two hours because the rains had made the forest tracks slushy and quite unnavigable. The bridge, deep inside the forest, was in a state of semi-collapse. Some of the thick logs had fallen into the stream. A few old logs had decayed and were now completely brittle. Forester Velayudhan instructed driver Basavaraju to stay in the vehicle while he led the group farther into the forest, away from the game road, to cut fresh logs to replace the damaged ones. A short distance from the bridge, the team climbed a small hillock to survey the area and choose the trees which could provide the required timber for the repair work.

The forest was calm. Mercifully, the day was now bright. Standing on the hillock, Vishakanta told himself that he should be able to finish the work quickly and return to Hanur by evening. He was looking forward to spending time with a few relatives who were visiting his family after a long time. He came out of his reverie when Velayudhan snapped at them to stop wasting time and get on with work. The men picked up their axes and began to hack at the base of the selected trees. Suddenly, five men wearing khaki uniforms and holding guns appeared from out of the bushes. The forester's team didn't recognize them, but the men looked and spoke menacingly enough to make them realize they might be in trouble. One of them seized Vishakanta's double-barreled gun and said, "We are Veerappan's men. Who are you?" Nobody answered. "Come with us. Veerappan is waiting." They began to push Velayudhan and his men in the direction of the bridge.

As they walked down the game road, Vishakanta began to get the sinking feeling that he wouldn't be home that evening to meet his relatives. Everyone was silent. Nearing the bridge, their fear turned to horror. Leaning against the parked van stood a man whom they immediately recognized as Veerappan. He looked at them expressionlessly. The driver Basavaraju stood on one side, his hands tied with a rope.

Veerappan began to slowly walk toward Velayudhan. "Weren't you the one who signed *a mahazar sheet* against me while serving in Gopinatham?" Velayudhan looked down, unable to meet his accuser's eye. Veerappan's memory was remarkable. Velayudhan had been a forest guard in his native village of Gopinatham, almost a decade ago, and had routinely signed official documents recording the occurrence of a crime.

"Chain all these fellows. Make sure they are kept together," Veerappan ordered one of his men. The ten foresters were pushed to the side and made to huddle together. Chains, the kind normally used to secure pet dogs, were run around their bodies and held tightly by three of the gangsters. Veerappan then began to march them toward Gummani Betta, half a mile away.

As the horrified men contemplated their future, Andani, for one, was convinced that his life was about to come to an end. He knew the ways of the bandit from as far back as 1969, having lived in the area for many years. "He won't spare any forest employee he lays his hands on," Andani told himself. The ghastly beheading of DCF Srinivas was proof enough of that.

They soon reached Gummani Betta, and Veerappan climbed on top of the hillock, from where he had a clear view of the forest that spread in all directions, as far as the eye could see. Perhaps he wanted to plan the route the group should take next. Or perhaps he was looking for bigger fish to catch. He didn't seem very happy that he had snared only the lower ranks of the forest department and no officers.

"Sit down, everybody," he said, gesturing with his hand. "The Karnataka government is causing me a lot of trouble. They are harassing me and my men. I will not tolerate this kind of behavior. Who do they think they are playing with? Your department is creating too many problems for me. The Tamil Nadu forest officers are a lot better. They respect me and even help me from time to time. I thought I could grab a few of your senior officers and make your government dance to my tune. Where are they? Why didn't they come with you today? What will

I do with fellows like you?" Everyone was silent; nobody dared say a word.

Veerappan then sat quietly for a while, contemplating his next move. Should he let these men go? Or should he wait a little longer to see if a bigger fish came his way? Ten minutes passed before he got up abruptly and disappeared behind a tree along with his trusted lieutenant, Sethukuli Govindan, who was carrying a cloth bag. He had made up his mind. The bag Govindan carried contained a small tape recorder, into which Veerappan recorded his demands.

"Take the van and get the rations," he told Tangaraj, a young member of the gang. There were nine of them altogether, including Veerappan. There was Sethukuli Govindan, "Tupaki" Sidda, "Meke" Rangaswamy, Madesha, Abru, Tangaraj, and Amburaj, besides Kumbhi, "Tupaki" Sidda's wife. Tangaraj hurried down the hillock to where the van had been parked, nearly half a mile away. About twenty-five minutes later he returned, gasping for breath. The van had got stuck in slush only a short distance away. Veerappan looked at Basavaraju. Without being told, the vehicle's original driver began to walk down the hillock with the inexperienced youngster in tow. It took them nearly forty minutes to get the rations hidden in the depths of the forest.

Some time later, the hostages were herded into the van. After everyone, including the gangsters, had got in, Veerappan ordered the driver to take the van to the Burude guesthouse, five miles away in the neighboring Bailur forest range. The guesthouse, built during the time of the British, was located deep inside the forest and was strictly off limits to anyone other than forest department officials. But Veerappan had little time for such niceties.

After a tense thirty-minute journey in an overcrowded van, which skidded perilously on the slippery and slushy game road, they reached the guesthouse at 7:30 p.m. There was not a soul in the vicinity of the building. The guesthouse obviously didn't have a full-time caretaker because of its location. It was cleaned and tended to only when an officer was on a visit. "Take all that you can. Blankets, water bottles, cooking utensils, and glass tumblers," Veerappan instructed the hostages. They began to realize they had a long ordeal ahead of them. Some of them even tore down the window curtains and packed them. They would come in handy as sheets to cover themselves in the night. Veerappan himself picked up two double-barreled guns and a handful of bullets kept in one of the rooms. He then divided the rations, consisting of rice, ragi, tamarind paste, salt, sambar powder, and the like into nine equal parts, tied them up in cloth bundles, and told the hostages each to carry a bundle.

By now, the moon was high up in the sky. The forest was enveloped in an eerie silence, punctuated only by the rhythmic chirping of crickets and the croaking of toads near a water hole. Turning to Basavaraju, Veerappan handed him the cassette. "Take this carefully to your deputy conservator—what's his name . . ." He scratched his chin, trying to remember. He was referring to Vijay Kumar Gogi, based in Chamarajanagar.

Basavaraju was as reluctant to leave his colleagues behind as he was to drive alone on the slippery game road in the dark night. "*Swami*, there is not enough diesel left in the tank. I cannot go that far," he protested mildly.

Veerappan stared at him. As he watched, Andani felt as though Basavaraju had incurred the wrath of the devil himself. But instead of doing anything to the driver, the bandit inserted a long stick into the diesel tank, removed it, and feeling its level of wetness, declared, "You're right, you are running low on diesel." He took out three hundred rupees from his pocket and gave it to the driver. "Take this and find a way to reach the place somehow." Basavaraju looked helplessly at his mates, reluctantly got into the cabin, and drove away into the darkness.

Veerappan, along with the hostages, began to walk in the direction of a Soliga settlement deep inside the forest, at a place called Keredimba. The stillness of the night was broken only by the heavy breathing of the terrified hostages and the dull thumping of their feet on the rough ground. As they neared the settlement of a few ancient-looking huts, dogs began to bark, sensing the intruders. But neither Veerappan nor his mates seemed unduly worried. The Soliga tribals had always been on their side, either out of fear or favor. The group passed the settlement silently. A little ahead was another village called Gombegallu. There too the dogs barked in the darkness, but to no effect.

It was around midnight when Veerappan decided to give the

hostages some rest. They were in the Boodipadaga area of the Biligirirangan hill ranges in Chamarajanagar district. The hostages were exhausted after the trials of the day and the long trek and were longing for a moment of respite. Veerappan addressed them. "Tonight we shall camp here. All of you try to get some sleep. But let me warn you, if any of you try to escape, I shall cut you to pieces. Do as I say and no harm shall come to you." His voice was emotionless, but he obviously meant every word. But the hostages were too tired to even contemplate escape.

The campsite was on a slight elevation, and bare of vegetation. Because there weren't many trees in the immediate vicinity, visibility was good. Verappan was a master when it came to selecting the right place to stay in the forest. While the elevation gave little chance for wild animals to make a sudden attack, the clearing allowed him to easily spot approaching intruders. Kumbhi began to collect twigs, leaves, and pieces of wood fallen on the ground, while "Meke" Rangaswamy arranged three large stones in a triangle, where he placed a huge round-bottomed aluminum vessel. A hurried dinner was prepared of rice seasoned with salt, a little turmeric powder, and a few green chilies. The hostages were ravenous and ate quickly. In a surprising act of hospitality, Veerappan had offered them their food before he himself ate.

After dinner the men lay down on the grass, covered by thin blankets taken from the Burude guesthouse. The hostages, unaccustomed to sleeping on the ground, had a restless night, but the others, including Veerappan, slept peacefully.

At 5 a.m. the next day, the hostages were rudely woken up and given twenty minutes to prepare for the journey ahead. They didn't know where they were being taken and they were too afraid to ask. For six hours they trekked through valleys and across streams, up hillocks and down small gorges, before they reached a place called Mooradi near Dodda Sampige, deep inside the Biligirirangan range.

The area gets its name from a huge sampige tree, whose trunk is so massive that six people with arms extended can just about encircle it. According to local legend, it was planted by the sage Agasthya more than three thousand years ago. Veerappan decided to camp here for the entire day.

On the third day, Veerappan moved the group to another camp

about six miles away. On the way, they spotted five men in the forest. Veerappan, apprehensive of their identity, sent two of his men to bring them to him. Only after he had ascertained that they were Soliga tribals living in the area did he breathe a little more easily. Before sending them off, he gave them five hundred rupees. This was obviously the way to ensure their silence, and was part of the usual precautions he took while moving through the forest.

Over the next few days, Veerappan shifted camps every day, with the obvious intention fo confusing the police if they happened to come after him. As they walked through the forest, they generally did not encounter other people. Finally, they passed through the forests surrounding the Honnemeti coffee estate and reached Tamil Nadu. Veerappan was visibly relieved. Now he was in "safe" territory.

On the morning of July 21, the camp, which was situated near a pond inside the forest, was visited by R. R. Gopal, the editor of *Nakkeeran*. He had come to negotiate the release of the nine hostages on behalf of the governments of Karnataka and Tamil Nadu. Veerappan himself had left the camp for a couple of hours to meet the intermediary alone.

Veerappan and Gopal went to a secluded spot near the camp and began to talk in low tones. Soon the discussion turned into an argument. The hostages noticed that Veerappan was always matter-of-fact, and at times even cold, with Gopal. What they discussed nobody in the camp, not even the others in the gang, could hear. Before leaving in the evening, Gopal spoke to the hostages and assured them that they would be released soon. Veerappan was demanding 250 million rupees as ransom, he told them.

For the hostages, the initial euphoria of seeing their "savior" began to dissipate as soon as Gopal left the place. They settled down reluctantly to life in the forest, at the mercy of a man whose moods swung from explosive rage to complete silence. Further, the hostages were not allowed to exchange even a word among themselves. The long hours of trekking silently in the dense forest, not knowing what the next day held for them, were beginning to take a toll on their health. Most of began to suffer from insomnia and lack of appetite.

Gopal came and went once more. For the hostages, the tension and uncertainty continued. They were getting weaker mentally and physically. They had not been able to shave or bathe since their ordeal began. Their mouths felt unwashed and gritty.

Veerappan seemed to revel in seeing them wither. He himself would shave quite regularly, especially prior to Gopal's visit. Also, as soon as Gopal arrived, the bandit would instruct the hostages to cry and fall at his feet, begging to be released. The little play-acting was necessary, Veerappan felt, for Gopal to convey to the authorities the precariousness of the hostages' lives.

Every time Gopal came to the camp, he brought with him two other men: his reporters Shiva Subramaniam and Subbu. Their luggage always consisted of four to five suitcases. While one suitcase contained food, such as bread, jam, biscuits, and other assorted snacks for the hostages, it was not clear what the others contained. Was it money? For the hostages, the snacks that Gopal brought were a welcome change from the almost tasteless sambar and rice they endured as captives. But for Veerappan and the other members of the gang, they were never to be touched. Who knew which slice of bread was poisoned and which biscuit didn't contain the usual wheat and sugar?

As the gang settled down in the Tamil Nadu forests, a pattern began to emerge. Once in three days, about eight to ten men would come to the camp, carrying rations in plastic bags. Days went by in this manner, and Veerappan began to relax a little. One day, he even decided to have a change of menu. His right-hand man, Sethukuli Govindan, shot a langur and brought it to the camp. Newer dishes were added to the menu. On one occasion it was venison, on another it was wild boar meat.

Whenever he had some time on his hands, especially toward the evening, Veerappan, his captives noticed, would retire with one of the two books he seemed to own and would soon be immersed. The books were Tamil editions of the *Ramayana* and the *Mahabharata*. When he was in the mood for it, he would read aloud from the epics with the whole gang sitting around him.

Fifteen days after his second visit, Gopal returned once again for the usual round of negotiations. After what seemed like ages, Veerappan announced that he would release six of the hostages. Perhaps for the first time, the hostages raised their voices. "If you are going to release us, then it has to be all of us. We refuse to have any of us left here." This show of unexpected solidarity surprised Veerappan, who had till then treated them with contempt, as if they were less than human. He did release one of the hostages, Raju, who had developed a serious infection from an insect bite at the back of his right ear. Even herbal medicines administered by Kumbhi and "Tupaki" Sidda had had no effect on his condition.

Meanwhile, Andani was a silent witness to the ripples of dissent in the gang. On one occasion, when he had gone a little distance from the camp to relieve himself, he overheard Madesha and Amburaj talking to each other. They seemed to think that Veerappan's stubbornness was complicating their lives. "We might as well surrender and spend a few years in jail. At least after that we would be free to lead a normal life."

It was now a month and a half since the hostages had fallen into Veerappan's hands, but there seemed to be no reprieve in sight. Gopal had come and gone as many as three times. Discussions had gone on for hours on end, but the hostages still didn't know what would happen to them ultimately. But things became clearer once Gopal arrived for his fourth rendezvous with Veerappan, twelve days after his previous visit. Immediately upon arrival, he huddled up with Veerappan for a long meeting, away from the campsite. Hours passed and there was no sign of the two men. The hostages were beginning to panic a little. They talked to each other in hushed tones, increasingly sure that their end was very near.

Finally Gopal appeared and said, "I have good news for you. I had a long discussion with him and have convinced him at last. Veerappan has agreed to release all of you." The hostages didn't know how to react. It was forty-four days ago that they had last breathed the air of freedom. Now they were about to be free again.

At about 8:30 p.m. on August 24, 1997, Velayudhan, Andani, Vishakanta, Dasa, Jadiya, Kumbha, Mahadeva, and Nanjanayaka were taken to a place on the fringe of the forest, close to the Punajanur main road, where two Ambassador cars were waiting. "You are free. Go and live well," Veerappan said, before disappearing into the forest again.

The group, including Gopal, reached Erode close to 2 a.m. They stayed at the house of a newsagent that night. The eight men still could not believe that they were free at last, and that their ordeal was finally over. They were taken in a bus to Chennai the following night. On August 25, at 10:30 a.m., they met with Karunanidhi in his chamber at Fort St. George. The CM expressed happiness at their safe release, although it had taken forty-four long days to achieve it. The former hostages were then kept under medical observation for forty-eight hours at a government hospital in Chennai.

Conservator of Forests (CF) (Mysore division) Sundar Naik and DCF (Chamarajanagar) Vijay Kumar Gogi had traveled to Chennai to receive their men. The nine men along with their officers later took the short flight to Bangalore and were presented before Karnataka CM J. H. Patel and Forest Minister Nagamarapalli at the Vidhana Soudha. There was relief all around that things had turned out all right.

For the nine men who had been Veerappan's hostages, life was suddenly very different. Not only had they seen Veerappan from close quarters, they had actually "lived" with him for forty-four days. For many days after their release, they remained the darlings of the media, chased by reporters and photographers. Accustomed as they were to working in the quiet of the forest, the attention and importance they were given was an unusual experience.

In a few weeks' time, the men returned to their duties and life became normal again. They chased poachers, repaired broken bridges, patrolled the forests in the night on half-empty stomachs, and walked miles in rain and sunshine. Although none of them ever came face to face with Veerappan or any of his gang members again, they have lived with that fear ever since.

## 14

# Mistaken Identity

On June 28, 1996, Shankar Bidri relinquished his post in the STF. J. H. Patel, who had taken over from H. D. Deve Gowda as the chief minister, appointed him chief of the state inteligence department. IG M. K. Srivastava replaced Bidri in the STF.

Early in 1997, the STF had found a diary with jottings in Baby Veerappan's hand. They stated that a man from Hollywood had made contact with him via the Coimbatore member of parliament (MP) to explore the possibility of making a film on Veerappan's life. The entry in the diary further said that the "film man" had been told that it was not possible to meet Veerappan, and that Veerappan himself would contact him if he felt the need for a film like the one on Phoolan Devi's life.

On April 22, 1997, the badly decomposed body of Baby Veerappan was found at a place called Arekadu Halla in the Punajanur forests, close to the Tamil Nadu border. The body, found near a campfire, bore a bullet wound in the chest. There were a few .303 cartridges lying nearby, but no weapon was found. Baby Veerappan had broken away from

Veerappan's gang by then and had his own group. His death was put down to gang rivalry.

By August, Veerappan seemed to have grown rather weary—the rigors of exile were finally beginning to tell on him. After the hostage drama, he must have decided that kidnapping was an easier way of having his voice heard in the upper echelons of the Tamil Nadu and Karnataka governments. During the second week of that month, he embarked on a long journey to the Moyar area, bordering Tamil Nadu and Karnataka, very close to the famous hill station of Ootacamund. The area derives its name from the river there, which empties into the cavernous Moyar Gorge. An inhospitable place, it is bordered by two famous wildlife sanctuaries, Mudumalai in Tamil Nadu and Bandipur in Karnataka. The continuous stretch of forests ranges from moist deciduous to dry deciduous and is home to vast herds of elephants, gaur, spotted deer, and sambhar, as well as tigers, panthers, wild dogs, and bears.

Walking through the dense forests, ridges, valleys, and gorges of the Western Ghats, Veerappan took almost one month to cover the distance from his hideout in MM Hills to Moyar. Accompanying him were Sethukuli Govindan, "Meke" Rangaswamy, Tangaraj, Amburaj, Appuswamy, and Madesha. They were on a mission. Veerappan had been told by one of his informers that the two national parks in the area attracted hundreds of tourists, including foreigners. He was shrewd enough to realize that taking a few white men hostage could have international ramifications and give him greater leverage to make demands.

Basavaraju and Mahadeva were small-time poachers and timber smugglers from the village of Hangala, five miles from the Bandipur National Park. They entered the forests sporadically, either in search of a deer to poach or a teak tree to fell. Some time in the third week of September, the two made their way toward Moyar, about eighteen miles from their village, through the forest on a poaching expedition. As they walked down a forest path they suddenly found themselves face to face with a man with a huge handlebar mustache. It was Veerappan. He growled, "Do you know who I am?"

The two poachers, taken by surprise, were so shaken they could hardly manage to squeak out their answer. "Yes, you are Veerappan," they said.

"Where are you from?" Veerappan demanded. "What are you doing here? Tell me about this place. How many tourists come to visit the sanctuaries? Do foreigners come here? Is it easy to procure rations here? If you tell me everything. I'll give you good money."

The questioning seemed to go on and on. Veerappan wanted to figure out the region's topography and also the kind of people who visited it—information which would be crucial to his plans. Basavaraju and Mahadeva began to answer Veerappan's queries with some trepidation. "*Swami*, a lot of tourists visit the two sanctuaries throughout the year. They come from all parts of India and also from other countries."

"Yes, yes, tell me more about those who come from other countries."

"*Swami*, they come here, stay in the forest lodges, go on a safari organized by the forest department, and go away." The two poachers were only stating the obvious. "And *Swami*, there is a maharaja who stays in Mangala village near Bandipur."

"Oh, really? Who is he? What does he look like?"

"*Swami*, we don't know his name. All we know is that he owns a big hotel there." They were referring to Gajendra Singh, the son-in-law of the last maharaja of Mysore, Jayachamaraja Wodeyar. Gajendra Singh was married to the maharaja's youngest daughter, Vishalakshi Devi, and owned a resort known as Tusker Trails, adjacent to Bandipur.

"Who else lives in the area apart from the maharaja? Where do the RFO and the other big officers like the conservators and deputy conservators stay? Do they stay anywhere near the sanctuaries?"

"*Swami*, the RFO stays inside the park. His name is Rajanna. But the others don't stay there. There are two men who are very big officers and they stay on the fringes of the forest in a small village called Melkamnalli. We see them moving around in a jeep in the area. They must be high-ranking government officers," said Mahadeva.

The poachers were in fact talking about two wildlife researchers and photographers called Krupakar and Senani. They had become a familiar sight to the people of both Mudumalai and Bandipur. The two men, both in their mid-thirties, were involved in a project on wild dogs and often contributed snippets on wildlife to the BBC. Although they were based in Mysore, they had built a small house just outside the precincts of the Bandipur National Park to facilitate their research. After their

trips into the forest on the trail of the elusive wild dogs, they would retire to their little house.

The mention of "high-ranking officers" immediately interested
Veerappan. "Tell me, how can I reach their house? Take me to that
area." He realized the dangers of trying to venture anywhere near the
maharaja's resort: it was bound to be full of people, both guests as well
as staff, and there was likely to be considerable vehicular movement
as well.

Mahadeva and Basavaraju led Veerappan and his gang toward
Melkamnalli through the Bandipur sanctuary. They passed Keknalla,
Ganjikatte, Hulikatte, and Kullanbetta before reaching the secluded
house of Krupakar and Senani from the Moolehole side of the forest.
They camped on a nearby hillock and waited for the arrival of the
two "officers." It was October 8, 1997, more than two weeks since
Veerappan's arrival at Moyar.

As the sun began to set behind the hill ranges, Veerappan heard the
roar of a jeep's engine in the distance. He sat up, alert. Soon headlights
came into view as the jeep made its way along the narrow track through
the bushes toward the house. It came to a halt, and two men got down
wearily with cameras slung around their necks and bags strapped to
their shoulders. "What a tiring day. I can't wait to have a good hot-water
bath," muttered Krupakar. They had spent the whole day scouring the
Bandipur forests in search of a pack of wild dogs they had earmarked
earlier. They went into the house and shut the door.

At 7 p.m., Senani came out of the house, feeling refreshed after a
bath. There were millions of stars in the clear sky. As he stood gazing
dreamily skyward, he noticed a shadow move. "Who is it?" he called
out. There was silence. The shadow moved toward him with the stealth
of a panther and in a moment a man was standing in front of him,
pointing a gun. In the dim light of the stars, Senani recognized him.
"Veerappan . . ." he whispered, and his heart began to beat faster.

"How do you know my name?" Veerappan thundered.

"Who doesn't know your name? The whole world knows who you
are," said Senani meekly. At the same time, the other gang members
rushed into the house waving flashlights. By their light, Senani could see
guns pointing at him.

Meanwhile, inside the bathroom, Krupakar was lost to the world as he poured mugs of hot water on his tired body. Suddenly he thought he heard some strange noises in the house. "Seni, what's happening? Who is it?" he called out to his friend.

"Take it easy, Krupa, it's Veerappan. Open the door and come out."

"We don't know anybody by that name . . ." Even before Krupakar could finish his sentence, there was a banging on the bathroom door. "Just a moment. Just a moment. I'm through, I'll come out."

Krupakar washed the soap off his face and rushed out of the bathroom in his underwear. A barrage of flashlights blinded him momentarily. Slowly, as his eyes focused, he saw three guns pointing toward him. Behind them were three men wearing caps and olive-green uniforms. "Where are the guns? Where are the guns?" the men kept prodding.

Why the hell are the police here? What guns are they talking about? They must be looking for someone else, Krupakar thought.

"What are you saying? I don't have a gun."

A little distance away, Senani had been cornered and was being questioned. In the intermittent flash of torchlight, Krupakar noticed a man with a monstrous mustache. It didn't take him long to realize who it belonged to. But before he could react, his hands were chained. A man stood by him with a gun.

Veerappan and Sethukuli Govindan were still questioning Senani. "Tell us, where have you kept the guns?"

"We don't have guns here. We don't carry anything like that." The other gangsters were rifling through the things lying in the room. Cameras, tape recorders, a small radio, books, files, and other assorted documents were strewn around. Krupakar noticed they had started to shove them carelessly into a gunny bag. He watched helplessly as they handled the precious equipment and books.

Veerappan was raving. "We know you are big officers in the government. I have found out everything about you. Don't try to lie to me. We must leave at once. It's already late. Come on, get going."

Krupakar and Senani were surprised. "Oh no, there is some mistake here. Someone has misled you. We do not belong to any government organization. Please try to . . ."

But Veerappan was in no mood to listen to explanations. "Get going, get going," he shouted. "If you listen to me, you'll be safe. Now take me to the forest officers' houses here. Go and knock on their doors. I'll do the rest. Take me to the Bandipur Divisional Forest Officer's house right now."

Senani tried to explain, *"Annai*, the DFO doesn't live here. He lives in Mysore and his office is in Gundalpet, nine miles away."

"Then take me to the ACF's house."

Krupakar now intervened, "I saw his house locked while I was passing that way in the morning today. He has gone to Mysore with the elephants in the camp here to take part in the Dussera procession."

He pointed to a bookshelf. "Look, we are not who you think we are. Can you see all those books there? They are books on animals and birds. I'll even show you our land records if you so wish."

Veerappan was unmoved. "I don't care if you are not government officers. Even if I get foreigners, I won't spare the two of you. You'll have to go with me." Krupakar and Senani were left with no option. Pulling on layers of clothes to keep off the cold, they started to slowly walk along with Veerappan and the others into the forest, their hands chained and held by two of the gangsters. There was a slight drizzle and the air was damp.

They began to climb the steep hillock. A few minutes passed. Nobody spoke. Suddenly there was a rustling noise. Pushing Senani aside, Veerappan lifted his rifle. "Elephant," he whispered.

"It must be a sambhar," said Senani.

Veerappan took four steps in the direction of the sound, finger ready on the trigger. There was a crashing sound in the bushes and suddenly all was quiet again. It was a gaur, which had fled the scene.

Walking in single file, the group covered a distance of two miles or so. Then they sat down to rest. Ten minutes later, the journey began again. In the dark, Krupakar and Senani had no idea where they were headed. They simply kept walking. After a while, Sethukuli Govindan stopped. Pointing to a grassy place, he said, "Tonight we shall rest here."

*"Annai*, this grass harbors a lot of ticks. We should look for a different place," said Senani.

"That's not a problem. We shall rest here."

It was 4 a.m. by the time everybody settled down to get some rest. An hour later, Sethukuli woke them up and said, "Let's go. It's time for us to leave."

Veerappan began to question Senani. "Do foreigners come to the forest to see the wild animals? What about big officers? Does the van carrying them have a firearm?"

"*Annai*, no one can predict. Sometimes they come and sometimes they don't."

Veerappan looked a little disappointed. "Anyway, if I get any foreigners, you'll have to translate my questions to them in English and then explain their answers to me. Is that clear?"

"All right, *Annai*."

Soon they reached a small pond called Hulikatte in the Bandipur game reserve. Veerappan walked across to a small bridge near the pond through which the game road passed and ordered his gang members to block the road with stones. He paced about restlessly with his gun anxious for the safari bus to come.

The place Veerappan had chosen to ambush the bus was hardly two miles from the main road to Ootacamund. Adjacent to the road was the forest department's reception center. All around this building were guesthouses for tourists and quarters for the forest staff, spread over an area of three to four acres. The place was busy, with tourists milling around and numerous vehicles in the parking lot.

Anwar Pasha, a driver, was having a busy day. He had to get his minibus ready to go on safari, with the STF commander Dr. Harshavardhan Raju and his family on board. The senior officer had not yet arrived from Mysore. Waiting to receive him were CF and Field Director, Project Tiger, Ekanthappa, DCF Rajgopal, ACF Thimme Gowda, and RFO Rajanna. Almost the entire top brass of the Mysore forest department was in attendance.

At about 8:15 a.m., a group of fifteen tourists from Kerala arrived at the reception center in two jeeps. Walking straight to the receptionist, one of the men said, "Could you please organize a safari for us? We have come a long way to see animals in the wild."

The receptionist called Anwar Pasha. "Pasha, this man wants to take his family on a safari. Would you like to take them?"

"Sorry. The DFO has asked me not to go anywhere." He approached another driver, named Sebastian. "Sebastian, I have a special program with the officers. I guess you should be taking these people into the forest."

Sebastian agreed. Around 8:30 a.m. he started on the journey along with the fifteen tourists, who were clearly thrilled.

Sebastian proceeded mundanely, unmoved by the exclamations of delight from his passengers. He'd been in the forest so many times that the animals and birds had ceased to have any impact on him. The bus wound its way slowly through the forest and neared the Hulikatte area. The sky was overcast and the forest was still.

Veerappan stopped his pacing when he heard the sound of the approaching van. The gang members, who were relaxing near the bridge, sprang to their feet and vanished into the bushes. As he neared the bridge, Sebastian noticed the stones placed across the road. "What the hell is this?" he mumbled to himself and jammed on the brakes.

On cue, Veerappan's men encircled the vehicle. Veerappan went straight to the driver's door and ordered Sebastian to get out. Taking him aside and pointing in Krupakar and Senani's direction, he asked him, "Do you know those fellows there?"

Sebastian was so unnerved that he began to stammer. "Yes, I know them. Th . . . th . . . they are conducting research on wild dogs."

Veerappan then turned his gaze on the van. "Are there any officers among you? Tell me before I shoot all of you dead. Be quick."

Veerappan looked disappointed when Sebastian shook his head. He walked up to Sethukuli Govindan, and they spoke briefly. "Go and sit with them," he ordered Sebastian, pointing to where Krupakar and Senani were sitting. Those inside the van were stupefied into silence. Nobody spoke a word or even attempted to move. Turning to one of his men, Veerappan whispered something in his ear. He got into the bus and emerged with a man carrying a camera. "Ask him where he is from," Veerappan ordered Senani. He turned out to be Dr. Satyabrata Maiti, a scientist working at the Indian Institute of Horticultural Research in Bangalore. Dr. Maiti, an avid wildlifer and a keen photographer, was a regular visitor to Bandipur and had hopped on to the bus at the last minute.

Veerappan then proceeded to "interview" all the men in the bus. "Where are you from? What is your salary?" He was anxious to discern whether any of them were government officers drawing a good salary.

Suddenly Veerappan turned his attention to Dr. Maiti. "Ask him to tell us all about himself," he said to Senani. "Where is he from?"

"I'm from West Bengal, but I work in Bangalore."

"Ask him if his is a government job."

"No, I work with an independent firm."

As Veerappan's questioning continued, Dr. Maiti revealed that he was drawing a salary of more than eight thousand rupees. Veerappan raised his eyebrows and said, "Oh, really, then let him come and sit here." Dr. Maiti was made to sit along with Krupakar and Senani. He had been "selected" as a hostage.

Veerappan called across to Sebastian, "Come here. Tell me, if this vehicle doesn't go back, will your officers come looking for it?"

"Er . . . yes," replied Sebastian.

"Then let us wait and watch."

Veerappan and his men settled down to wait for the search party to arrive. The minutes ticked by, But there was no sign of another vehicle. Everybody in the bus was silent, their fear evident on their faces. A child started to cry. Veerappan gestured to one of his men. "Give the child a packet of biscuits." They continued to sit there, waiting patiently for someone to come in search of the tourists.

Back at the reception center in Bandipur, panic was slowly beginning to spread. The minibus had left at 8:30 a.m. and had not returned even at 10:30 a.m. Normally the duration of the safari was one hour. If a vehicle did not return even after an hour and a half, the forest staff would go looking for it. Delays were usually caused by either a mechanical problem or a tire puncture.

At 10:30, Anwar Pasha volunteered to go and find out what had happened to the bus. Three other drivers, Mujeeb, Moin, and Prakash, a water pump operator, Raju, and a cleaner, Krishnappa, joined him on the drive. Balu, the CI's driver, also wanted to go, but Pasha persuaded him to stay, saying, "It is better if you stay back. If you join us there won't be any driver left here. At least you can bring the officers to the spot if something is really wrong there."

Pasha and the others hopped onto the jeep. They were in a boisterous mood, talking loudly and laughing. Strangely, they talked about Veerappan. "If we are ever able to get Veerappan, I shall organize a grand meal of chicken biryani," joked Pasha.

"I shall garland all of you if you capture him soon," replied Mujeeb.

As they neared Hulikatte, Pasha noticed the minibus. "Ah, there it is. Wonder what happened." He stopped the jeep a few yards behind the bus. There was no trace of either the tourists or the driver. They had been herded to a spot a little away from the game road. "Where on earth have these people disappeared?"

Getting off the jeep, Pasha surveyed the area as he lit a *beedi*. He had hardly taken a few puffs when Veerappan's men surrounded the jeep. Veerappan first made sure they were not carrying guns, then he began to question them. "Who are you? Where are the officers? Why haven't they come?"

Pasha was trembling like a leaf. Looking at him, Veerappan growled, "Tell me who among you is an officer."

Pasha could speak Tamil better than the others, so he answered. "*Periavare,* all of us here are drivers. None of us is an officer. Believe me." He continued, "*Periavare,* this man Moin here, and that man, Mujeeb, are temporary drivers. They are on daily wages. Only I, Krishna, and Raju are permanent employees." No one mentioned Prakash's designation or type of service. He had dropped flat on the floor of the jeep and hidden himself at the first sign of trouble. Fortunately, none of the gangsters had noticed.

Veerappan proceeded to record his demands on an audiocassette. He spoke into the tape recorder with practiced ease. The demands pertained mostly to his terms for surrender. He then took Pasha and Moin aside and asked, "How do I make sure your officers come to the spot now?"

"*Swami,* this is a Project Tiger zone. If they are told that there is a tiger lying dead in the forest, they are bound to rush to the spot. This is the only way to ensure they come here."

Veerappan seemed to like the idea. He nodded in agreement. Pasha turned to Mujeeb, who was standing transfixed, and spoke to him in Kannada in a low voice. "Rush to the DCF and tell him that we have been caught by Veerappan." When Veerappan came within earshot, Pasha quickly added, "Go tell the officers that a tiger is lying dead near Hulikatte. Ask them to come here immediately."

Mujeeb and Moin took off at such great speed they raised a cloud of dust on the game road. Veerappan was satisfied that his quarry would land soon enough. He ordered all the tourists to get into the bus. They heaved a sigh of relief and rushed toward it. But when Dr. Maiti attempted to board the bus, Veerappan shouted, "Where does he think he's going? Ask him to get off. Let him come and sit here." It was then that the scientist realized he was on the list of hostages.

Reaching the reception area, Mujeeb and Moin rushed to the Gajendra guesthouse, where DCF Rajgopal was seated along with the other officers. Calling him aside, they broke the news about Veerappan's presence in the forest. The two were gasping for breath and stuttering in fear. Rajagopal stood like a statue. How had Veerappan dared to come to Bandipur, which was teeming with cars and tourists? As the news spread among the other officers present, they started to leave Bandipur, jumping into their jeeps and cars as fast as they could. Dr. Harshavardhan Raju had had a providential escape. He had been all set to go on the safari.

AT HULIKATTE, hardly two miles away, Veerappan waited for the officers to arrive. An hour passed. It was becoming clear that the officers would not be coming. Veerappan then handed Sebastian the cassette in which he had recorded his demands and said, "Go and tell your DCF that he has to hand over the tape to the CM by this evening."

Falling at Veerappan's feet, Sebastian began to cry, "*Swami*, I'm grateful to you for having spared me. I shall do your bidding at any cost. Thank you so much for letting me go."

As he hurried toward the vehicle, as though he had been given a fresh lease of life, it began to dawn on Pasha, Raju, and Krishnappa that they were being left behind. Pasha rushed toward Veerappan and fell at his feet. "Periavare, I'm an unfortunate fellow. My wife died recently. There is no one to take care of my small children. I beg of you to let me go. I beg of you, please."

Krishnappa and Raju followed Pasha's example. "*Swami*, we are not well. We have problems at home. We are poor people and our families will be left in the lurch without us. Please let us go." But Veerappan sat like a rock, unmoved.

The outbursts of the three men touched Krupakar and Senani.

"*Annai*, let them go, please. They are small men. The government will not budge if you take such people hostage. We are willing to be with you for as long as you want. Please let them go."

Veerappan simply said, "Let's wait and watch for three or four days." Dr. Maiti sat without displaying any feelings.

After Sebastian had left with the tourists, Veerappan shouted, "Let's get going. We have a distance of one hundred and twenty-five miles to cover. It's already late." They began to walk deeper into the forest, between the lantana bushes, along a track used by elephants. All the hostages were in chains. They walked in single file without a sound. It had rained a little the previous night and the ground was slightly wet. It was the duty of the man walking last to smooth the footmarks and erase any clues to their presence.

After traversing the forest track for about three miles, Veerappan decided to halt for the night. It was around 6 p.m. There was a small stream flowing nearby. Judging by the large quantity of provisions lying there, it was clear that the place had been chosen earlier, and preparations made for their halt. There was a bag of rice, dal, tea powder, *beedis*, a bag of puffed rice, and some short eats. "Make some tea," he told "Meke" Rangaswamy, the gang's official cook. Veerappan distributed some puffed rice to everyone and ate some himself. This was the first meal of the day for all of them, including the hostages. Before long, dinner was ready. Krupakar and Senani, who had got used to life in the forest, slept without any difficulty. But the others, especially Dr. Maiti, had trouble sleeping. The night wore on and a fire burned. As the embers glowed brightly in the dark, two of the gangsters kept a night-long vigil.

The next morning there was no trace of Veerappan. He emerged later from the direction of the stream, clad in a pair of shorts, his forehead smeared with holy ash. The ever-present gun dangled from his shoulder. Facing north, he closed his eyes and folded his hands in prayer. After a while, he opened his eyes and sat down on the grass. He began to speak. "How I wish I had captured a few foreigners. Things would have been totally different then."

Senani made bold to say that things would have been worse. "*Annai*, you must understand that foreigners are basically very delicate. They cannot take the rough and tumble of life in the forest. They would have died from drinking the water here."

"*Annai*, if you had taken a few white men and women, America and England would have dropped bombs on Bandipur. They don't care what happens to the forest as long as they rescue their people," added Krupakar.

The men chatted over a lunch of dal and sambar. Veerappan was curious to know what educational qualifications these two wildlife researchers had. "I have a degree in engineering," said Senani.

"I have studied business management," said Krupakar.

Although Veerappan did not understand exactly what these two disciplines entailed, he seemed impressed. "It is clear that you fellows are well read. So what the hell are you doing in the forest running behind wild dogs?" he laughed.

As they were speaking, there was a rustle in the bushes. Veerappan and the others in the gang instantly dived to the ground and lay flat, guns on the ready. They gestured to the others also to lie still, hugging the ground. But it was only a gaur making its way to the stream for a drink.

When some hours had passed, Veerappan called out to Amburaj, "Where are you? Get me the radio. It's time for the news in Kannada."

The kidnapping was one of the lead items on the news. The words "bandit," "sandalwood smuggler," and "ivory poacher" were liberally used in descriptions of Veerappan. Veerappan, who did not understand Kannada, wanted to know what was being said, and Pasha, who could speak Tamil the best among the hostages, was forced to translate.

Veerappan's eyes burned with rage. The grip on his rifle tightened. He was livid. "So these bastards use such words to describe me, do they? Do you know the kind of things they have done to my family? They have ruined my people and set fire to our village. There has been so much injustice, so much high-handedness. They think they can do anything just because they are in the government. Now they have the gall to call me names." The rant continued for a long time.

Although the gang was known to be in the Bandipur area, there was no mention of any police action. In fact, Home Minister Roshan Baig had given clear instructions to the STF chief Dr. Raju not to undertake any combing operations in the forest for fear of jeopardizing the lives of the hostages. Veerappan, guessing that this would be the government's stand, decided to stay in the same place for the next two days. He could go about his day without any apprehension of a sudden attack.

On the third day, Krupakar and Senani were amused to see Veerappan immersed in an issue of the *National Geographic*. It had been "confiscated" in the raid on their house on the night of their kidnapping. With Veerappan was Sethukuli Govindan. The two seemed to be engaged in serious discussion. Veerappan was pointing to something in the book. "This should be about ninety pounds."

"Oh, no, maybe seventy-five pounds."

The two researchers, who were sitting nearby, overheard the conversation and were bewildered. Suddenly Veerappan called Senani to his side. "How much do you think this is?" he asked, thrusting the magazine under his nose. He was pointing at a picture of a bull elephant.

"About nine to nine and a half, I suppose."

"What do you mean? Can't you see how well grown it is, and you still say it is just that much?" Senani took a closer look and said, "Ah, it must be about eleven to thirteen thousand pounds."

"What?" Veerappan jumped up. "Have you gone crazy?" He pushed the magazine a little closer. "Take a good look before you say anything." It was then that Senani realized that the two bandits were guessing the weight of the tusks of the African elephant in the picture.

"*Annai*, whenever we see an elephant, it is standard practice to try and assess its height and body weight, and not the weight of its tusks," he explained.

In the afternoon, Krupakar saw two of the younger members of the gang, Madesha and Amburaj, holding a book. It was a richly illustrated book on Indian and African elephants titled *The Sacred Elephant*. He spent the rest of the afternoon explaining various aspects of wildlife around the world to the two mesmerized youngsters. Veerappan looked at the three of them and smiled. Turning to Senani, he asked, "How many tuskers do you think there are in Bandipur?"

"To the best of my knowledge, there must be five or six. The majority of the male elephants have been poached. It is quite rare these days to see adult tuskers."

Senani then ventured to ask Veerappan a serious question. "We have read in newspapers that you have killed nearly two thousand tuskers. Is that true?"

Veerappan began to explain that he had been made a scapegoat in most incidents of poaching. "The minute it becomes clear that I'm in a particular area, local poachers take advantage and poach elephants with impunity. Very conveniently they point a finger in my direction, saying I was the man who killed the elephants. I can tell you there are more than twenty-five gangs operating in the forest areas bordering Karnataka and Tamil Nadu. Within three days of my coming here, I saw a terrified tusker which was being chased by four Malayalis deep inside the forest."

In the days that followed, Krupakar and Senani talked to Veerappan often about his life in the forest. But to the other hostages, Pasha, Raju, and Krishnappa, their conversations with Veerappan appeared danger-ous. "Please do not ask him any more questions," they begged one day. "He might get angry and finish us. Please, try and understand. It is a question of life and death for all of us here." Dr. Maiti alone remained aloof, mainly because he could converse in neither Tamil nor Kannada.

MEANWHILE, IN MYSORE, hardly fifty miles from Bandipur, prepara-tions had begun for the annual Dussera procession. Almost the entire state cabinet including the chief minister had converged on the royal city. Krupakar and Senani were slightly worried. What if the journalists covering the procession asked Patel questions about the kidnapping? What if Veerappan began to think that they were eminent men? What if the CM made a "soft" statement to the press? Then their captivity would be extended.

Senani approached Veerappan. "*Annai*, journalists in Mysore must have asked the CM lots of questions and pressured him to make a state-ment on the kidnapping. And he might have said something just to please them, without meaning it." Even while the two were talking, Amburaj walked up to Veerappan with the radio in his hand. It was time for the news in Kannada from AIR, Delhi.

Patel had requested Union home minister Indrajit Gupta to send in the army to put an end to the hostage crisis. This would be the government's ultimate weapon against Veerappan. Senani continued, "*Annai*, the Centre (the central government of India) has agreed to send the army to capture you. See, there is no talk of considering your demands at all. Moreover, this forest is not like the other forests where you normally roam. It is not very dense. The visibility is very good here. You can see for miles around. If the army enters this place, you'll be in great trouble. We know you are capable of escaping any onslaught. But we are definitely going to be killed in the crossfire. Even if the army kills us, people will say that it was you who was responsible for our deaths. Just imagine what that will do to your reputation."

Krupakar and Senani had learned by now that Veerappan took pride in his image as a bandit who was feared by the world at large. They pressed on, "*Annai*, there is already a feeling that you do not like Kannadigas and you are on the side of the Tamilians. If we die here, some people will take advantage and attack the Tamilians living in Gundalpet and Chamarajanagar. Even in Bangalore, Tamilians will be hounded. As you know, in such situations, only the poor are affected. They will have to go back to Tamil Nadu, leaving their homes and belongings behind, just to save their lives. We're sure you don't want anything like that to happen, do you?"

If Veerappan was perturbed, he was shrewd enough not to show it. With a wave of his hand he said, "No, no, nothing like that will happen."

Veerappan decided to shift camp. They climbed two hillocks, crossed a few streams, and reached a place called Kullanbetta, about five miles away, near the Kerala border. They set up camp near a stream and spent the day quietly. The next day, toward afternoon, Veerappan switched on the radio as usual to listen to the news in Tamil. "Former Tamil Nadu chief minister Jayalalitha and Janatha Party president Subramaniam Swami have said that Chief Minister Karunanidhi is hand in glove with forest brigand and killer Veerappan. . . . They have urged Union home minister Indrajit Gupta to send the army to put an end to Veerappan. . . ."

Veerappan, filled with rage, switched off the radio abruptly. Clenching his fists tightly, he strode about in chilling anger. "So they want the Centre to send the army to capture me, huh? I'm considered a criminal, am I? What about those bastards the politicians? What kind of people are they? They are worse than me. They say I have killed one hundred and thirty people. Why only one hundred and thirty? Put the figure at one forty. But haven't the police dogs massacred more than two hundred people, all in the process trying to capture me? So the equation is balanced now. What's the big fuss about? The police have not been able to touch even a hair on my body for the past fifteen years. Five hundred million rupees have gone down the drain. So many villages have been turned into graveyards. In spite of this, they haven't been able to even sight me properly, let alone catch me. What did the BSF do? Were they able to catch me?"

Veerappan was screaming by now. He was almost hysterical. Pasha, Raju, and Krishnappa cowered in fright. Dr. Maiti, Senani, and Krupakar moved away from his sight and remained silent. After what seemed like ages, he seemed to calm down a little. Then "Meke" Rangaswamy walked up and in a return to banality announced that they were out of cooking oil and dal.

Veerappan looked at him. "Don't worry, I shall go to the nearby town tonight and get you everything. This mustache can open any door anywhere," he boasted, stroking the luxurious mustache.

A week went by. Dr. Maiti's wife had made an emotional appeal to Veerappan over radio to release her husband and the others. The hostages held a semblance of hope that they would be released. The "rapport" built in particular by Krupakar and Senani was making life with Veerappan a little easier. Veerappan began to open up a lot more. He regaled them with stories of his life as a young boy in his native village of Gopinatham; of the exploits of his grandfather and father, who were ace hunters, and how he would spend most of his time with older men listening spellbound to their tales of valor whenever they went hunting. On one occasion Veerappan said that every time he looked at Senani, he was reminded of his brother Arjunan. "My brother was a tall and lean man like you. He was such a brave man, and a wonderful sharpshooter. You know how the police bastards deceived and killed him?"

He opened his bag and took out a bullet. There was something inscribed on it in red paint. "Read this," he said, turning to Pasha, who was sitting a few feet away.

"Periavare, I can speak Tamil but cannot read," Pasha said.

Veerappan held the bullet high so that everyone could see it. Running his forefinger across it, he read, " 'Shankar Bidri.' I have preserved this bullet so that I can put it through his head. I would have finished him if he had stayed on in MM Hills. But the coward ran away."

Veerappan was a firm believer in fate. "Look, there is nothing in our hands. We are all destined to do the things we do in life. How else can you explain your kidnapping by me? It had to happen and it did, didn't it?"

He narrated an incident from his past, when he was thirteen years old. "I had gone to the forest near Gopinatham along with three of my friends to shoot wild boar. I was carrying a very old muzzle-loader. Toward noon we fell asleep under a tree, exhausted by our efforts to find a boar. Suddenly, one of my friends screamed. I opened my eyes and was shocked to see darkness around me. We had slept for so long that it was night. A huge elephant had placed its trunk on his stomach. I tried pushing the trunk aside. The enraged elephant lifted me and hurled me to a distance of nearly forty feet. I fell into a rocky stream facedown. My face was splattered with blood, but I was alive. God had willed that I live. If this is not fate, what is?"

Taking his cue, Dr. Maiti read Veerappan's palm, professing to be a palmist. "He shall live for another ten years," he declared.

"What is he saying?" asked Veerappan.

Senani was quick to answer, "*Annai*, he says you'll live for another twenty years without any problems."

As the hostage drama dragged on, Veerappan began to get fidgety. He moved everybody to a place close to Mastimukhi, where they had camped on the first night. Ten days had gone by. There was still no definite word from the government.

The governments of Karnataka and Tamil Nadu had rejected most of Veerappan's demands. He had demanded money as rehabilitation aid for his associates and weapons for himself. This had been struck down. The Karnataka government said his accomplices in Mysore jail would not be released immediately as he demanded, although their trial could be expedited. The two governments also wanted him to serve at least two years in jail before they would consider his appeal for clemency.

Veerappan wanted to be housed in an open-air jail. The Tamil Nadu government accepted this and even began to scout for a suitable place. They went so far as to promise him police protection. Karnataka on its part agreed to transfer all the cases relating to him to a court in Tamil Nadu. This was one of his major demands. Bearing in mind the manner in which his brother Arjunan had met his end, he feared brutal treatment from police if he was taken into custody in Karnataka.

Meanwhile, Karnataka home minister Roshan Baig had a meeting with K. Kasturirangan, chairman of the Indian Space Research Organization (ISRO). "Sir, is it possible to use satellite imagery to track Veerappan? The only hope we have of locating him in the dense forest is with the help of such sophisticated technology." The famous scientist, however, was skeptical. The government then explored the possibility of using MI-8 helicopters to track him down. But it was not easy to conduct air sorties in this terrain with its ridges, valleys, gorges, and hillocks.

Veerappan, on his part, was getting increasingly despondent. Toward evening on the eleventh day, he called Pasha to him. "Why do you look so depressed? Is something wrong?"

"It's just that I remembered my little son and felt a little sad. I wonder how he is, without me."

Veerappan took out a photograph from his shirt pocket. "Look, this is my daughter. I haven't seen her in years. Now how should I be feeling?" Then, staring at Pasha, he asked, "For how long was Rama in the forest?" Pasha looked back at him blankly. Without waiting for an answer, Veerappan said, "Fourteen years. And for how long have I been in the forest? For twenty-five years. Even if I want to surrender and live the rest of my life like all the others, the police won't allow me to. Is this not unfair? Tell me." Pasha had no answer.

The next morning, the Tamil news informed them that the Karnataka chief minister had set October 25 as the deadline for Veerappan to release all the hostages. He threatened military action if Veerappan did not comply. The hostages were happy that some pressure was being exerted on the bandit. Veerappan looked perturbed. His men had already begun to fear they'd be forced to live indefinitely as fugitives. Chances were diminishing that the two governments would accept the terms for surrender.

That night, as everybody slept, Veerappan got up suddenly. Swathed in a shawl and holding his gun, he began to speak loudly. "Will they send the army to catch me? The BSF went back with egg on its face. What could it do to me? Nothing. What have I done, after all? I have only avenged the killings of innocent men and women. Am I asking for the whole country to be given to me? All I'm asking for is a pardon, only a pardon. Whatever happens, I will not budge. I shall keep these men with me even if it takes two months. I don't care." The hostages listened in silence.

The following day, Veerappan and Sethukuli Govindan held a secret meeting. All the other gang members, except Rangaswamy, followed them. They went a little away from the camp and huddled together. Sethukuli Govindan was the first to emerge, two hours later. "We are going to release all of you," he said in a matter-of-fact tone. The time was 6 p.m.

"*Annai*, then we should leave immediately. It is still quite bright," said Senani.

"Oh, no, not at this hour," interjected Pasha.

Veerappan and Madesha assured them that they would be free the next day. "You can leave tomorrow. We shall leave at about eleven o'clock after lunch. You must wait till three o' clock before finding your way back. Is that clear?" He obviously feared a police attack and wanted to get a head start on his way out of Bandipur.

On the fourteenth day of the hostages' captivity, Veerappan and his men prepared to leave as planned. The bandit gave an audiocassette to Krupakar to be handed over to the CM, in which he had reiterated his demands. At about 11 a.m., they had a little rice and sambar to eat. After leaving some food for the others, they began to walk away. Within minutes, they were lost from view amid the trees and shrubs. The hostages were free at last. They sat on the grass unable to fully comprehend their newfound freedom until Pasha stood up and said, "We should leave immediately. Let us not wait. If we delay our departure, it will begin to get dark and we will definitely encounter elephants on our way. It would be such an irony to die in an elephant attack after having been given a new lease on life by Veerappan. Come on, let's get going."

The others agreed, and they began to walk in the opposite direction to the one taken by the Veerappan gang. They would turn around and look across their shoulders every now and then to see if Veerappan was testing them by hiding behind a bush or a tree. Fortunately, there was no trace of him, and they heaved a sigh of relief. The whole day they wandered around the forest trying to find their way out. They would follow a path only to see it ending near a water hole, then another and another. Toward evening, they spotted a familiar landmark.

"Look, that is Bolgudda there," shouted Pasha. It was a hillock on which the forest department had built a guesthouse deep inside the forest. Once they reached Bolgudda, it was easy to find their way to Krupakar and Senani's house near Melkamnalli. The trek had taken them nearly eight hours.

After a refreshing bath, they set out in the darkness, on the periphery of the forest, toward the Ootacamund road. A slight drizzle had started by then. They had reached the main road and were walking in the direction of Bandipur when they noticed the bright headlights of a vehicle at a distance, coming from behind. The vehicle overtook them and stopped. The doors were flung open and four men jumped out. They were Sebastian, Prakash, Vasu, and Moyar Raju. They hugged Krupakar, Senani, and the others and wept for joy. It was the same jeep in which Pasha, Krishnappa, and Raju had gone looking for the tourists on the day that they fell into Veerappan's trap.

Their ordeal had finally come to an end.

# PART V

# 15

## Prize Catch

On the *amavasya* (new moon) night of July 30, 2000, Veerappan undertook his most daring act to date. In pitch darkness he and his men arrived in Gajanur, a little village in Erode district in Tamil Nadu, close to the Karnataka border. Veerappan knew that here he would find his latest and most famous target—Kannada cinema's greatest icon, Rajkumar.

In a career spanning nearly fifty years, Rajkumar acted in more than two hundred films. His first role was in the 1954 G. V. Iyer film *Bedara Kannappa*, in which he played a mythical, god-fearing hunter named Kannappa, who lived in the jungles of Kalahasti near the famous temple town of Tirupati. By this time, Rajkumar was already well known as a stage actor, having quit school to take up acting under the guidance of his father, Singanallur Puttaswamiah. A stage actor himself, Puttaswamiah had a major influence on his son's life with his powerful portrayal of characters from Hindu mythology and legend.

Rajkumar, then known as Muthuraj, went on to play roles ranging from the venerable Buddha to the local version of the flamboyant secret agent James Bond in films with historical, mythological, and social themes. Over the years, his portrayal of virtue and heroism on the screen began to color perceptions of his real life. In 1981, it became clear he had an influence over the people of Karnataka. That year, he addressed gatherings across the state, urging the government to implement the V. K. Gokak Committee Report, which had recommended that Kannada be one of the languages of study in schools and colleges. Needless to say, he succeeded and action was taken on the report quickly.

Rajkumar's talents as an actor and a singer brought him a host of awards. Prominent among them was the prestigious Dada Saheb Phalke Award, which he won in 1995. He also received the Karnataka Ratna, the highest award conferred by the Karnataka government, and the Padma Bhushan, bestowed by the central government. In 1993, he capped his musical career by winning a national award for the song "Naada mayaa . . ." from the film *Jeevana Chaitra*.

Such is Rajkumar's popularity in Karnataka that his fans staged a dharna in front of his house when he announced a hiatus from acting in 1996. Forced to reconsider his decision, he returned to films. The first film he made subsequently, *Shabdhavedi*, in which he played a sincere police officer hell-bent on eradicating the drug trade, was a smash hit all over Karnataka.

On July 28, 2000, Rajkumar, along with his wife, Parvathamma, headed for Gajanur, 150 miles from Bangalore. In his seventies now, Rajkumar found himself increasingly drawn to the peace and quiet of his native village, far from the high-profile celluloid world he had become accustomed to. Accompanying the couple were their son-in-law Govindaraj, a trusted family friend named "Vodda" Nagaraj, their old servant Nagappa Maradagi, and a relative, Nagesh.

Rajkumar had recently celebrated the completion of a palatial farmhouse set on seventy acres of farmland, opposite the old and rather decrepit building that is home to his late sister's family. He had built the farmhouse so that he could stay for longer periods in the village he so dearly loved. When he was there, he would walk alone over long distances on his estate, taking in the salubrious air and reminiscing about his childhood days.

Raju, one of Rajkumar's most ardent fans from nearby Chamarajanagar, came visiting that night. He was excited to see his idol after such a long time. "*Namaskara Anna*," he said, folding his hands. "I have brought some mutton biryani prepared specially for you. I would be honored if you would taste it."

Rajkumar smiled. "When you have brought something for me with so much affection, do you think I'll say no? Come, let's all eat together." After dinner, Rajkumar settled down to watch television, contentedly chewing a betel nut. Earlier in the day he had spent hours with a group of fans, the relatives of his friend Jayasimha, who were visiting India on a holiday from the United States.

It was dark that Sunday night, so dark that it was difficult to venture out anywhere outside the house without the help of a flashlight. Not a leaf stirred on the trees around the house. All was still and calm. The village of Gajanur had gone to sleep, and there was no one to be seen on any of the narrow stretches of dusty road that crisscrossed the area.

For lack of space in the old house, Govindaraj, "Vodda" Nagaraj, Nagesh, Nagappa, and the driver Hanumanthu were to spend the night in the newly built but still unfurnished bungalow.

As the men made their way toward the house, Nagaraj, who was walking in front, suddenly found himself seized and held from the back. Startled, he tried to wriggle out of the restraining grip. "Who is it? Let go of me," he cried in irritation.

A gruff voice replied, "I'm Veerappan. Don't you know me?"

Nagaraj and the others were struck dumb. Veerappan placed a finger on his lips and gestured to all of them to keep absolutely quiet. They complied without as much as a murmur.

"Where is Rajkumar?" he asked Nagaraj. The tone was cold and brusque. Nagaraj was too numb to answer immediately. His mind seemed to have gone blank. He stammered in fright.

"Tell me quickly," Veerappan hissed in a low voice. When Nagaraj continued to stammer, Veerappan hit him on the chest with the butt of his rifle. One of the others in the shocked group shakily pointed in the direction of the old house.

Veerappan gestured to them to sit on the ground, close together. Then he seemed to change his mind and said, "All of you kneel down. Don't try to escape or do anything silly like that. I shall put a bullet through your head if you try any games with me. . . . Guard these fellows carefully until I return," he told five of his men. He then quietly made his way to the old house. With him were Sethukuli Govindan and six others.

Clad in military fatigues and carrying his rifle, he slowly entered the porch of the house. Inside, he could see a group of people sitting on the red-oxide floor of the small hall, the walls of which were overcrowded with old black-and-white photographs of Rajkumar's parents, and of the handsome star himself in his younger days. Everyone was watching television. Rajkumar sat comfortably with his legs resting on a small wooden stool.

Veerappan waited for a moment, observing the peaceful scene. Turning to Sethukuli Govindan, he said, "I shall go inside. You and the others stay outside. Let there not be too much panic in the house."

When he walked into the house, there was a concerted gasp of fright and disbelief. Veerappan approached Rajkumar directly. "Get up and come with me. I'm taking you along because I have some issues to sort out." He tied the actor's hands tightly at the back with a thick plastic rope. Turning to Rajkumar's nephew Gopal, his wife, Premmamma, and their three children, he said, "Keep silent. Don't make any noise, just stand still. I shall shoot him dead if any of you makes a noise or shouts for help." He then handed over an audiotape to Parvathamma. "Take this to your chief minister, Krishna. Let him listen to it. He'll know what I'm looking for. Don't worry about your husband. I'll make sure no harm comes to him while he is with me in the forest."

The whole operation took just five minutes. Veerappan led Rajkumar out of the house with the other gangsters providing cover from all sides. The actor seemed to be calm and composed. "I don't know what they want from me. All of you keep calm. There is no point in getting panicky. No harm will come to me," he told Nagaraj and the others outside. But his voice betrayed a slender hint of tension.

Veerappan ordered Rajkumar to identify the five men who were kneeling outside. "Who is this fellow?" the bandit asked, pointing to Nagaraj. Perhaps he thought Nagaraj, with his burly build, was one of the actor's bodyguards. He looked at Nagaraj closely. "Tell me truthfully. Who are you?"

"I'm a close friend of Rajkumar's family and a physical education teacher by profession. I live in in Mysore . . . and . . ." Veerappan abruptly waved his hand as if to say stop, and looked in the direction of Rajkumar. The actor nodded meekly, confirming the fact.

Meanwhile the others, including Govindaraj, maintained total silence. Veerappan and his gang, all armed with rifles, began to herd the hostages to one side, one after the other. Rajkumar, Govindaraj, Nagesh, and Nagappa were pushed together. Nagaraj, who was made to stand a few feet away, ventured to speak to Veerappan. "*Swami*, I'm a diabetic. If you permit me, I shall go to the house and bring my medicines."

Veerappan thought for a second, then told him to move back. He had decided not to take Nagaraj hostage, perhaps concerned that his medical condition would hamper the gang's movement in the jungles. "Go away. Don't come with us. We don't want you," he said.

Then the driver, Hanumanthu, started pleading to be taken along with Rajkumar. "*Swami*, please take me with you. I won't be able to live without my master," the man almost wept.

Veerappan pushed him away, saying, "Take your master's wife wherever she wants to go. She will need you to drive the car."

The night wore on. Unaware of the strange happenings in their midst, the villagers in their homes slept peacefully. The inmates of the old house, including Parvathamma, stood in a state of dazed silence. They had been warned by Veerappan not to make even the slightest noise, let alone shout for help. "I shall shoot Rajkumar dead if any of you even think of raising an alarm. Keep quiet," he had ordered before leaving.

Govindaraj's watch showed 9:25 p.m. Veerappan, with the biggest catch of his criminal career, began to hurry toward the jungle. Crossing the uncultivated fields that lay beyond the building, he and his gang vanished into the darkness.

# 16

## Shock and Panic

Parvathamma and the others rushed out of the house a few minutes later, only to be greeted by pitch darkness. There was no sign of Veerappan or her husband. She called out to her driver, "Hanumanthu, Hanumanthu, where are you? Come here quickly." She kept her composure and didn't raise an alarm. The others, including Nagaraj and Gopal, were still in shock and could only look around vacantly. Minutes later Parvathamma got into her Ford along with the driver. "We have to get to Bangalore immediately. Drive as fast as you can." Hanumanthu started on the impossibly weather-beaten road that leads out of Gajanur, toward the Satyamangalam–Mysore highway, en route to Bangalore.

An hour into the journey, Parvathamma instructed the driver to stop in Mysore at the house of Bhasyam Swami, a mystic and astrologer known to her family. It was nearly midnight when she knocked frantically on Bhasyam's door. "Swamiji, Veerappan has kidnapped my husband. He barged into our house in Gajanur and took him away. I don't know what to do. Please help me."

Bhasyam went into a huddle with his brother Seshadri. Then he assured Parvathamma that no harm would befall her husband. "God is on your side. Take it from me, he'll be released unharmed within a week or ten days."

By 3:30 a.m., Parvathamma reached Bangalore. She drove straight to the residence of the CM, S. M. Krishna, whom she had telephoned earlier from Mysore. She handed over the audiocassette given by Veerappan to Krishna.

Home Minister Mallikarjun Kharge and Director General of Police (DGP) Dinakar had been phoned and were hurrying to the CM's residence. Home Secretary Prakash was also called in. The Tamil Nadu CM Karunanidhi was informed of the incident and promised to help the Karnataka government in handling the crisis. Later, Krishna created a high-level crisis management team that included Kharge, Dinakar, Prakash, Transport Minister Sageer Ahmed, Chief Secretary B. K. Bhattacharya, and Rajkumar's son Shivaraj, who was a Kannada film star in his own right.

The next morning dawned bright and clear in Bangalore. But within a few hours, the city was plunged in gloom. The news was broken to a disbelieving city by Udaya TV, a private Kannada channel, on its 8-a.m. news bulletin.

Krishna left for Chennai along with senior government officials, including Additional Director General K. R. Srinivasan, who had been named as the liaison officer to hold consultations with his Tamil Nadu counterpart. Questioned by media personnel before he boarded his aircraft, he told them, "We have yet to learn the exact nature of Veerappan's demands. We do not have too many details at the moment. All I can say now is that Veerappan has taken Mr. Rajkumar hostage."

Raghavendra, Rajkumar's other actor son, became the official spokesperson of the family. "On behalf of my family, I appeal to the entire state to maintain peace. We won't be able to achieve anything if we let emotions take over our actions," he said.

In Bangalore, the political and business capital of Karnataka, normal life came to a standstill. Schools and colleges were closed for the day. Hotels, shops, offices, business establishments, and even banks followed suit. Rumor mills worked overtime, churning out the most bizarre stories. A few of Rajkumar's fans were said to have committed suicide by slitting their throats in public near Kalasipalya. Another rumor had it that three men had attempted self-immolation in Munireddipalya.

Cellular as well as land lines were jammed for over two hours after the news broke, with people making frantic calls to either confirm the news or get more details. The state government immediately pressed into service twenty-eight companies of the KSRP, twenty-four companies of the City Armed Reserve (CAR), and one company of the Rapid Action Force (RAF) to preserve order.


THE KANNADA FILM INDUSTRY was thrown into a state of acute panic. There was chaos in front of the offices of the Karnataka Film Chamber of Commerce. As film stars and producers gathered to discuss the ramifications of the incident, a group of Rajkumar fans broke down uncontrollably. "Our *Anna* has to be brought back safely. Otherwise we won't live." Hundreds of people began to crowd in front of the offices, some to participate in the events inside and a few others to simply get a ringside view of film actors and actresses who they thought were bound to make an appearance. Police constables on duty seemed unprepared to control the crowd, which was swelling by the minute.

Kannada actors Saikumar Dodanna and Jayanthi, who had acted with Rajkumar in innumerable films, huddled together. Hamsalekha, who had scored the music for Rajkumar's latest film, *Bhakta Ambareesha*, which was still in production, looked morose. Knowing Veerappan's admiration for Rajnikanth, the immensely popular Tamil actor, he suggested mournfully, "Rajnikanth may be able to play a decisive role in ensuring Anna's release. Rajni is a great fan and friend of his. Only he can put sense into Veerappan's head."

In the meantime, Jayanthi addressed the huge crowd gathered outside. "Do you want Rajkumar back or not?" she yelled into a megaphone. "Yes, yes," the crowd chanted in response. "Then please try and remain calm. That is what he would want you to do."

Film star turned politician Vasanth Kumar Bangarappa, whose sister Geetha is married to Rajkumar's son Shivaraj, said the government was doing everything it could to get Rajkumar released. Film Chamber president K.C.N. Chandrashekar, after an hour-long meeting with members of the industry, announced, "No production, distribution, or exhibition of films shall take place in Karnataka until Rajkumar returns safely." The Kannada film industry had shut down in sympathy.

There were scenes of disorder all over Bangalore. Those who were lucky enough not to have ventured out before the news broke stayed at home, glued to their TV sets. Others who were not so lucky were stranded at airports, railway stations, and bus stands as public transport was thrown into chaos. There was tension in Mysore, but no major rioting or violence was reported.

In Talavadi, 150 miles from Bangalore, a crowd of more than a thousand people, composed of Rajkumar's fans and prominent citizens of Chamarajanagar, marched to the police station and locked it in protest against what they perceived as an unpardonable delay in conducting investigations on the part of the Tamil Nadu police. In Gajanur, at daybreak, groups of people began to gather in front of the actor's house. They came from the nearby villages of Talavadi, Naithalpura, Hiripura, Gatwadi, Iggalur, Talamalai, Hasanur, and even Chamarajanagar. There were people from as far away as Mysore and Kollegala, which was a good sixty miles from Gajanur.

Media personnel belonging to news organizations ranging from the big national dailies, magazines, and TV channels to the smallest local dailies of Chamarajanagar also rushed to Gajanur. By 11:30 a.m., the nondescript village had become the cynosure of the country. The cars bringing in media persons and fans had turned the grounds in front of Rajkumar's ancestral house into a huge parking lot, and the house itself became the nerve center for news.

The Tamil Nadu police, headed by Erode DSP Tamarai Kannan, arrived on the scene toward noon. A posse of gun-toting policemen was made to stand guard, a little too late, in front of Rajkumar's ancestral home. All it achieved was to keep the milling crowds at bay. The man who was responsible for this situation was already in his hideout deep in the jungles of the Dimbam range, far out of the reach of the police party that had descended more as a matter of routine than with any serious investigative intent.

IG (Southern Range) M. K. Srivastava addressed reporters about the immediate course of action. "There is nothing I can say about the incident. Decisions are being taken at the CM's level. Until then, we all have to wait."

Journalists who had descended in droves began their own investigations. "At what time did it happen?" "From which direction do you think Veerappan came?" "Do you think he had planned the whole thing for a long time?" "Did Rajkumar put on his slippers before leaving?" "Which part of the forest do you think Veerappan would have taken Rajkumar to?" "How far is the forest from here?" "How many men were there with Veerappan?" "Where do you think Rajkumar will be kept in the forest?"

For Rajkumar's family, who had spent the previous night without any sleep, the persistent questioning was getting annoying. While the women confined themselves to their rooms, it was left to Rajkumar's nephew Gopal and Nagaraj, one of the key eyewitnesses, to fill in the details. Nagaraj still had on the shirt he had worn the night before, with the mark of Veerappan's rifle butt on the front.

CHIEF MINISTERS KRISHNA AND KARUNANIDHI, after a ninety-minute meeting, decided to consider Veerappan's demands with an open mind. Karunanidhi revealed that an emissary would be sent to negotiate with Veerappan in deference to his wish "to meet an emissary to discuss some of the problems I face," as he had said in the audiotape.

News spread that a mob had attacked the offices of four prominent Bangalore-based Tamil dailies, Dina Malar, Dina Thanthi, Dina Sudal, and Kalai Kathir. Although there was no major damage to either men or material, the incident only compounded Bangalore's law-and-order situation, which was threatening to explode out of control. It also shattered the myth that the Karnataka capital was one of the most cosmopolitan cities in the country. Tamils living in Bangalore, Mysore, and the border villages began to get jittery, fearing reprisal from radical Kannadiga elements.

The police were put on high alert. Congress president Sonia Gandhi called Krishna to discuss the problem, and offered to seek the help of Union home minister Advani in bringing the situation under control. Union information minister Pramod Mahajan promised Central help to both Karnataka and Tamil Nadu.

Toward evening that day, the Tamil Nadu CM announced, "Gopal, the editor of the well-known Tamil biweekly *Nakkeeran*, has been chosen as the emissary of both the states. He shall go into the forests to negotiate with Veerappan soon. It is our firm belief that the crisis will be resolved at the earliest."

The media attention shifted to Gopal, who said he regretted that Veerappan had returned to his old ways after a lull of nearly a year and a half. "I really don't know what the motive behind the kidnapping is. I will have to reacquaint myself with the workings of Veerappan's mind. I shall do my very best to secure Rajkumar's release."

Two days after the incident, the Karnataka CM's office announced that Gopal had set out to meet Veerappan, who was holed up somewhere in the dense Dimbam forests. The route was supposed to be a closely guarded secret. All that was known was that he would be going by way of Perambalur, twenty-five miles from Tirichinapalli. (It was here that one of *Nakeeran*'s correspondents, Selvaraj, had been hacked to death a week earlier by unknown assailants, presumably in retaliation for a story he had filed for the biweekly.)

Not wanting to take any chances, the Karnataka government promptly withdrew all STF operations against Veerappan. In order to demonstrate its willingness to facilitate serious negotiations with Veerappan, it then went a step further and withdrew all personnel manning the forest, all police, and all sales-tax checkposts along the route from Dimbam to Chamarajanagar through Hasanur and Punajanur. If the checkposts remained, Gopal's entry into and exit from the forests would have been greatly hindered, the government reasoned. Later in the day, Home Minister Kharge announced at a press conference that all criminal charges against Gopal had been withdrawn. He had been charged with having worked against the interests of the state by establishing links with a wanted criminal and not revealing to law-enforcement authorities his whereabouts. But in view of the changed circumstances and also the role he was playing, the state government reconsidered. The same government that had come down heavily on Gopal for alleged antinational acts was now appeasing him for its own protection.

Gopal, it was thought, would take a while to meet Veerappan, because he was bound to change his hideouts often while holding hostages. Meanwhile, Tamil superstar Rajnikanth offered to negotiate with Veerappan. "I am always willing to carry out any responsibility given to me. If the TN government wants me to enter the forest and speak to Veerappan, I'm willing to do so." But his well-meaning statement was not considered. Gopal was thought to be a better risk, given his rapport with Veerappan.

Meanwhile, peace was slowly returning to Bangalore. Straw and paper effigies of Veerappan were burned in a few places, but apart from that, nothing violent occured. S. R. Govindu, head of the All-Karnataka Rajkumar Fans' Association and a producer himself, declared firmly that "the association shall not allow any of its branches around the state to turn violent. Peace has to be maintained. There is nothing we can achieve by resorting to violence."

The government announced that public transport services would resume the next day. Eight platoons of the Central Reserve Police Force (CRPF) were deployed in the city. One company of the RAF staged a flag march in some of the sensitive areas, such as Kalasipalya, Kamaraj, and Magadi. Schools and colleges remained closed for the day.

The morning of August 2 brought news that Gopal was making headway in his attempts to meet Veerappan. The arduous drive from Chennai to Dimbam had been tiring, but this was no time for rest. His trusted lieutenants and colleagues Subbu, Shiva Subramaniam, and Balasubramaniam were with him. Around 6:30 a.m., the team reached Talavadi, a stone's throw from Gajanur. Four men, who had covered their faces with mufflers, were standing idly near a tea kiosk. As Gopal's white Tata Sumo screeched to a halt, they looked in its direction. Gopal's bewhiskered face appeared at a window.

As Gopal got down from the vehicle, they started to walk slowly toward him. They had been awaiting his arrival for the past hour. The four men got into the Sumo, and they started off in the direction of Naithalpura, bordering the forests, five miles away. They made a surreptitious entry there, en route to Veerappan's hideout inside the Jeergalli forests in the Satyamangalam belt. Gopal had with him a letter which authorized him to negotiate on behalf of the Tamil Nadu government, written by the CM. It was almost a foregone conclusion that negotiations would be protracted. Veerappan was unlikely to give up his prize catch easily.

That evening, an audiotape reached Chennai, via Pondicherry, ostensibly by courier. Veerappan's voice, when they listened to it, was unusually confident: "You will do well not to underestimate me. Unlike in the past, I now have both men and resources at my command. My hand has now been strengthened. If you do not take me seriously, you shall be doing so at your own peril." Representatives of both governments were puzzled. What did Veerappan mean by saying that his hand had been strengthened? Who were those men he referred to?

Back in Bangalore, Rajkumar's family tried reaching out to him over the radio. It was decided that the best way to at least get messages to him would be by using the services of the Bangalore station of AIR. Government intelligence sources had clearly said that Veerappan was known to listen to the radio regularly. So Parvathamma and her sons Shivaraj, Raghavendra, and Puneet went on air. "Please take care of yourself at any cost. Do not worry about us. We have a lot of wellwishers here who are coming to our aid. Please do not forget to take your medicines on time. It is very important for you to maintain your health," said Parvathamma in a choked voice.

"Appaji, how are you? We're all very eager to see you. Do not get upset by anything in the forest. We are taking good care of Amma. Just don't worry. We are all praying for your early release. We hope to see you soon," said his sons. According to H. R. Krishnamurthy, the station's director, there was every reason to believe that Veerappan and Rajkumar would have heard the broadcast. The Bangalore station's transmitters are powerful enough to reach the dense parts of the forest. But Veerappan himself gave no indication of having heard, either then or later.

There was speculation all around whether the aged film star would be able to withstand the harsh conditions in the forest. The seventy-one-year-old Rajkumar suffered from pain in the knee joints. This was bound to hamper his trek through the inhospitable terrain. Predictably, there were as many theories as there were questions. While some felt that Veerappan would take good care of "Anna," others were sure that he would be put to untold hardship in the forest. "Our Anna has to make do with monkey meat as long as he stays in the forest with that scoundrel Veerappan. Oh, what a shame," whispered an ardent fan in Mysore, as if fully aware of the menu in the bandit's camp.

Meanwhile, heavy rains in Dimbam became a cause for concern and hindered Gopal's progress through the forest. The vagaries of nature were obviously beyond government control, but the functioning of schools and colleges in Karnataka was not. It was decided to extend their closure by another week as a precautionary measure.

The Kannada film industry continued to incur huge losses. The main gates of the ninety-five cinemas in Bangalore city and the remaining 1,505 around the state were locked. The loss to date was a whopping thirty million rupees. The wealthy producers could perhaps afford to bear the loss, but not so the nearly two thousand daily-wagers registered with the Karnataka Film Workers' Association. For most of them, not working meant going hungry. But even they did not seem to mind. Of paramount importance was the safe release of their beloved Anna.

Ironically, a few years earlier, in 1989, a Kannada film on Veerappan, produced by Chandulal Jain, had done exceedingly well at the box office and had gone on to win a state award for the second-best film in Kannada for that year. Devaraj, the actor who portrayed the bandit, had shot into the limelight then. But now, the real Veerappan had brought the entire industry to a dramatic halt.

On August 8, three days after Rajkumar was kidnapped, Bangalore, though tense, was largely peaceful. A few hours into the day, Tamil TV channels went off the air all over Karnataka. Sun, Raj, Raj Digital, Vijay, Jaya, Pudhugai, and the Tamil channel Doordarshan were all blanked out by the cable operators. With a huge Tamil population in almost all the major cities, not to speak of the numerous small towns and villages in the border areas, the state was generally considered to be tolerant and broad-minded. But the kidnapping of the Kannada icon by a fugitive who iden-tified himself as a Tamil and portrayed himself as an oppressed member of a minority community had clearly affected the level of tolerance.

TAMIL MIGRATION TO KARNATAKA can be traced back to the eleventh century, when the Srivaishnava saint-philosopher Ramanujacharya fled

Tamil Nadu to escape Shaivite persecution during the Chola period. He reached Melkote, a small village thirty miles north of Mysore, and there he began to preach Vishistadvaitha. In due course, he built a temple dedicated to Lord Cheluvanarayanaswami.

The patronage of the Mysore kings, especially Mummudi Krishnaraja Wodeyar, to arts and music during the latter part of the nineteenth and the early part of the twentieth century also brought many Tamils to the state. The setting up of the Kolar gold fields in 1851, fifty-eight miles from Bangalore, and a large number of public-sector undertakings in the state much later resulted in thousands of Tamil families moving to Karnataka, mainly from Dharmapuri and Tiruvannamalai in north Arcot district. Moreover, until the linguistic reorganization of states in 1956, large areas in the Kollegala–MM Hills belt were under Coimbatore district in Tamil Nadu. As a result, there was a constant intermingling of Tamils and Kannadigas in these areas.

INSIDE THE FORBIDDING DIMBAM FORESTS, Gopal was preparing to conduct talks with the bandit. The actual rendezvous was unknown to the outside world. He was carrying clothes and medicines for Rajkumar and the other three hostages. The air in Karnataka was thick with uncertainly. Krishna decided to take a helicopter ride to the famous temple on the Malai Mahadeshwara Hill to seek the favor of Lord Mahadeshwara, who reigns over Veerappan's territory. Rajkumar's youngest son, Puneet, and senior police officials accompanied him. On returning to the capital, Krishna promptly went to Rajkumar's mansion in the posh Sadashivanagar area. "*Namaskara*, I went to MM Hills to offer my prayers to the lord for the early release of your husband," he told Parvathamma. "Please accept the prasada. And please do not worry about Sri Rajkumar's safety. We are making every possible effort to see that he is released soon."

Meanwhile, it became known that as recently as May 2000, Arkesh Gowda, an SP with the CRPF who had served in the STF, had warned the Karnataka government that Veerappan might be plotting to kidnap Rajkumar. The report also stated that Veerappan's hit list included Dr. Sudarshan, a Magasasay award–winning medical practitioner working for the upliftment of tribals in the forests surrounding Biligirirangana (BR) Hills, and former minister Nagappa and MLA Vatal Nagaraj, both of whom are from Chamarajanagar district, part of the poacher's operational area.

Arkesh's report was based on an incident that occurred in mid-1998. The Green Group, a twenty-two-member team of the Karnataka STF headed by SP Ravindra Prasad, had gone to the Argyam forests between Kadambur and Makanpalya in Tamil Nadu on an exhaustive combing operation after receiving information that Veerappan was holed up in the area along with his men. While conducting the operation, they chanced upon two men inside the forest, who fled as soon as they spotted the police. When the STF party rushed to the spot, they found a bag containing sixty-five to ninety pounds of top-quality rice, medicines, camphor, dried meat, cooking utensils, and, surprisingly, fifteen pairs of jeans. But Veerappan was nowhere near the hideout.

They searched the place thoroughly and found a small diary written in Tamil. Ravindra Prasad, who could read the language, was shocked to discover jottings on the various strategies that could be adopted to kidnap the Kannada actor Rajkumar from his house in Gajanur. Also listed were the names of other eminent men in the area and even the registration number of the official jeep of another STF officer, DSP Suresh. Ravindra Prasad had said jokingly to his team, "Boys, you might have to prepare for a major operation in the near future, going by what this diary contains."

THE MUCH-AWAITED NEWS from the forest came on August 4 in the form of an audiotape, sent from Veerappan's hideout, again through an unknown courier. As Karunanidhi listened to Rajkumar's voice, he looked a little relieved. "I'm happy here. I'm well and being cared for comfortably. Please maintain peace, my dear and near ones. I shall be in your midst as soon as possible. I'm waiting for that moment to arrive." The voice was unmistakably Rajkumar's.

However, Gopal had yet to meet Veerappan. The fury of the southwest monsoon raging in the Western Ghats was hampering his progress.

Parvathamma responded to Veerappan's audiotape in a broadcast over AIR. "Veerappan avargale," she began in Tamil. "Please consider me as your sister and take care of my husband. He is not too well. So please make sure that you give him medicines every day. We feel lonely without him. Try to understand our plight."

# 17

## Veerappan's Dictate

U nlike his earlier negotiations for surrender, Veerappan's demands this time were politically charged. He made ten demands, and nearly all of them had clear political overtones.
Evidently the criminal who until now had kidnapped randomly and only for ransom had suddenly assumed the role of a political
messiah of the Tamil masses.

Inside the Vidhana Soudha, where the tape was played, Veerappan's
voice rang out authoritatively: "Implement immediately the interim
award of the Cauvery Water Disputes Tribunal and the release of 2050
million cubic feet of the river water to Tamil Nadu. I also want you to
give adequate compensation to Tamil victims of the 1991 Cauvery riots
in Bangalore and parts of south Karnataka."

The fourth demand went even further. "Tamil should be granted the
status of the second administrative language in Karnataka. I want this to
happen at any cost." The fifth demand was seemingly innocuous and
easier met: "The statue of Tamil poet-saint Thiruvalluvar should be installed prominently in Bangalore. When people look at his statue, they'll
know how rich Tamil culture is."

He continued: "The Karnataka government should lift the High Court's ban on the functioning of the Justice Sadashiva Commission instituted to inquire into atrocities on villagers by the STF of the two states while trying to catch me. All the fifty-one persons booked under TADA [Terrorist and Disruptive Activities (Prevention) Act] and languishing in Mysore jail should be released. I know they are all innocent and have been framed by the police. Along with these fifty-one persons, five members of the TNLA [Tamil Nadu Liberation Army] should also be released from Chennai jail."

Ironically, Veerappan did not include his own brother Koose Madiah, who was lodged in Coimbatore jail, in the list of people he wanted released. His reluctance to seek his brother's freedom could have been due to intragang rivalry. Or perhaps, now that Veerappan was assuming the role of Tamil savior, he felt that his brother, if united with the gang, could pose a stumbling block on ideological grounds.

"I want the government to immediately release compensation to nine scheduled caste and tribal persons murdered by the STF a few years ago. The procurement price of tea leaves also should be increased in order to solve the financial crisis of the Tamil Nadu tea industry. Lastly, you should find a solution to the problems of the workers of Manjolai tea estate [a private plantation in Tirunelveli]."

How had a semiliterate villager, who had spent his entire life roaming the dense jungles, almost cut off from civilization for the past fifteen years, suddenly become an expert on some of the most intricate and far-reaching political issues in southern India? All the demands except one, pertaining to the release of his alleged associates from Mysore jail, had absolutely no personal relevance to Veerappan, as far as anyone could see. Curiously, too, there was no mention of any ransom amount to be paid for the return of Rajkumar. It was clear that Veerappan was speaking on behalf of someone else—a person, or an organization.

It was not long before the role of the TNLA came into sharp focus. Ilavarasan, a lawyer who had appeared for Tamil extremists in the past, explained, "Veerappan has been in touch with Tamil ultras since 1998. There is nothing surprising about the involvement of armed radical groups in the present hostage drama, since he and his gang have been working in tandem with such groups for over two years now." The

TNLA, a Marxist-Leninist outfit of Byzantine complexity, was started in the mid-1980s by Tamizharasan, an engineering school dropout and former member of the banned People's War Group (PWG) of Andhra Pradesh. It subscribed to the goal of Tamil nationalism. In September 1987, Tamizharasan and his men robbed a bank in Tamizharasan's own village, Ponparappi. But before they could escape, angry villagers lynched Tamizharasan and four other gang members.

It was after this gruesome incident that thirty-six-year-old Sengottavan, popularly known as Maaran, had taken over as the head of TNLA. Son of a man named Singaram, he came from Mullangudi, a small village near Kumbakonam in Tanjavur district. As a college student in the late 1980s, Maaran had been drawn to the issue of Tamil nationalism, and he began to build a following among the educated, unemployed Tamil youth, mostly from lower-middle-class backgrounds. He established contact with Veerappan in late 1997, at a time when the bandit was keeping a low profile. The relationship was symbiotic to begin with. For Veerappan, Maaran and his men came as a much-needed replenishment to his depleted ranks. For Maaran's outfit, the dense forest was the safest possible place to hide in. The TNLA also provided equipment such as night-vision glasses and large-caliber rifles that transformed the bandit's arsenal.

There are reasons to believe that the TNLA has, over the last three years, been steadily creating and expanding its base in the Satyamangalam jungles with the intention of destabilizing the state administration. Iman Ali, supposedly a Bangladeshi, is said to have trained the TNLA in the jungles how to handle explosives and guns. The link man is supposed to be Shamshulla, a Chamarajanagar-based timber merchant, now on the run, who had regular business contacts in the coffee estates of Bejalatti, Atikane, and Bedguli, from where he procured timber. Interestingly, Shamshulla's brother-in-law Jamshed is now in Coimbatore jail for his alleged role in the bomb blasts that rocked the city in February 1998.

Some of the other political parties that appeared to benefit from Veerappan's demands, particularly the one pertaining to the tea industry, were the Puthiya Tamizhagam (PT), which was mainly composed of Dalits, and the Vanniyar-supported Pakkali Makkal Katchi (PMK). These parties wanted to extend their network to the western districts, where tea estates are located. The thousands of tea-estate workers, mainly Vanniyars and Dalits, were a valuable vote bank to both parties.

The PT, founded by Dr. Krishnaswami, now an MLA, and the PMK, headed by Dr. Ramadoss, have long been sympathetic to the pan-Tamil cause. The PMK first aligned itself with Veerappan, a Vanniyar himself, when the issue of granting him amnesty was first discussed three years ago. With the sympathies of both the PT and the PMK lying with the so-called Tamil cause, it was not surprising that they had also been vocal on all fronts, including propagating the struggle of the LTTE.

All this is not to suggest that the PMK and the PT, or their leaderships, are hand in glove with the TNLA. Individual leaders in these two parties may have had links with TNLA leaders at various levels and at various times, but there is no evidence of anything more concrete.

IN 1998, VEERAPPAN AND HIS GANG, along with members of the Tamil National Retrieval Troops (TNRT), the political wing of the TNLA, had attacked a police station in Vellithiruppur in Tamil Nadu's Erode district. Three of those arrested—Satyamurthy, Manikandan, and Muthukumar—were sent to Chennai jail under the National Security Act (NSA). They now figured in the list of five extremists whose release Veerappan sought as one of the conditions for Rajkumar's freedom.

Muthukumar is reportedly the head of the TNRT. A native of Palani, he is supposed to have been trained by the LTTE and has been known to smuggle gasoline to Jaffna. He was among the first extremists to build a link with Veerappan.

Satyamurthy, from Kamarajapuram in Pudukottai district, started his political life as a Dravida Munnetra Khazhagam (DMK) activist. With a diploma in textile technology and a reputation as a forceful orator, he became involved with TNRT after college, and is known to have once taken a doctor to Veerappan's hideout to care for him.

Manikandan, also from Kamarajapuram, was a member of the student wing of the PMK before he was made second in command of the TNRT. He is also known to have been trained by the LTTE in the Vanni jungles near Jaffna.

The other two men on Veerappan's release list were "Radio" Venkatesan and Ponnivalavan, also of the TNLA. Venkatesan, who had earned the nickname "Radio" for his skill in making transistor bombs, is the son of a retired tehsildar in Kudanthai village in Tanjavur district. Ponnivalavan, a native of Sethiyathope in Cuddalore district, was involved in a 1997 raid on the armory of the Andimadam police station in Perambalur district, and had earlier faced TADA charges for a 1993 attack on the Kullanchavadi police station. This was one of TNLA's major successes; they made off with a large cache of arms. Veerappan and Sethukuli Govindan were cited as the absconding accused in the Vellithiruppur police station raid case. The case is still pending in a magistrate's court in Bhavani.

NEW DEVELOPMENTS WERE BEGINNING to emerge in the hostage drama, but Krishna did not seem to have any contingency plan to secure Rajkumar's release. "There is no need for anything like that. I'm confident the talks between Gopal and Veerappan are taking place in a very cordial manner. Let's wait awhile longer," he said repeatedly. The Karnataka government went about its task of negotiating Rajkumar's release with as much confidence as a blind man walking through a minefield, while the whole state waited gloomily for fresh news from the jungle. In Bangalore, the overcast sky and the sporadic spells of rain didn't do much to enliven the mood.

News was expected on the evening of August 9. One of Gopal's colleagues who had accompanied him to the jungle was returning with Veerappan's response to the government. He was also bringing an audiotape with Gopal's own message, which was likely to throw light on Veerappan's response, as well as a few photographs. This would be the first message from Gopal since he had left Chennai eight days ago.

The audiotapes arrived in Chennai the next day. *Nakkeeran* assistant editor Kamaraj, after receiving them from his colleague Subbu, handed them over to Karunanidhi. The CM listened to Rajkumar's voice. "I am being looked after well here. Please do not worry about me. I shall see you all soon. I'm enjoying the atmosphere of the forest and seem to have forgotten food and sleep. It is so enchanting," he informed his family and fans. To the two governments he said, "I will consider it my good fortune if Chief Ministers Krishna and Karunanidhi react favorably to Veerappan's demands and fulfill them at the earliest." There were three photographs in which Rajkumar and the other three hostages were seen standing alongside Gopal. Portions of a tent could also be seen. But Veerappan himself was not in any of them.

Gopal's message said, "It was a Herculean task for me to locate Veerappan's hideout. Being delayed by the rain, the insect bites in the forest, the cold, the long treks up steep hills—all this was terrible. It took me six days to get there. I shall emerge from the forest in a day or two."

In Bangalore, Krishna called a high-level meeting to review the latest developments. Later he told waiting media, "The government will formulate its next move only after it receives the bandit's reaction." Questioned about the absence of Veerappan in the photos, he shot back, "Why should we bother about him? We are only concerned about Rajkumar, and he is in the photographs." The government's surrender to Veerappan's whimsical demands was beginning to assume absurd proportions. A criminal's charter of demands was being accorded the dignity and importance of a well-composed political manifesto.

In the meantime, almost every astrologer in Bangalore worth his chart was doing his best to discover the exact time of Rajkumar's birth. This was supposed to facilitate accurate predictions about the near future and the date on which one could expect his release. Astrological permutations and combinations were being worked on furiously, but the all-important time when the famous star was born could not be ascertained. S. K. Jain, noted astrologer and television personality, was hard at work in his office, like most of his clan. "Rajkumar was born on April 24, 1929, in the same area from where he was kidnapped. At the time of his birth, the village where he was born received copious rains after a long dry spell. The villagers who rejoiced at the happening concluded that the child was indeed a blessed one," he pronounced.

"Rajkumar was born under Swathi Nakshatra on the day of Chitta Purnima [full moon]. Aries, the sign under which the birth took place, had the unique congregation of five planets. Rajiv Gandhi, too, had a similar configuration in his sign, Leo. Such a thing is considered rare and the person born thus is bound to scale glorious heights as has been proved in both cases. If the exact time were known, we would know if Rajkumar's lagna is Meena lagna or Mesha lagna. If it is Meena, then this is a dangerous period for him. But if it is Mesha, then he will not only return triumphant but also make sure that Veerappan's mind undergoes a change for the better."

Jain approached Parvathamma to get a copy of her horoscope in an attempt to fix the actor's exact time of birth, based on the period in which their marriage was solemnized. The astrologer, who counted among his clientele famous film stars, athletes, and politicians, made it clear that he could reveal all if only someone would furnish him with the elusive time of Rajkumar's birth. "Since there are no details relating to Veerappan's birth, I'm helpless. Otherwise, I could have put together the horoscopes of the captor and the captive and predicted the future," he said.

On August 11, K. R. Srinivasan telephoned Krishna with the news that Gopal was returning to Chennai from the forest. Krishna, along with Kharge and Prakash, flew to Chennai in time for Gopal's arrival. But the news Gopal brought took them all by surprise. Veerappan had come up with four new demands and this time had given an eight-day deadline for the government to respond to them.

Foremost among the new demands was that the Cauvery water dispute between Karnataka and Tamil Nadu be referred to the International Court of Justice at The Hague. Veerappan had said that the Cauvery River Water Authority, with the prime minister as chairman, should not be involved.

He also wanted the Tamil Nadu government to pass immediate orders for the release of the five TNLA and TNRT extremists in jail.

His third demand reflected his emphasis on the Tamil minority issue. "I direct the Tamil Nadu government to enact laws making Tamil the medium of instruction in schools up to tenth grade. I also want the government to provide shelter to rape victims of Vaachatti and Chinnampatti villages, where the STF went on a rampage." Veerappan had listed the new demands on a sheet of paper and signed it on behalf of himself, the TNLA, and the TNRT.

After a meeting between the two chief ministers, Karunanidhi announced that they would release the five extremists "In the interests of the people of both states." But when a reporter asked the identity of the five men, Karunanidhi replied, "I do not remember them." He did, however, touch upon the other aspects of Veerappan's demands in a little more detail. "With regard to Veerappan's demand that the Cauvery water dispute be taken to The Hague, I'm clear that it is not possible. Someone is misguiding Veerappan. Making Tamil the medium of instruction in schools is a legal issue. The government's order to make Tamil the instructional medium up to fifth standard has been quashed by the state High Court and the matter is pending before the Supreme Court." Karunanidhi continued, "The rape incidents occurred during the earlier AIADMK regime and the High Court had ordered necessary compensation to the victims."

Gopal's mission had opened up a channel of communication with the brigand and reassured Rajkumar's family and the people of Karnataka that the superstar was unharmed and doing well. Within a week he was to carry the government's response and clarifications to Veerappan. He told the media, "Veerappan has expressed satisfaction with some of the earlier responses. But he is now posing as a Tamil nationalist."

Karunanidhi's retort was quick. "That is purely Gopal's opinion."

Gopal revealed that Veerappan had sought neither general amnesty nor a ransom for Rajkumar's release. "Is it true that you carried suitcases full of money to Veerappan's hideout?" asked a television journalist.

"No. I have done nothing like that." He nevertheless confirmed that Tamil extremists were with Veerappan now. "Veerappan fancies an extremist role for himself. This is the main difference since the last time I met him. He sounds like a dictator, calls himself a Tamil extremist, talks about calling a high-level committee meeting and even mentions the name of Che Guevara." Reacting to this, a senior police officer laughed, scoffing at the bandit's newfound interest in international revolutionary movements.

There now seemed to be a new method in Veerappan's madness.

Gopal had other tales to tell of the jungle. He spoke of the difficulties he had to face in order to meet Veerappan. "The pouring rain threatened not to stop at all. We spent three nights in a tribal hamlet, cold and numb because of the inclement weather. The insect bites made my skin itch continuously and the lack of sleep drove me mad. I got a message from Veerappan on August 7 at about five p.m. that arrangements were being made to take me to his hideout. As darkness fell over the forests, his men started leading my team and me to the place. The journey seemed endless. Finally we halted for the night. The next morning we set out early. I felt they were taking me through a circuitous route with the obvious intention of confusing me. After hours of walking, I got to meet Veerappan and Rajkumar. We exchanged pleasantries but I noticed that there was a big change in Veerappan's personality. He is blunt, cold, and quite rigid in his utterances now. Rajkumar was happy to see me and thanked me for taking such a risk and going there."

Soon afterward, the Karnataka government released twenty million rupees in deference to Veerappan's demand, as compensation for those affected by the Cauvery riots in 1991. The Justice Sadashiva Commission of Inquiry, created to look into alleged atrocities committed by the STF on Veerappan's trail in the mid-1970s, was allowed to continue with the probe by the High Court. As for unveiling Thiruvallavur's statue in Bangalore, this was made contingent on whether a statue of Kannada philosopher-saint Sarvajna's statue could be installed in Chennai—someone's bizarre idea of a barter.

A certain segment of the media was angry at the way in which the two governments were handling the issue. In a particularly hard-hitting, acerbic piece in the *New Indian Express*, columnist T. J. S. George wrote, "The Ten Commandments of Veerappan go beyond Moses himself. They seek to make fundamental alterations in the basic postulates of democracy; in the way things are done in India. Issues on which the courts and national commissions are exercised are now seen as issues that must be settled in the style of shotgun marriages. This is not just politics pure and simple; it is politics purely and simply dumb. . . . Extremism begets extremism. Every cause has a lunatic fringe, which precisely because it is loudly lunatic in its ways, often ends up setting the agenda for others. . . ."

On the eve of Independence Day, the president of India, K. R. Narayanan, decided to speak his mind on the events in Karnataka and Tamil Nadu. In his address on national television, he voiced his concern over the "unholy alliance" between criminals, politicians, and important people in society. In an oblique reference to Rajkumar's kidnapping he said, "It is time that civil society and lawful government asserted their authority and primacy over daredevil heroes of crime and banditry." This was clearly an indictment of the virtual surrender of the Karnataka and Tamil Nadu governments to Veerappan. The president also chastised the "sensation-crazy" sections of the media. "There is a crying need at every social and political level to speak out against crime and violence of all kinds. Even such rhetoric is absent in India today. On the other hand, there is a tendency to romanticize them."

Regardless of the president's views, Home Secretary Prakash took off for Chennai toward afternoon that same day to hand over to Karunanidhi copies of the state government's orders relating to Veerappan's demands. The TN government was also likely to issue orders for the release of the five Tamil extremists the following day.

In the Assembly, AIADMK supremo Jayalalitha thundered that army action was necessary to put an end to Veerappan's menace. "I was silent all this while as I did not want to hamper the ongoing rescue attempts by the two governments. But the sorry spectacle of two chief ministers tamely succumbing to Veerappan's demands is too outrageous to be borne any longer. The whole matter would have been over by now had the police of the two states mounted a commando operation to free the hostages. The criminal deserves to be mowed down mercilessly. If the two chief ministers cannot do it, they should resign at once."

In Mysore, there was another little drama unfolding. A few members of the Karnataka social activist group Dalit Sangharsh Samithi had decided to take upon themselves the task of getting Rajkumar released from Veerappan's clutches and were on their way to Talavadi. The police swung into action and arrested them. This led to a heated argument between Rajkamur's self-styled rescuers and the police officers, who obviously felt that there were others better equipped to deal with the hostage crisis than a bunch of youngsters whose enthusiasm had clearly overtaken their reason.

Meanwhile, there was action of a different sort taking place in the law court complex of Mysore. A seventy-six-year-old man, gaunt and haggard-looking, his body bent with age, was initiating legal proceedings in the court of the district and sessions judge Rajendra Prasad, who, incidentally, was also the special judge designated to hear the TADA cases against the fifty-one alleged associates of Veerappan who were lodged in Mysore jail.

The old man, who walked with a tripod walking stick, was Abdul Kareem, father of SI Shakeel Ahmed, who had fallen to Veerappan's bullets in 1992 while hot on his trail.

A police officer who had retired as a DSP, Kareem had a no-nonsense reputation and could not be taken lightly. With Kareem, no favors were requested and none granted. After Shakeel's death, he had become increasingly bitter about the system that allowed a man like Veerappan to flourish. "It is the nauseating machinations of vested interests that has ended up lionizing a vermin and making a hero out of him. Anyone with even an iota of self-respect would hang his head in shame at how Veerappan is being exalted. Is this a country with great traditions of democracy or a third-rate banana republic without a constitution?" he railed.

Veerappan's abduction of Rajkumar and the subsequent demands for his release further enraged Abdul Kareem. "It would be a travesty of justice and a crude mockery of the rule of law if the government allowed the accused to get away. It is not just a question of my son's sacrifice to the cause of catching Veerappan. It is about the disgusting acts of moral turpitude being committed by those in power who do not seem to care for the validity and sanctity of law. If I don't succeed in stopping this charade at the local court's level, I shall approach the Supreme Court," he told a journalist who interviewed him.

"Not even a schoolboy would buy the story that it is difficult to catch Veerappan because of the tough terrain and the lack of support to the law enforcers from local villagers in his area. The police have been grossly inefficient in their ways, and at times even scared to venture into the forest to get him. It's such a pity that they cannot even think of a convincing alibi. After all, an excuse has to sound credible, doesn't it?"

The Kareem family lives in the upmarket Yadavagiri area, home to Mysore's upper classes. Abdul Kareem had been allotted a house there in the mid-1970s by the City Improvement Trust Board (CITB) and had raised a loan from the Police Cooperative Society to buy the property. Now he was contemplating selling the house in order to mobilize funds to continue the legal battle. "Of what value is a house if you compromise on your ideals? I shall not let anything come in the way of my prayer for justice," he said.

Kareem's comrade-in-arms was his other son, Jameel Ahmed, a lecturer in political science at the Mysore University. A thin man with a salt-and-pepper beard, he was as much a fighter as his father.

Abdul Kareem's advocate, Umesh, filed an application before the judge. "Your Honor, I challenge the Karnataka government's decision to withdraw TADA charges against the fifty-one accused. It is my view that it has not been done in the best interest of the law. It is unfortunate that the government has made such a decision only to accede to the whims of a bandit and not with any genuine inclination toward the dispensation of justice. The state has completely failed in apprehending Veerappan and is now being made a victim of his blackmailing tactics. The offenses committed by the bandit and his associates are too heinous to be taken lightly. Many would suffer if the cases are withdrawn. . . ."

The judge admitted his plea.

Earlier, Special Public Prosecutor Ashwini Kumar Joshi had sought the withdrawal of TADA charges against the fifty-one persons in jail. "My Lord, it is my humble submission that the charges against the accused do not hold good as the government, in the changed circumstances, has decided to withdraw all cases against them. Therefore, the prosecution does not see the necessity to press the case further. . . ."

Judge Rajendra Prasad adjourned the hearing to August 16. This was to become the start of a long-drawn-out battle, with serious legal and ethical dimensions, between Abdul Kareem and the Karnataka government.

# 18

---

# Legal Tangle

O n August 17, the focus shifted to Mysore, where an unusually large crowd had gathered outside the courts. The air was thick with expectancy. Rajkumar's release hinged to a great extent on the outcome of the day's proceedings in court.

Excitement peaked at the sight of the two blue police vans bringing the fifty-one accused into the court complex. Among them were Simon, "Mese" Madiah, Chinna Thambi, "Watchman" Kaliappa, Bhilawendra, and Veeraswamy. These six stood accused of some of the most heinous crimes committed by the gang in the early 1990s in MM Hills.

Simon had supposedly been the brain behind the Sorakaimadu bomb blast on April 9, 1992, when twenty-two people, including fifteen policemen, had been killed. Soon after this incident, in May 1992, the six gangsters were said to have taken part in the attack on the Ramapura police station, in which they had shot dead five sleeping constables at point-blank range before fleeing with arms and ammunition looted from the storeroom.

On August 14 of the same year, two of the most determined police officers ever to go after Veerappan and his gang, SI Shakeel Ahmed and

SP Harikrishna, were lured into a trap and shot dead near Meenyam. The six gang members lodged in Mysore jail were said to have had a hand in this incident too, as well as in the ambush at Rangaswami Oddu.

The fifty-one accused were booked for crimes ranging from murder and rioting to possessing explosives and illegal firearms under Sections 143, 144, 147, 148, 149, 341, 307, and 302 of the Indian Penal Code to be read with Sections 3, 4, and 5 of the Indian Explosives Act and Sections 3 and 25 of the Indian Arms Act. Along with this long list, Sections 3, 4, and 5 of TADA were also invoked.

None of these were charges that could be easily dismissed, no matter what the urgency of the situation. But the Karnataka government, which had filed charge sheets running into hundreds of pages against the accused, was now clearly eager to forgive and forget. Justice was being bartered at the altar of political expediency.

People ran toward the vans to get a closer look at the men and women said to have been part of Veerappan's gang. Journalists tried to get a quote or two from the accused through tiny peepholes on the sides of the vans before they could be taken inside. The police had a tough time quelling the thronging crowds and bringing some kind of order to the court premises. The prisoners were quickly shepherded out of the vans and marched single-file, surrounded by a police cordon.

Among the journalists were two foreigners, Helen and Christopher, who were recording the event on video. They were in India shooting a film on elephants in the Mudumalai game sanctuary when Rajkumar was kidnapped. A friend of theirs who worked for Channel Four in the United Kingdom had requested that they cover the event. This they did enthusiastically enough, with borrowed equipment, after being briefed on Veerappan's background by a few obliging local journalists. To these two "BBC reporters," it was amusing to see advocates and press reporters holding forth profoundly and self-consciously on the legal and ethical aspects of Veerappan's case.

When the hearing began, Special Public Prosecutor Joshi submitted to the court that the cases against the accused should be dropped "in the larger interests of the public, especially those living in the areas bordering Karnataka and Tamil Nadu, as violent reprisals to Rajkumar's kidnapping could erupt at any time."

In his deposition, Umesh responded, "Your Honor, it would not be in the interest of upholding justice if the prosecution's plea is considered. I request you to give me time to establish my client's *locus standi* in the case and also the validity of his objections to the dropping of TADA charges."

His plea was considered sympathetically. Advocate Venugopal, who was representing a few of the accused, argued, "The petitioner cannot object to the withdrawal of TADA charges as all the accused are in jail for alleged murder and can always be tried by a regular court, other than the one designated to hear TADA cases." After hearing arguments for half an hour, Judge Rajendra Prasad adjourned the hearing to the next day.

On August 17, Ramakrishnan, part of Kareem's legal team, began his arguments in the packed courtroom. Quoting President K. R. Narayanan's address to the nation on the eve of Independence Day, that it was time for lawful government to assert its authority "over daredevil heroes of crime and banditry," he pleaded that the court should seriously consider the consequences of allowing criminals like Veerappan to overturn the might of the law.

"If these men and women are released without adherence to the due process of law, it will set a very unhealthy trend in this country where thousands of others will also want to circumvent legal procedure to get out of jail. Your Honor, may I remind the court that a review committee must be set up by the Centre before TADA charges can be dropped, as it is imperative for the state to take the central government's concurrence. Police officers Shakeel Ahmed and Harikrishna were shot dead by Veerappan in 1992. Some of the accused presently in jail have been charge-sheeted in the case. Arms and ammunition on Harikrishna's person were taken away in the attack. This amounted to looting central government property, as Harikrishna was an Indian police service (IPS) officer whose service rules made it clear that he came under the purview of the central government, no matter in which part of India he was posted. So I urge this court to direct the state to take the union government's permission before charges are dropped."

Special Public Prosecutor Joshi began his counterargument. "The state government was not bound to involve the Centre as Harikrishna was serving as an officer in the Karnataka unit and hence the said properties were vested with the state." When one of Kareem's advocates, Manjunath, claimed that the public prosecutor was acting on orders from the state to withdraw all charges against the accused, Joshi was livid. "I am nobody's agent. I'm acting on my own volition. The prosecutor is free to decide not to press charges against any accused. In the current changed circumstances, in which the government itself has decided to drop the cases pending against the accused, I've taken the view that there is no reason for further argument. As for the setting up of a review committee in TADA-related cases, such a necessity did not arise."

The court rejected at this juncture a similar petition filed by Putte Gowda, the father of Jagannath, one of the police officers who had also been killed by Veerappan. "At the time of Jagannath's death, TADA had not been invoked and hence the petitioner has no *locus standi*," said the court. Even as everybody waited with bated breath to hear the pronouncement on Abdul Kareem's petition, Judge Rajendra Prasad postponed his judgment to August 19—the same day that Veerappan had set as his deadline.

In an attempt to allay apprehensions over the approaching deadline, the Tamil Nadu government announced that Gopal would meet the bandit at any cost before August 19. In another development, the Chennai High Court dismissed a writ petition filed by an advocate, G. Krishamurthy, urging the court to direct the TN government not to accept the "illegal" demands of Veerappan.

A division bench composed of Acting Chief Justice N. K. Jain and Justice K. Raviraja Pandian said, "The court is not inclined to interfere in the government's decision, which as made in public interest." In his petition, the advocate had contended that as the four hostages were being held inside Tamil Nadu, the DGP was duty-bound to rescue them and not trade extremists for their release. A designated court also dropped TADA charges against one of the five Tamil extremists.

Gopal could now enter the forests and meet Veerappan, secure in the knowledge that the five extremists were eligible for bail, and the fifty-one others in Mysore jail would in all probability be able to seek bail in the next couple of days.

Advocate Ramakrishnan, however, was not ready to accept defeat.

He served a legal notice on the Union home secretary under Section 80 of the Civil Procedure Code, invoking Article 355 of the Constitution, which made it mandatory for the Centre to intervene in the governance of any state faced with threats from either external aggression or internal disturbance. He was convinced that the only way out was to ensure that the STF operations were taken over by the Centre. "That is the only hope we have of getting Veerappan, dead or alive," he said. But there was no response from Delhi.

In Bangalore, the CM instructed Home Secretary Prakash to facilitate the release of the fifty-one accused against whom TADA charges had been withdrawn. But in Chennai, a small complication had arisen. The five ultras were refusing to seek bail and were insisting that all cases against them be withdrawn immediately. Karunanidhi immediately convened a high-level meeting to discuss the legal implications of such a move.

On August 19, the Karnataka government got a reprieve for the first time since the hostage crisis had erupted. Judge Rajendra Prasad upheld the prosecutor's plea to drop TADA charges. "The prosecution has made out sufficient grounds to drive home the point that there is no basis for it to press the charges against the accused. . . . They are now eligible to seek bail. . . . I also uphold the special public prosecutor's contention that Abdul Kareem has no basis to object to the withdrawal of the charges as it is being done in the larger interests of the state and to offset the heavy atmosphere prevailing in the wake of Rajkumar's kidnapping. . . ."

Overruling Kareem's objection, he further cited in his judgment an earlier decision of the Patna High Court: "The verdict of the Patna High Court allowing victims' relatives a say is not binding, as the Karnataka High Court's ruling was very specific on the issue of *locus standi*. Further, I uphold the prosecutor's contention that those released on bail earlier did not go back to their old ways and that there has been a marked decline in criminal activities in Veerappan's area. . . ."

In a sixty-one-page ruling, the judge withdrew charges under Sections 3, 4, and 5 of TADA. Cases under Section 18 of the same act had been transferred to the court of the Principal Sessions judge. The accused could finally consider the possibility being free after having been inside the dingy confines of their cells in Mysore jail for periods ranging from six to eight years. No sooner had the judge finished than seven of the accused filed for bail. Their plea was to be heard on August 21 by Rajendra Prasad, who was also the principal and sessions judge.

Abdul Kareem was silent as the proceedings continued. He chose not to comment on the judgment.

Meanwhile, with the TADA issue out of the way, the government awaited Gopal's word from the jungle.

THE REVOKING OF TADA charges against the fifty-one prisoners was seen as the first concrete move on the part of the Karnataka government toward the release of Rajkumar and the other hostages. But by August 20, there was still no news from Gopal.

Nine days later, Abdul Kareem faxed a petition to Justice Anand, the chief justice of India. The standing counsel of the state in the apex court was informed of the development.

Meanwhile, Judge Rajendra Prasad ruled that the hearing of the bail applications would take place on August 24. The counsel for the accused had been able to move only twenty-six bail applications, with the remaining twenty-five to be moved on the day of the hearing itself. Chennai too faced a few legal bottlenecks. The TN government did not know what to do with four of the five Tamil extremists who had refused to seek bail in the hope that they would be completely exonerated of all charges and released. The Karunanidhi government was up to the task—it was getting ready to release all five extremists unconditionally, the modalities for which were being worked out. There was news that the fifty-one accused in Mysore jail were also contemplating demanding the Karnataka government to drop all criminal charges against them.

Talks between Gopal and Veerappan had started by now. But it was unlikely that Rajkumar would be released within the next couple of days, as the hearing on the bail applications was slated for later. Since the state government had already cleared the way for the granting of bail, the court proceedings were considered a mere formality. The government had also alerted its advocates in Delhi about handling the proceedings in the Supreme Court in the event that Abdul Kareem's petition came up for admission.

While the two governments were busy finding their way through the legal maze, the Tamil film industry observed a one-day token strike, demanding the early release of Rajkumar and his companions.

On August 23, Kamaraj at *Nakkeeran* announced that Gopal had sent some photographs from Veerappan's hideout. The final decision on withdrawing all the charges against the five Tamil ultras was to be made only after a clear message was received from Gopal. The Centre had by then agreed to withdraw charges concerning offenses committed by the five on central installations such as radio stations and television transmitters.

Gopal returned to Chennai the next day, early in the morning. His second mission had not been successful. An immediate settlement was not in sight, for Veerappan was unhappy with some of the responses of the two governments. On reaching Chennai, Gopal drove straight to Karunanidhi's residence and handed over an audiocassette and two videocassettes to him.

Veerappan was apparently bitter about the tardy progress being made in releasing the TADA detainees from Mysore jail. His unhappiness was exacerbated by the judge's decision to post the hearing of the bail pleas for August 28 after all the fifty-one accused had filed applications. Although the state had not filed any objections, the judge was reluctant to make a hasty decision in such a sensitive case.

Following the court's ruling that TADA charges did not stand any longer, there was little ground for prosecuting the accused. The state said in its application to the court, "The prosecution submits that under the peculiar circumstances of the case and the fact that the accused have been in jail for seven years, and those accused already out on bail having not repeated any of the previous offenses nor committed new ones, the honorable court may pass suitable orders on the bail applications filed by the accused. The court may impose conditions as may be deemed necessary in the circumstances of the case." In Chennai, the designated court extended the remand of "Radio" Venkatesh, one of the Tamil ultras, till September 13. This further antagonized Veerappan, for whom the release of these five men was obviously first priority.

In Chennai, Jayalalitha filed an application in the Chennai High Court seeking to lift the interim injunction, granted on the 23rd, restraining her from making any "defamatory" statements against Gopal and his role as negotiator in the Rajkumar crisis.

In their meeting in Chennai on the 25th, Krishna and Karunanidhi made a key decision: to provide compensation to villagers affected by the STF operations to capture Veerappan during 1992–93. The money was to be distributed among the victims as and when the Justice Sadashiva Committee, set up by the National Human Rights Commission (NHRC) in 1999 to probe the alleged STF excesses, submitted its findings. There had been many accusations of police abuses of power and even atrocities during that time, when the operations were at their peak. Veerappan had demanded that a million rupees be paid to rape victims and 100,000 to the next of kin of those killed. He had also wanted the officers responsible for such excesses to be punished.

In the second cassette, Veerappan had also put the same figure on his earlier demand for compensation to victims during the 1991 Cauvery riots. "I want the Karnataka government to release one million rupees to rape victims and the next of kin of those killed, and half a million to those injured or rendered homeless. I also direct the government to immediately disburse compensation to all those who had filed applications before the interstate commission formed by the two governments, following a Supreme Court directive. I'm totally unwilling to accept that compensation has already been paid to victims as per court directives. I demand further payments on the basis of the commission's findings." With at least ten thousand applications pending before the commission, the Karnataka government would need to spend more than two billion rupees to fulfill this demand.

Krishna's response was indignant: "The bandit has complained that the two governments were not serious about paying the compensations owed to the affected villagers. This is not true. Successive governments have paid compensation according to NHRC recommendations. Apart from the thousand-million-rupee corpus, we are ready to meet any extra financial burden if the situation so warrants. The decision to drop TADA charges against the fifty-one accused was reached after considering the volatile situation in the state in the aftermath of Rajkumar's kidnapping. If I may quote a precedent, even the cases against farmers in the Bagur-Navile tunnel agitation demanding compensation for crop losses were withdrawn."

The CM was actually drawing a parallel between a proven criminal's list of unreasonable demands and a relatively harmless farmers' movement. On the issue of according Tamil the status of a second language in Karnataka, Krishna was sarcastic. "Veerappan has begun to realize lately the existence of a constitution in the country." It was another matter that the two governments themselves, in their great hurry to placate him, were throwing all constitutional tenets to the winds.

In Rajkumar's ancestral village, from where he had been kidnapped twenty-seven days ago, his anxious relatives had begun to depend on cowherds and woodcutters who ventured into the jungles routinely for information about his probable location. Not surprisingly, the family had ceased to rely on what visiting journalists told them; there seemed to be as many theories about Rajkumar's whereabouts as the number of reporters covering the story. One day, Basaviah, a woodcutter, informed them that he had seen a fifteen-member gang in the Mudiyanoor jungles. In the group was a man clad in a white shirt and dhoti, as well as a few others who did not look as if they belonged with the gang. The place where they had seen them was not more than twelve miles from Gajanur. Telltale pieces of burned wood, scalded grass, and the remnants of ash had also been found. Such bits of information comforted the troubled family to some extent, for they were now increasingly worried about Rajkumar's health. His appearance in the videos that Gopal had brought back suggested that he wasn't very well. They pinned their hopes on Gopal's next meeting with Veerappan. Gopal himself was upbeat about this third meeting. "I will not return from the jungle this time without Rajkumar."

Most others also felt that he would succeed this time. Speculation was rife that the bandit would release the hostages on the night of the new moon, so that he would have the cover of total darkness to melt away into the depths of the jungle, safe from any sudden police attack.

Meanwhile, in Mysore, a large crowd of curious onlookers, advocates, and members of the Kannada film industry had begun to gather in the court complex, even before the courts could open for the day. There was anticipation in the air that Veerappan would release Rajkumar soon after his fifty-one associates were let off.

Among those waiting the outcome of the hearings were popular Kannada film stars Ambarish and Vishnuvardhan. The latter was visibly uncomfortable at the attention they got from the adoring crowds. He smiled weakly and waved halfheartedly every time an excited fan shouted out his name. Ambarish was in no mood to acknowledge the adulation either. In the shade of a tree, the two actors talked with the producers "Rockline" Venkatesh, S. R. Govindu, and Manju. At stake were tens of millions of rupees invested in the many films that were lying idle in various stages of production when news of the kidnapping broke out.

One of the defense lawyers assured the film industry representatives that there was no cause for tension; that he had secured bail for the prisoners. Still they were taking no chances. The film producers, Vishnuvardhan, and Ambarish—who is also a sitting member of Parliament—had come prepared to provide surety to the accused. The total cash surety for all the fifty-one amounted to more than a million rupees, but that was a price worth paying to reopen the film industry.

Toward afternoon came the long-awaited decision. The judge had granted bail to all the fifty-one suspected associates of Veerappan, against whom the government had earlier dropped TADA charges. He had ordered that the accused be freed from jail after executing a personal bond of ten thousand rupees and a surety of a like sum, or a cash surety of twenty thousand rupees each. He had also overruled Ramakrishnan's pleas to wait until Abdul Kareem's special leave petition was brought up in the Supreme Court, which was to occur at about 10:30 a.m. the next day.

"Your Honor, please put the proceedings of this court on hold and reserve the orders on the bail applications until the outcome of my client's petition in the Supreme Court is known tomorrow. Here is a copy of the fax communication of Mr. Kareem's advocate in the Supreme Court, Chava Badrinath Babu, sent to advocate Umesh here a few hours ago," Ramakrishnan pleaded. But the judge was in no mood to listen.

"The Supreme Court advocate's communication from Delhi to his Mysore colleague is of a purely personal nature. How do you expect me to react?"

The judgment brought relief to the state government and the film industry. There was jubilation among the advocates who had supported bail for the accused. Ambarish, Vishnuvardhan, and the three producers returned to their hotel and promptly hit the bar to celebrate.

But as they prematurely celebrated their Anna's release, they forgot that there was a mountain of paperwork involved before the accused could be released on bail. Their complacency was to cost them dearly.

Soon after the verdict, the Karnataka government made the shocking decision to withdraw all cases against not just the fifty-one accused presently in jail, but also seventy others already out on bail. Krishna, looking grim, announced the decision. "The government has passed orders to drop all charges against the one hundred twenty-one persons said to be Veerappan's associates. This has been done in the larger interests of the public. The public prosecutors in Mysore have been told to file applications to drop all criminal charges against the accused. If the charges are dropped, the suspected associates of the bandit will not face cases under the relevant sections of even the Indian Penal Code. However, cases against absconding persons, including the bandit, will continue to be pressed."

The Tamil Nadu government had already indicated that it was willing to withdraw all charges against the five Tamil extremists. Karunanidhi had said he was "waiting for final word from Gopal before implementing the decision." In Chennai, "Radio" Venkatesan justified Rajkumar's kidnapping: "It was necessary to shock the government, make them see our point of view and realize the injustice being dealt out to the people of the state."

The next morning, at about 10:30, Special Public Prosecutor Joshi received a call from the chief secretary that was to change the course of events dramatically. The Supreme Court, he was informed, was furious with the state government for having dropped all charges against Veerappan's associates. It had taken serious notice that they had been granted bail, and had directed the district court to stay the execution of its orders till 3 p.m.

As everyone waited anxiously for 3 p.m. to hear the outcome of the stay, news came that was to jolt the prosecution further. The Supreme Court had directed that the stay be extended until September 1.

A journalist telephoned Abdul Kareem to inform him that the Supreme Court had admitted his petition. On hearing the news, the old man finally broke down. He was too overjoyed to express himself in any other manner. "My stand has been vindicated. I'm so grateful to Allah and the Supreme Court for having considered my plea. Justice has won over the forces of evil. It is the happiest day in my life. No matter what happens from now on, I can die a peaceful death."

It was advocate Ramakrishnan who was responsible for the turn in the case. The previous night, at about 10 p.m., he had telephoned Abdul Kareem's counsel, Chava Badrinath Babu, and convinced him that they still had one chance left to try to stop the district court's judgment from being implemented. The Supreme Court, as a matter of course, allots a little time each day at the start of routine proceedings before the chief justice draws up the list for the day to hear any urgent or serious matter. Taking advantage of this procedure, Ramakrishnan persuaded Babu to inform Chief Justice Anand that the Mysore court had rejected Kareem's plea. In a rare instance in India's judicial history, the Supreme Court took cognizance of a plea and stayed proceedings in a lower court without even hearing the petition. It had been a nerve-racking photo finish.

How Kareem found an advocate to represent him in the Supreme Court is a story in itself. Manjunath, a junior of Umesh, Kareem's counsel in Mysore, had gone to Delhi in February 2000 as part of an advocate's delegation to protest against the Centre's move to amend the Advocates Act and the Civil Procedure Code. While in Delhi, he met a man named Chava Badrinath Babu, who introduced himself as an advocate practicing in the Supreme Court. The two men exchanged business cards. Like most routine encounters with strangers, this one was quickly forgotten. When the old man decided to approach the Supreme Court, it became imperative to find someone to represent him there. Kareem didn't know anybody, nor did his counsel Umesh. It was then that Manjunath, after much rummaging around in his drawer, fished out the dog-eared business card of Chava Badrinath Babu and made an urgent phone call to Delhi. Manjunath explained the issue in great detail, and to everyone's relief, Babu agreed to represent Kareem in the Supreme Court.

Soon after the stay became public knowledge, a slumbering Ambarish was rudely woken up by the shrill ringing of his cell phone. "*Anna*, there is terrible news. The Supreme Court has stayed all proceedings in the Mysore court for two days. Once it understands the facts of the case, it's bound to come down heavily on the government. By the looks of it, we are doomed." The counsel for the accused didn't know how to pacify their clients in jail, or their relatives outside who had journeyed all the way to Mysore from their remote villages on the Karnataka–Tamil Nadu border to bring the prisoners home.

Actor Sundar Raj, producers S. R. Govindu, Venkatesh, Manju, and a few of their friends gathered in Ambarish's hotel room to take stock of the situation. "How about going to Abdul Kareem's house and requesting him to withdraw the case in the Supreme Court? Maybe that will help," suggested Sunder Raj.

Producer Manju shot back, "Maybe we should have bundled Kareem into a car and taken him away to some secret place before he could do all this."

A journalist who was present in the room and who knew Kareem well advised Ambarish not to try going to his house. "He wouldn't even open the door of his house to you. Moreover, it's impossible for even Kareem to 'take back' his case in the Supreme Court. It's against judicial procedure. Even if he did so, the Supreme Court is likely to take up the case *suo moto*."

On the evening of August 29, the star-studded team, headed by Ambarish, finally left Mysore, convinced that there was nothing it could do to solve the impasse. As the Tata Safari drove out of the imposing gates of the Kings Kourt hotel, Ambarish couldn't help thinking that the time had not yet come for Rajkumar to be released from Veerappan's clutches. Two days later, he was to be proved right.

# 19

## Long Suspense

On September 1, 2000, the Supreme Court stayed the release of the fifty-one TADA detainees indefinitely. A reconstituted three-judge bench, composed of Justices S. P. Bharucha, D. P. Mahapatra, and Y. K. Sabharwal, patiently heard the arguments of Advocate General A. N. Jayaram and Solicitor General Harish Salve after they filed a counteraffidavit on behalf of the Karnataka government. They argued that the decision to facilitate bail for the fifty-one TADA detainees was made in the face of the chaos that ensued, especially in the border areas of Karnataka and Tamil Nadu, after Rajkumar's kidnapping. "It would have serious and far-reaching implications on the lives of the common people residing there if riots broke out between Tamils and Kannadigas. The situation is quite explosive. The Karnataka government understands the legal ramifications of its decision, but there is no other choice before it."

Justice Bharucha listened intently, his hands cupping his chin. Finally he looked at Harish Salve and said, "We take strong exception to the Karnataka government's attempt to stir up the issue of law and order in the event that the accused are not released. We make it amply clear that it is the government's responsibility to maintain law and order. If it cannot do it, then let it make way for someone who can do it. The stay on the release of the accused shall continue until further orders. The Mysore court is hereby directed to conform to our decision. You are trying to accord more sagacity to the district judge there than we are willing to grant him."

In Bangalore, Krishna convened an all-party meeting to discuss options in the context of the Supreme Court's decision. Addressing the media, he said, "The state's counsel has been directed to press for an early disposal of the special leave petition. We cannot afford to waste time at this crucial juncture. The government understands the matter completely and appropriate steps are being taken."

The next day, Solicitor General Harish Salve applied to the three-judge bench of Justices K. G. Balakrishnan and Santosh Hegde and Chief Justice Anand to consider fixing an early date for the hearing, "in view of the urgency and seriousness of the matter." The court was unanimous in saying, "We direct all parties concerned to complete pleadings in the next ten days and then file an application pleading for an early hearing date." It was becoming evident that the court was in no mood to play along with the government.

Meanwhile, the Tamil Nadu government was preparing an affidavit to counter the Supreme Court's decision. It had decided to cite Section 321 of the Criminal Procedure Code, which empowers state governments to withdraw pending criminal cases with prior sanction of the trial court. The citation included the famous Baroda dynamite case involving the present defense minister, George Fernandes. Fernandes had been accused of subversive activities during the 1975 Emergency declared by Indira Gandhi's government. But at the end of the Emergency, after he became part of the Morarji Desai cabinet, the case had been dropped. Another precedent was a case involving Karunanidhi himself. The MGR-led AIADMK government in Tamil Nadu had charged him and a few others in 1978 with attempting to murder Indira Gandhi after she had left office, while she was touring the state. The case was subsequently dropped.

Meanwhile, as the governments tried every trick in the book to sway the Supreme Court, they waited for their emissary Gopal to return to

Chennai to tell them what had happened in Veerappan's "court" in the Satyamangalam forests. Matters were complicated by a statement made at this critical juncture by DGP Dinkar, who was known for his directness. In an interview to a website, Rediff.com, he said that there had never been any political will to capture Veerappan. "When J. H. Patel was the chief minister, he was never interested in doing anything about the Veerappan issue. What could be expected of a man who shamelessly said that he was only interested in wine and women? Only yes-men were appointed and good policemen were banished to the attic," he said.

On September 6, Gopal arrived in Chennai with a warning for Krishna: "No police action should be initiated against Veerappan. Otherwise the lives of the hostages will be in danger. Veerappan will undoubtedly shoot them dead." Although Rajkumar was safe, the Supreme Court's decision to stay proceedings had gotten in the way of negotiations. "Veerappan knows what the Supreme Court means, but he is very adamant. All that he told me was, 'Release my men and then take Rajkumar.' "

The Karnataka High Court added a new dimension to the case when a division bench, composed of Chief Justice Ashok Bhan and Justice R. Gururajan, passed orders on writs filed by Assistant Commissioner of Police (ACP) Muthuraya and a few others, staying the proceedings of the Justice Sadashiva Commission.

In Delhi, Union minister of state for home I. D. Swami offered to send in paramilitary forces to capture Veerappan and put an end to the issue. But neither state government responded. As in the past, there seemed to be a distinct political reluctance to engage with Veerappan actively. Each time there was talk of the army or other competent forces stepping in, some reason or another was hurriedly found to prevent it. Or, as in this case, the possibility was ignored.

After the next meeting of the two chief ministers in Bangalore, they informed the waiting media, "We are going to argue the merits of our case in the Supreme Court, then wait till our case is decided before any further action is taken to secure Rajkumar's release. We are confident that the problem will soon be solved."

The politics of language, implicit in Veerappan's demands, were articulated unexpectedly during the press conference. When Krishna spoke in English, a few reporters commented that he should be speaking in Kannada. "I cannot do that because Mr. Karunanidhi will not understand me," Krishna responded.

"But Mr. Karunanidhi always makes it a point to speak only in Tamil, no matter where he is," a reporter replied.

"Sorry, whatever you say, I will speak in English. Otherwise what is the point of his coming here all the way from Chennai?" asked Krishna.

When it was Karunanidhi's turn to speak, he predictably spoke in Tamil. "My law minister, Aladi Aruna, will translate my replies into English," he said. Karunanidhi's stubbornness was interpreted as an example of Tamil chauvinism, which had by now become a subject of debate all over Karnataka.

There had for some years been a sense of discontent between Kannadigas and Tamils, in places like Bangalore, which offered abundant employment opportunities, especially to the hardworking and enterprising Tamil labor class. Kannada Rakshana Vedike chief Janakere Venkataramiah's call to "all Tamils in Karnataka to get out" only fanned the embers of dissatisfaction. No sooner had Venkataramiah articulated his demand than anti-Kannada posters appeared in places like Thozhudur, Pennadam, and Thuthukudi in the Cuddalore district of Tamil Nadu. In the battle against discrimination, Veerappan, who seemed to be simultaneously defying the government in Karnataka and proclaiming his Tamil roots, was deified as Maha Veeran ("Great Warrior"). The posters also made it clear that no Kannadiga, not even senior IAS and IPS officers in Tamil Nadu, would be spared if anything improper happened to Tamils living in Karnataka.

As a strange side effect, anti-Veerappan cassettes began to flood the market in Karnataka. The smaller music companies recognized a market for such tapes, which had a common theme—badmouth Veerappan, glorify Rajkumar, and attack the Karnataka and Tamil Nadu governments for having mismanaged the kidnapping episode. The titles were far from serious: "A Diamond in the Hands of a Monkey"; "What Does a Donkey Know of Fragrance"; "Karnataka's Ruby in the Forest"; and "The Pearl That the Forest Bandit Stole." It is estimated that each of these cassettes sold over 25,000 copies.

On September 11, 2000, the Tamil Nadu government filed its counteraffidavit before the Supreme Court, hoping that the court would be suitably impressed with its citations. In Delhi, Chief Justice Anand had sent Abdul Kareem's petition to a three-judge bench headed by Justice Bharucha. The other two judges were Justices S. N. Phukhan and V. R. Patil.

When the matter came up for hearing on Tuesday, Justice Bharucha asked Chava Badrinath Babu whether Kareem had filed his replies to the statements of the two governments.

Badrinath Babu explained that the replies could not be filed because he was not given enough time. A lot of the material he needed to study was in Kannada, and the translation work proved to be laborious and time-consuming.

He was granted till October 9 to file replies and was told the court would take up the matter on October 11. So the release of the detainees was delayed even further.

The postponement of the hearing came as a blow to Rajkumar's family. The strain affected his wife the most. On September 20, Parvathamma had to be rushed to Mallya Hospital after complaining of chest pain. As the news of her illness spread, people started gathering outside the hospital. There were rumors that she had died of a heart attack. But by late evening, her condition had stabilized. The next day, almost the entire Kannada film industry went in a silent procession to Governor Rama Devi's office and presented a three-page memorandum urging for an immediate end to the crisis. Popular stars Vishnuvardhan, Ramesh, Ravichandran, Ambarish, Devaraj, and Sashikumar, along with a host of technicians, producers, directors, and actresses, walked with the bearded Shivaraj, Raghavendra, and Puneet in a show of solidarity. In the forecourt of the governor's mansion, S. R. Govindu announced that there would be a Karnataka *bandh* on September 28 "to draw the attention of the Centre to the crisis."

Shivaraj Kumar addressed the crowd of nearly two thousand: "If Mahatma Gandhi is the father of the nation, Appaji is the father of Karnataka. Let the lawmakers, the politicians, stay in the forest for a day or two and find out how difficult it is to live there before they condemn another man to fend for himself in the wild. We shall even go on a hunger strike if necessary. But my only request is, let us observe the *bandh* peacefully. The effect should be felt in Delhi." There were loud cheers and clapping.

Meanwhile, a Public Interest Litigation (PIL) opposing the release of the TADA detainees by the Tamil Nadu government was filed in the Supreme Court. The petitioner was a Delhi-based advocate named B. L. Wadhera. Replying to the PIL through an affidavit, Tamil Nadu deputy home secretary A. S. Dharmaraj said, "We had informed the Karnataka government almost a year ago about the possibility of Veerappan kidnapping Rajkumar. The Karnataka police assured us that their Tamil Nadu counterparts would be informed whenever Rajkumar was slated to visit Gajanur. But when he visited his native village on July 27, no notice was given."

As the desperate situation became more prolonged, Rajkumar's family made an announcement that it would undertake a fast to press for his immediate release. Meanwhile, heavy rain in the dense Satyamangalam forest area was hampering Gopal's progress.

On September 27, ten thousand policemen were deployed throughout the state in anticipation of the *bandh*. About three thousand security personnel, including commandos of the RAF, were told to take up positions in Bangalore. The *bandh* coincided with the inauguration of the world-famous Dussera festivities in Mysore, which attract thousands of tourists from all parts of the country and abroad. Any disruption of the opening ceremony would be a terrible embarrassment to the government. Home Minister Kharge said that all precautionary measures had been taken and announced that as many as fourteen hundred known troublemakers had been taken into preventive custody throughout the state.

The government's tension was dissipated to a large extent by a cassette containing a message from Rajkumar, which arrived in Chennai late that afternoon. "As all of you are aware, the Dussera festival will commence on the 28th. Our state needs the blessings of Goddess Chamundeshwari. We all are aware how auspicious and significant the festival is for the people of Karnataka. I request all of you not to do anything that will bring disrepute to me and cause inconvenience to the people at large. If you have any value and respect for my words and concern for my life, please ensure that the *bandh* is observed in a lawful manner," he appealed.

Shivaraj and his brother Raghavendra responded to their father's message with a broadcast over AIR, Bangalore. "*Appaji*, let us assure you that we shall abide by your wishes. We promise that the state of Karnataka shall not resort to any unlawful means to register its protest at the delay in your release. The day shall pass smoothly as you have requested. Please don't neglect your health. We are desperate to see you soon." The station broadcast the message three times, every two hours.

Rajkumar's appeal had the desired effect. The *bandh* was peaceful. In the four southern districts of Bangalore, Mandya, Mysore, and Chamarajanagar, considered the most sensitive ones, people preferred to stay indoors. Business establishments lowered their shutters and so did schools and colleges. But in coastal areas like Mangalore and Karwar, the *bandh* did not evoke any response. Life went on as usual.

September 28. It was the night of the *amavasya*. Darkness had settled like a thick blanket on the forest. Visibility was almost zero. At Veerappan's hideout, two tents were pitched at a distance of twenty feet from each other, near a cluster of thick bamboo. A faint light emanated from a weather-beaten kerosene lamp in front of the tents. Veerappan and his men were away performing a special *pooja* at a forest temple to the goddess Kali. Propitiating the goddess, known for her appetite for blood, was a ritual they performed every new moon night. Rajkumar and his three companions sat in one of the tents, fidgeting and feeling listless. Three men with guns in their hands sat on guard, smoking *beedis*. Veerappan and his companions returned from their *pooja* late in the evening. They were tired after their long trek through the forest, and after a frugal meal of rice and sambar they retired to sleep.

Only Nagappa, inside his tent, lay awake. At about 2 a.m. he rose carefully and looked around the tent. He couldn't see the others in the darkness, but he could hear their snores. Cautiously, he tiptoed out of the tent. The guards seemed to be sleeping too. Nagappa knew that if his movements awakened Veerappan or any of the others, he would be ruthlessly chopped to pieces. Once outside the tent, he dropped caution and charged into the darkness.

Nagappa had no idea where he was headed. There were no landmarks to guide him, and the forest was frighteningly intimidating in the night. But he scrambled through the thicket blindly, knowing that he had to put as much distance as possible between him and the sleeping men. The forest path was uneven and rough. Once, he stumbled against a tree stump and fell. He picked himself up and hurried on. A few minutes later, he hit his head against a tree trunk and fell backward violently. He could not afford to waste even a moment to turn back and see if he was being pursued. He crossed the ravines, the streams, and the hillocks as if seized by a demonic will to keep going.

Nagappa was panting and sweating with exhaustion when he finally stopped to take stock of his location. The first rays of the early-morning sun were beginning to filter through the thick canopy of trees. He knew that he had to keep going as quickly as possible in order to escape Veerappan's wrath. As he limped on, dragging himself through the dense vegetation, suddenly he saw a dirt road snaking its way through the forest. Nagappa decided to follow it. Nearly twelve hours later, he found himself standing on a tarred road, sure sign that he was close to civilization.

Nagappa's luck continued to hold that fateful day. He had reached Bannari, a small village with an STF outpost at the head of the Satyamangalam forest belt. But he did not go to the police for help. Accosting a villager, he begged him for some money. His voice was cracking with fear. His hands were trembling as he folded them in a namaste. "*Anna*, I beg of you. Could you please give me a few rupees? I need to take a bus to my village. I don't have anything with me at the moment. Please help me. Don't say no. I shall fall at your feet." Nagappa was panting as he spoke. His tired eyes looked desperately at the stranger. The villager was kind. Taking out fifteen rupees from his pocket, he handed the money to a grateful Nagappa.

A few minutes later, Nagappa boarded a bus headed for Talavadi, twenty-two miles away. Finally, at about 4:30 p.m., he tottered into Rajkumar's ancestral village from where he had been taken hostage fifty-seven days ago, exhausted to the point of collapse. Thirsty, hungry, and disheveled, with his clothes torn in places, he looked like a man back from the dead.

Rajkumar's nephew Gopal, who was relaxing on the veranda of his house, could not believe his eyes. He jumped up and shouted in uncontrollable excitement, "Nagappa is here, Nagappa is here. Look, he has returned."

Nagappa's eyes were misty. He began to sob with joy and relief. "Anna is doing fine. Anna is all right. There is no need to worry too much about his health," he kept saying.

The news of Nagappa's escape spread quickly in the surrounding villages of Naithalpura, Iggalur, Talavadi, Mudiyanoor, Hiripura, and Gatwadi, and from there to Chamarajanagar and Mysore. The Erode SP, Tamraikannan, and his counterpart in Chamarajanagar, Anne Gowda, rushed to Gajanur. After a few basic questions, Nagappa was whisked away to Anne Gowda's residence in Chamarajangar.

The police wanted to keep Nagappa away from the media until they had debriefed him. But journalists who had got wind of his escape milled around the SP's residence. After they had waited for a few hours, their patience began to run out. Tempers were rising and there was a lot of shouting. "Show us Nagappa. Allow him to talk to us. Why are you hiding him from us? Are we not entitled to meet him and talk to him? You cannot muzzle the media in this manner."

Finally Nagappa was presented to the journalists. He came up with a rather improbable reason for his decision to escape from Veerappan's hideout. "I heard Amma's voice over the radio a few times. I just could not bear to hear her beg for her husband's release. I felt so bad that I decided to run away from there, come what may, just to see her and talk to her." Nagappa had obviously escaped in order to save his own life. But he was shrewd enough to concoct a story that made Parvathamma the focal point, to avoid incurring the wrath of Rajkumar's family and fans who felt "betrayed" that he had abandoned their Anna in the forest.

One of the rumors that made the rounds immediately after Nagappa's escape was that Veerappan and his men had been discussing the possibility of beheading one of the hostages and sending the head to Krishna as a ploy to shock the government into accepting their demands. They had decided to make Nagappa the sacrificial goat because he was considered the most dispensable of the four hostages. Nagappa, it was said, overheard the discussion and decided to flee.

Karunanidhi expressed surprise over Nagappa's escape and stated emphatically that there was no question of sending the STF to storm Veerappan's hideout based on what Nagappa told them, because there was no guarantee that the bandit would be in the same place. There was no explanation offered for why a trained police force could not gain access to a place that was obviously not too far from the main road and from where even a man like Nagappa, without any understanding of the forest terrain, could escape.

A day after Nagappa's escape, an audiocassette reached the office of the president of the Tamil Nationalist Movement, an outfit sympathetic to the LTTE, in Chennai. Veerappan made his impatience clear. "Whether the hostage crisis ends amicably or not is entirely in the hands of the two governments. We are adamant that our demands should be met at any cost because we are fighting for a revolutionary cause. We placed twelve demands in good faith, but you are delaying the matter by saying that somebody or the other is stalling your moves. You must understand that there is a limit to our patience." Strangely, there was no mention of Nagappa's escape or its ramifications.

Meanwhile, Parvathamma, who had been in the hospital for eight days, was discharged on September 29. And in the early hours of Saturday, September 30, Gopal returned to Chennai from Veerappan's hideout after the fourth round of negotiations with the news that Veerappan was furious at Nagappa's escape. According to Gopal, but for this unforeseen event, Veerappan might have come around to an agreement.

Nagappa, in the meantime, had reached Bangalore on the afternoon of the 29th. After a medical checkup at Mallya Hospital, the police sent him into virtual hiding. They obviously did not want journalists pressing him for his views on the kidnapping and details of his escape. The government was treading on thin ice and felt that it could not afford any more complications. There was also the issue of protecting him from the wrath of Rajkumar's fans who felt betrayed by him. But the official word was that the government didn't want Nagappa to complicate issues with conflicting reports in such a delicate situation.

ON OCTOBER 11, as Gopal prepared for his fifth trip into the forest, the Supreme Court came down heavily on the two governments for surrendering to the whims of the bandit. Advocate Chava Badrinath brought up the report sent to the Karnataka government by Arkesh Gowda to prove that the government, despite being informed of the threat to Rajkumar, had done nothing to protect him.

Justices Bharucha, Mohapatra, and Sabharwal showed their surprise at this, and taking a cue from the mood of the court, Badrinath Babu pressed home his advantage. "Your Lordships, allow me to also bring to your notice that the special public prosecutor, since 1994, had been repeatedly opposing any relaxation in the bail conditions to the accused already on bail, and grant of bail to those under judicial custody bail. How is it that he has chosen not to oppose the granting of bail to them now?"

The court finally ruled that the two governments had clearly acted in haste to appease Veerappan. "The special public prosecutor has not thought carefully before moving his application to drop TADA charges against the bandit's associates. The actual reasons for moving the applications to drop charges were never told to the designated court in Mysore. The government is pulling wool over the court's eye. It is perfectly clear that everybody has acted in fear of Veerappan. This is most unfortunate."

Justice Bharucha was so angry that he chastised the Karnataka government even more harshly: "You have not stated before the Mysore court the fact that it is Veerappan who is dictating terms to you. You have conveniently used the ground that you are dropping TADA charges in the larger interests of the public. One factor, which cannot escape anybody's attention, is that acceding to Veerappan's demands may release the film star, but the day after tomorrow another will be abducted and the same drama will be enacted."

The court was further informed that both Karnataka and Tamil Nadu had incurred an expenditure of over 250 million rupees every year on the STFs constituted to nab Veerappan. Although the bandit had killed over 138 people, including thirty-eight policemen, the governments remained helpless to stop him. The usual reasons cited were the mountainous terrain and the dense forests in his area, which were difficult to conquer.

The response of the bench was to examine the problem from two angles: "One, there is a man who has been an outlaw for the past ten years and the STF set up for the purpose has not been able to arrest him. So what are the genuine efforts that were made to nab him? Second, what is the genuineness of the apprehension that there would be flames of linguistic unrest in the two states if something happened to

Rajkumar? For this, what is the material on record? Mere filing of affidavits by bureaucrats will not do to show that it is based on reality. The government has to show this to us through primary reports."

The bench decided that the court required more documents from the governments to rule on the case. They directed the two governments to place before the court, in sealed covers, details of the two meetings between the chief ministers regarding Veerappan. The deadline was set for October 17. The solicitor general appearing for Karnataka was also instructed to place in a sealed cover the details of any alternate plan to secure the release of Rajkumar.

Unfortunately, it turned out that the minutes of the meeting between the chief ministers had not been recorded. Or, what was more likely, the governments had no desire to place on record their plans to placate Veerappan.

IN CHENNAI, hectic behind-the-scenes parleys started for the drafting of three new entrants into the negotiating team. Word had come from Tamil extremist Maaran and his followers, who were holed up in the forest along with Veerappan, that three of their supporters should accompany Gopal on his next trip. "We want to make it clear to the governments that we need our men to talk to us. We shall go by what they have to say about the situation outside. We shall talk to someone in whom we have total faith."

The fact that Gopal had repeatedly failed in his mission to get Rajkumar released had become a cause for worry because he was the only one everyone seemed to trust as negotiator. At this juncture, a Bangalore-based Tamil organization, Karnataka Tamizhar Peravai, under the stewardship of Shanmuga Sundaram, entered the fray.

Shanmuga Sundaram, an important Tamil figure in Bangalore and the owner of a large fleet of lorries, had approached Kolathur Mani in Salem almost twenty days earlier. Mani is an influential DMK leader in the Veerappan belt, and is known to be a supporter of the LTTE too. "The situation is quite bad in Karnataka. If something is not done immediately, it could have serious consequences. A lot of innocent lives will be lost. If there is someone who can convince Veerappan, it is you.

Why don't you make an effort to meet him and persuade him to release Rajkumar?" Sundaram asked Mani.

Veerappan, it was said, knew Mani's father well and held him in high regard. Finally, Kolathur Mani met Veerappan sometime around September 26 and persuaded him to accept the president of the Tamil Nationalist Movement, Nedumaran, and two others—Professor Kalyani and Sukumaran—as emissaries so that a mutually acceptable decision could be reached. Professor Kalyani is a college teacher from Villupuram known for his radical leanings, and Sukumaran is a TNLA sympathizer based in Pondicherry, who is also active in the local unit of the Public Union of Civil Liberties (PUCL).

With these three men drafted into the negotiation team, it was hoped that Veerappan could be made to see reason. Nedumaran and his colleagues were said to have better bargaining power than Gopal, as the Tamil extremist elements seemed to be controlling proceedings in Veerappan's camp. Nedumaran was expected to "talk it out" with them. The government did not seem worried that the new emissaries swore allegiance to the LTTE. "Whether they are sympathizers or not, we are only concerned about the safe release of the hostages. That is the only thing on our minds," said the home minister.


GOPAL, ACCOMPANIED BY THE NEW TEAM, left for the hideout. On the evening of October 16, Veerappan formally released a hostage: Govindaraj, Rajkumar's son-in-law. Gopal, Nedumaran, and the other two emissaries accompanied him out of the forest. While the others left for Chennai, Govindaraj was taken to Bangalore. He reached the city in the early hours of the morning and drove straight to Rajkumar's residence, where Parvathamma and the others received him.

Govindaraj looked frail after his seventy-seven-day ordeal. Sporting a salt-and-pepper beard, he spoke in a labored voice at a crowded press conference in Bangalore later in the day. He spoke of a fresh demand that Veerappan had made. "Veerappan has sought an assurance from the governments that no commando action will be initiated against him after he releases Rajkumar and Nagesh. He will release them only after his associates are released from jail. He is very adamant about it. He feels

that the governments have committed themselves and they have to fulfill their promise. I was released only after Anna impressed upon
Veerappan that my health was failing. I am a diabetic and a heart patient. I also suffer from high blood pressure. I just don't know how I
managed to survive in those terrible conditions in the forest. I have not
brought any cassette from Veerappan. Anna told me before I left that he
would be in our midst soon."

When the emissaries reached Chennai, there were already signs of
conflict between them. Rajkumar was still not a free man. The
Nedumaran camp said that unlike Gopa, he was sent to meet Veerappan
by the TNLA, not the government. Gopal claimed that it was
Nedumaran's presence that made Veerappan change his mind at the last
minute about releasing Rajkumar. Govindaraj later met Chief Minister
Krishna along with Rajkumar's three sons. After listening to Govindaraj,
Krishna convened an emergency cabinet meeting at 3 p.m. to discuss the
bandit's latest demand. The Supreme Court was also to resume hearing
the case later in the day.

In the Supreme Court, the three-judge bench of Justices Bharucha,
Mahapatra, and Sabharwal began hearing the case. Dr. Wadhera, who
had filed a special leave petition on behalf of the former DGP of
Tamil Nadu, Walter Dawaram, rose to speak. "Your Lordships may
please be informed that the TN government has not filed any documents substantiating its grounds to release the five TNLA men in
its custody. If any special documents were indeed produced before
the lower court, the same were not made available to the petitioner."
Justice Bharucha directed the Tamil Nadu government to produce
the documents made available to the public prosecutor when he sought
the release of the detainees from the TADA court. The bench also
expressed its concern over the links between Veerappan and Tamil
secessionist elements.

Justice Bharucha was acerbic in his observations. "We are extremely
distressed. There is no doubt that anybody would be affected by the relationship that has blossomed between Veerappan and secessionist elements in the Satyamangalam forest area. We wonder how he escaped
from custody in 1986. Securing Rajkumar's release is no lasting solution
to the problem called Veerappan. He has been indulging in kidnapping

and will continue to do so unless he is apprehended and dealt with in accordance with the law."

The judge was severely critical of the governments' move to release Veerappan's associates. "Do the two governments understand the effect their action will have on the witnesses in the cases, on society, and the morale of the police force in general and the STF in particular? As far as we are concerned, the onus lies with the two state governments to satisfy us as to why one man, who has committed so many atrocities, has not been apprehended for the past so many years. He has committed so many killings, and what happens if his associates are allowed to join him in the forest? We will take into account the fact that Tamil Nadu has confirmed, through its affidavit, Veerappan's association with extremist elements. It seems certain to us that Veerappan will continue with his life of crime and it is very likely that those crimes will have antinational objectives."

When the hearing resumed the next day, Solicitor General Harish Salve tried to impress upon the court that withdrawing charges against the TADA detainees, some of whom were over seventy years old, would be less grave than allowing Rajkumar to remain Veerappan's hostage. But the judges were unmoved. "State precisely on what basis the Karnataka government came to the conclusion that Rajkumar would be freed after the fifty-one TADA detainees are released on bail. Why has the government ignored Veerappan's other demands, such as making the Tamil language compulsory in Karnataka schools, releasing Cauvery water, and erecting the Thiruvallavur statue in Bangalore, and focused only on this demand that his associates should be released?"

Salve was stumped. All he could do was promise to return with an affidavit after consulting Chief Minister Krishna.

Salve also argued that the court could certainly question the manner in which the application was made before the designated court in Mysore, but not the state government's decision to negotiate with Veerappan. However, he admitted that Veerappan now had links with secessionist elements, and that made the matter more serious. "But the government made its decision in peculiar circumstances, Your Honor. In spite of that, all the pros and cons were weighed."

In reply, Justice Bharucha demanded evidence to show that was in fact the case.

On October 19, the court met for the third consecutive day to hear the case. The judges were firm in their view that the two governments had erred in their decision to facilitate the release of the TADA detainees on bail. Justice Bharucha was unstoppable. "The special public prosecutor's affidavit calls for the withdrawal of TADA charges, which would allow the accused to file necessary bail applications, and consequently be released. It is thus clear that the Karnataka government and the special public prosecutor envisioned a package which included the withdrawal of the TADA charges against the accused. This indicates complicity with the accused. We deprecate the conduct of the Karnataka government and the special public prosecutor. You think you are performing some deed in great public interest and so you can abdicate all your responsibility? Further, it is unpardonable that despite having received specific information that Rajkumar might be kidnapped from his farmhouse in Gajanur, the Tamil Nadu government did not take any step to prevent this."

Senior counsel V. R. Reddy, appearing on behalf of the Tamil Nadu government, tried to argue that there was no occasion for the government to provide security to Rajkumar, since he did not inform the state police of his visit, and moreover, the police force of the area was busy handling the agitation of tea plantation workers in the nearby Nilgiris area. But his argument had little effect on the judges.

Justice Bharucha said, "The greatest danger is that if the prisoners were released, the government would then have to face not Veerappan alone, but a lethal alliance between his gang and secessionist elements. If these people associate with Veerappan, and in that terrain, who knows what plan will be hatched, what arms would be procured and what training would be imparted. The Mysore court's order of August 19 is appalling. It was made out of pure fear. Therefore we are not inclined at the moment to release the TADA detainees on bail." The court was adjourned till October 31.

ON A VISIT TO RAICHUR a few days later, Congress president Sonia Gandhi expressed her displeasure that Nedumaran, an LTTE supporter, was selected as an emissary of the government. Given the antipathy of the Gandhi family toward the LTTE, her censure was not surprising. Krishna claimed in his own defense that he was not consulted before Nedumaran was chosen. But Karunanidhi said that Krishna not only knew about it, he had interacted with Nedumaran once before too. The controversy took center stage for a while, pushing the focus away from Rajkumar—and Veerappan.

## 20

## The Homecoming

As the hostage crisis continued, the two governments became increasingly evasive on the matter. In the absence of any action, Rajkumar's family went back to the one medium they thought might get Veerappan's attention—the radio. The usual messages of concern for his well-being were aired. Veerappan was once again begged to change his mind and let the aging actor go. This time his grandchildren, Vishu and Ashwini, were made to speak too. *"Thatha,* everybody is celebrating Deepavali. But we will celebrate only once you come back. How can we be happy when you are in the forest? Please come back as soon as possible. Take care of your health and don't worry about anything."

In Chennai, a different game plan was being tested. Nedumaran, Kalyani, and Sukumaran drafted a nine-page memorandum to the NHRC to intervene in the Supreme Court case. They wanted the commission to present before the court human rights violations by the STF and also the plight of the TADA detainees who had suffered as a result. The memorandum said, "There has been gross violation of human rights in the villages in Veerappan's area. Prisoners who have been languishing in jail without trial and also the families of those killed in 'encounters' have undergone terrible misery over the years. So many have faced sexual abuse and torture. The Justice Sadashiva Commission's inquiry into all this has to be reopened. It would be a statutory lapse on the part of NHRC if it did not do anything about this. The commission's intervention now would protect the rights of the fifty-one persons in custody since 1993 and also the seventy others who were granted bail but are forced to sign at the Ramapura police station every week. . . ."

Back in the Supreme Court, advocates were bracing themselves for another round of battle. The court wanted to know what the Centre was doing in the matter. Representing the Centre was Additional Solicitor General Kirit Raval. "Your Lordships," he began, addressing the same three-judge bench headed by Justice S. P. Bharucha. "It is not as if the Centre is unenthusiastic about what has happened. We will respond as and when the request for assistance comes from the two states. The imposition of president's rule cannot be contemplated at this stage."

Justice Bharucha replied, "The court is not suggesting anything. But surely there are steps that the Centre can take. It might be very legally sound for the Centre to say that law and order is a state subject, but what we are seeing is the birth of an independent state, a foreign nation. As citizens and judges we are anguished. Would you say you shouldn't act even if an independent state comes into being?"

Kirit only reiterated what Harish Salve had said before. "If anything were to happen to Rajkumar, the two states would have to deal with a serious law-and-order problem, Your Lordships. It would leave deep scars on the minds of the people."

"The court shall not agree to this line of argument. The two state governments have not been reasonable in handling the issue. They can come back to this court only if they have anything concrete to substantiate their reasoning. Our prima facie conclusion is that the two states have acted in panic and without thinking things through. The court would like to confine itself to this case, but we would be dishonest if we didn't say at least briefly what we have seen. The court reserves its orders." Mysore advocate Venugopal's plea for bail for the accused was also rejected.

The Karnataka government chose not to comment on the Supreme

Court's decision to reserve its orders. It was now clear that a favorable verdict was out of the question. The government had no more options left, except perhaps to launch a commando operation to free Rajkumar. But Krishna did not want to do anything to jeopardize the actor's life, let alone his own as a politician. He said, "The time is not ripe for alternative action. We have to keep continuing the negotiations with Veerappan. Whatever we decide should have the sanction of the Tamil Nadu government as well."

November 6 marked Rajkumar's one hundredth day as Veerappan's captive. There was still no sign of the drama ending. For the emissaries, it was time for yet another trip to the forest. The governments' standard line had become "We shall continue negotiations until Rajkumar is released." But what stage the negotiations had reached and when he would be finally free were questions for which no answers were forthcoming. Politicians on both sides of the border had taken refuge in the fact that the Supreme Court had not yet passed its final verdict.

The much-awaited Supreme Court verdict came on November 7. Justices S. P. Bharucha, D. P. Mahapatra, and Y. K. Sabharwal were unanimous in their decision that none of the TADA detainees should be released. They passed severe strictures on the Karnataka government and castigated the conduct of Special Public Prosecutor Ashwini Kumar Joshi in withdrawing from the prosecution without even perusing the records. The court also quashed a Tamil Nadu trial court's order dropping TADA charges against "Radio" Venkatesh. The Tamil Nadu government's decision to revoke detention orders against Tamil extremists Sathyamurthy, Manikandan, and Muthukumar was also quashed.

The Supreme Court raised eight pertinent questions for which there were no clear-cut answers from either of the two governments:

Was there evidence to show that the police feared civil disturbances, which would justify the dropping of TADA charges against Veerappan's associates?

What, in the assessment of the police, was the risk of leaving Veerappan free to commit future crimes, and how did it weigh against the risk to Rajkumar's life?

If charges were dropped, what was the likely effect on the morale of the law-enforcing agencies and the witnesses?

What was the likelihood of reprisals against the many witnesses who had already deposed against the accused?

Was there any evidence to show that Veerappan would release Rajkumar even if some of his other demands were not to be met at all?

Was there any evidence to suggest that Veerappan would be satisfied with the release of only the accused persons?

Was there any evidence to suggest that after the accused had secured their discharge from TADA charges, Veerappan would release Rajkumar?

Given that the two governments had been pursuing Veerappan for ten years, was this a ploy to keep him out of the clutches of the law?

The judges had been clinical in their assessment of the case. Justice Y. K. Sabharwal took over from S. P. Bharucha in criticizing the special public prosecutor's conduct. "The public prosecutor has to be straight, forthright, and honest and has to admit that the real arrangement was to ultimately facilitate the release of the accused from judicial custody by not opposing their bail applications after the withdrawal of TADA charges. The intention is well established."

He then went on to ask, "In such circumstances, why the camouflage? Why is it not stated in the application filed before the district judge under Section 321? In fact, it is a deceit. No court of law can be a party to such camouflage and deceit in judicial proceedings. The application was not made in good faith. True, the power of the court under Section 321 is supervisory. But that does not mean that while exercising that power, consent has to be granted on mere asking.

"It doesn't appear that anybody considered that if democratically elected governments appear to their citizens to be lawbreakers, would it not breed contempt for law? Would it not invite citizens to become a law unto themselves? It may even lead to anarchy. The governments have to consider and balance the choice between maintenance of law and order and anarchy. . . ." The fate of the two governments was sealed.

Soon after this, the Tamil Maanila Congress (TMC), the main opposition to the Karunanidhi government in Tamil Nadu, started saying that Nedumaran should be dropped from the team negotiating with Veerappan because of his pro-LTTE links. The leader of the Opposition,

S. Balakrishnan, stated bluntly that "Nedumaran is an antinational. Not only should he be removed from the negotiating team, but also arrested. If such men are given opportunities to be active in society, we will be doomed."

Stung by the criticism, Nedumaran decided to withdraw from the mission. "I'm not going to the forest. Balakrishnan is a great patriot and is wiser than me. He can easily tackle Veerappan and secure Rajkumar's release. I chose to be the emissary purely on humanitarian grounds. I have no ulterior motives."

A Kannada film industry delegation led by actor-MP Ambarish hurriedly left for Chennai to try to persuade Nedumaran to undertake the trip to the forest once again. PMK chief Ramadoss, Shivarajkumar, and "Rockline" Venkatesh joined Ambarish. They pleaded with Nedumaran not to be offended by what was said about him. Saying he was their only hope, they begged him to relent for the sake of the people of Karnataka and also for Rajkumar. Nedumaran finally agreed, and the process of negotiation started again.

Chief Minister Karunanidhi justified Nedumaran's role in the Assembly during a three-hour discussion on an adjournment motion on the hostage issue. He said, "I am neither supporting nor denying the charge that Nedumaran is close to LTTE supremo Velupillai Prabhakaran. Nedumaran's organization is not banned here. What is the harm if he is willing to go and talk to Veerappan? All of us want Rajkumar released, don't we? It is a well-known practice to remove a thorn with another thorn."

Finally, around November 9, Nedumaran drove to the periphery of the Talamalai forests along with Professor Kalyani and G. Sukumaran. This was to be the final throw of the dice. Shanmughasundaram joined the team from Bangalore. Along with him were two others, Ramkumar and a Tamil woman named Bhanu, who lived in Bangalore. Ramkumar was the son of retired Karnataka DGP Ramalingam. Both Ramkumar and Bhanu were in the granite business and had key links with people in the Satyamangalam belt, Kolathur Mani.

Surprisingly, Gopal was left out of the negotiations this time. Although Veerappan himself did not have anything against the journalist, Maaran and his men preferred not to have him around.

Nedumaran and his team reached the hideout toward nightfall. The sixth round of talks with Veerappan began. "Both the governments will honor their commitment of ensuring that all the TADA detainees in jail in Tamil Nadu and Karnataka are released after following the due course of law. This has become necessary due to the Supreme Court's intervention. Believe us, their interests will be looked after," Nedumaran began. Veerappan and the others listened.

Shanmughasundaram explained to Veerappan the sensitive situation in Karnataka, especially Bangalore. "Please understand that there will be a strong anti-Tamil backlash which could even turn violent if there is any further delay in Rajkumar's release. There will be a lot of problems for the common man and your own image among your people will be tarnished. Please make up your mind and put an end to this. The people have waited for too long to see this issue come to an end."

Bhanu, the lone woman in the team, was masquerading as a doctor. She had been told to "examine" Rajkumar in Veerappan's presence and tell him that all was not well with the actor's health. It was hoped that this would force the bandit to release him. Bhanu played her role well. She told Veerappan that Rajkumar's heart condition was deteriorating.

Veerappan, who had been silent all this while, finally spoke. He asked the team to return after a few days, by which time he would have made a decision. Five days later, he announced that he had decided to release Rajkumar and the second hostage, Nagesh. "They are free to go," he said. And in the early hours of Wednesday, November 15, the 108-day story finally came to an end. The bandit ended the episode melodramatically by "honoring" Rajkumar and Nagesh with a pair of shawls brought from Erode before allowing them to go.

This was the public version of the story. But it is rumored that nearly 300 million rupees were paid to Veerappan and his men to secure Rajkumar's release, and that quantities of gold were given along with the cash. It does seem unlikely that a man as shrewd and unbending as Veerappan would give up his prize catch so easily, especially as he requires money to survive in the forests with his men. With extremist elements like Maaran joining him, large sums of money had become more necessary. It is said that while a portion of the ransom amount came from Rajkumar's family, most of it was "collected" from big businessmen in Bangalore, mainly in the liquor trade.

An hour's drive took the former hostages and their rescuers to the farmhouse belonging to one of Kolathur Mani's friends near Erode, about eighteen miles away. That afternoon, Chief Minister Krishna made a formal announcement in the Assembly about the release: "Rajkumar has been released at last. The darkness of amavasya has been dispelled." Members thumped their desks, welcoming the announcement. Krishna went on, "I take this opportunity to thank the people of the state, the Tamil Nadu government, the emissaries, the media, the Karnataka Film Chamber, and the Opposition parties for their sincere cooperation during the crisis. The abduction was most unfortunate, but the government has learned a lesson. We should not allow such things to happen again. I request the people to continue to maintain law and order even after Rajkumar returns to Bangalore."

Outside, fireworks lit up the sky as Rajkumar's fans danced deliriously on the streets. "Victory to Rajkumar," they shouted. Crowds thronged the streets, animatedly discussing the circumstances of the release. Some of them distributed sweets to passersby.

The Karnataka government decided to send a helicopter to Coimbatore for Rajkumar, Nagesh, and the others. On the afternoon of November 16, close to four thousand people gathered at the Jakkur airport. There was a tremendous sense of excitement and anticipation in the air. As the helicopter touched down, the barricades erected to keep the crowd at bay gave way. The police watched helplessly as thousands ran to greet their idol.

In a gesture reminiscent of his screen persona, Rajkumar knelt down and touched the ground reverentially. He looked around and waved. "It's as if I'm visiting a new world," he said in awe. As the policemen wrestled with the crowd, Rajkumar got into a car that took him to the majestic Vidhana Soudha in a seemingly never-ending convoy.

Under the ornate canopy of the massive stone building stood a beaming chief minister, along with Mallikarjuna Kharge. In the background, loudspeakers belted out old hits from Rajkumar's films. As he was led up the huge stairway to the banquet hall, the media were in full attendance. Scores of cameras flashed to capture the moment. Television cameramen vied with each other to get the best angle. Dressed in his trademark white shirt and dhoti, Rajkumar looked sunburned, but otherwise well.

He was pensive when he spoke about his experience in the forest. "I feel new to this world, as if I have landed from some other planet," he said. "It is amazing to think that I spent so many days in the forest. What can I say about that place? It was forest after forest for us . . . no towns, no people . . . sometimes elephants would come near our camp. Veerappan and his men were like relatives to us. There was no other choice, we had to accept them as our relatives.

"As I lived in the forest, I would sometimes be haunted by memories: of my people, my family, the children, and the grandchildren. Many questions would arise. How do I spend time? Are there any escape routes? Why does day break? Why does night set in? Everything was tiring. But we had to carry on. We had to somehow while away time. Initially we had felt that we would be released within ten or twelve days. We would listen to the radio every day as the radio messages would make us feel secure."

"Gopal came some four or five times. But he could not do anything. And then Nagappa escaped. That man's escape put us in trouble. What would happen to us? Veerappan had a big group. What if they shot us? We could have done nothing. One group had gone out when the incident took place. After returning, they tied our hands. It was a very anxious moment. I told them, 'Release the boys and shoot me. I'm old. I have seen everything in life. Good people, good friends, good times, opportunities to mingle with great people . . . shoot me. I have nothing else to look forward to in life. Kill me if you want. . . .' But Veerappan came up to me and said, 'Don't worry. Nothing will happen to you.' "

Rajkumar revealed that it was Veerappan himself who had suggested that Nedumaran should be asked to take part in the negotiations. "Veerappan said that if Nedumaran came to the forest and spoke to him, he would consider releasing us. That is when I sent a recorded message to the Tamil Nadu chief minister. A few days after the cassette was sent, we were happy to see this man who looked like a yogi, a Maha Purusha, coming to visit us. We had changed some fifty to sixty hideouts in the forest. In some places, we would stay for a day or two. But in certain other places, we would stay on for ten or twelve days. We were all very tired. My son-in-law, Govindraj, who is basically not too well, began to develop problems. I asked Nedumaran to persuade Veerappan to release him. Soon after this, Govindraj was released. Before leaving, Nedumaran said that we would also be released soon. It was such a relief to hear this.

"As the days went by, we settled down to our life in the forest again. Then one day in the afternoon I was amazed to hear a woman's voice. She introduced herself as Dr. Bhanu. She had come with Ramkumar and Mani. I was surprised to hear her speak in Kannada. 'Don't worry, we have come to get you released,' she told me. 'We shall definitely do it in the next five or six days. We have made all arrangements.' They returned after four or five days. I don't know what they did, but we were released. To me, the lady came as a *devathe*."

Rajkumar then went on to explain how he was made to pretend that he was not feeling well. He finally said, "Veerappan is a man with some humaneness. Otherwise, he wouldn't have presented us with shawls and new clothes before sending us off."

Rajkumar's comments about the man who had held him hostage for 108 days were more sympathetic than bitter. There was no sign of anger, no desire to retaliate, no recognition, almost, of the fact that Veerappan was a criminal and a ruthless killer.

Perhaps in this lay Veerappan's real victory.

# Epilogue

Four days after Rajkumar was released, Karunanidhi announced the resumption of STF action. "The STF's strength has been increased. It will now consist of one extra DIG, three SPs, and additional personnel," he said. ADDL. DGP H. T. Sangliana (KSRP) Bangalore was appointed as the chief of the Karnataka STF.

Sangliana, a 1967 batch IPS officer, is a Mizo known as much for his daredevilry as for his honesty. He is said to have once stopped the car of Karnataka CM Devaraj Urs and asked him to reimburse the money spent on a wreath that had been bought at his behest—which, as anyone living in India knows, is absolutely not done, unless you want a transfer to the most remote corner of India. Sangliana's career has been the inspiration for two hit films in Kannada, eponymously titled *Sangliana I* and *II*.

Shankar Bidri, the former STF commander widely known as Veerappan's scourge, has also been drafted into the newly structured STF, after a long layoff. Soon after J. H. Patel became chief minister of Karnataka in 1996, he had weaned Bidri away from the STF and appointed him as the chief of state intelligence. Bidri, based in Bangalore, is presently an IG with the KSRP.

Along with these two officers, in the new team is Kempiah, a DIG in the Karnataka police who had led the hunt for Sivarasan, prime suspect in the Rajiv Gandhi murder case.

Soon after the team was formed, it was decided it would launch a joint operation against Veerappan, under the overall command of Tamil Nadu IG K. Balachandran. After a meeting between Chief Minister Krishna and Union home minister L. K. Advani, it was announced that the BSF would assist the operations. Sophisticated weapons and even helicopters were readied. Seven STF platoons—twelve belonging to Tamil Nadu and five to Karnataka—started combing operations in the Satyamangalam jungles, where Veerappan and his men were said to be hiding. Before embarking on his mission, Sangliana declared, "We are very confident of catching him this time. A new strategy has been worked out, which is bound to yield solid results in the next few days." The police officers pored over the area's maps, the helicopters went on sorties, the commandos trekked the jungles, guns on the ready, but as usual, there was no trace of Veerappan.

By the middle of January 2001, there was word that Veerappan and his men had sneaked into the jungles of Kerala, unable to bear STF pressure in their home territory. The Kerala police scoured the Siruvani jungles in the Agali and Mannarghat ranges in Pallakad district, and it seemed briefly that success was just around the corner, but finally nothing came of it.

On February 2, there was an exchange of fire with the Veerappan gang, not in Kerala, but in the Sambandikadu forest area between Coimbatore and Pallakad. One gangster was said to have been injured. The STF intensified its operations in the Valayar and Chemmanthimala jungles of Kerala bordering Tamil Nadu. Amid the drone of helicopters and the thudding of four thousand police boots on the jungle floor, combined with the panting of sniffer dogs, it seemed that Veerappan and his men would be caught at any moment. "Veerappan is fighting his last battle. We have effectively closed all his escape routes. He will be caught soon," said Tomin Thachankery, SP, Pallakad division. But, except for seizing 290,000 rupees in cash, ten bags of food, three mobile phones, medical kits, and batteries from the area, there was no other progress. The mobile phones clearly indicated that the bandit was again being aided by outsiders.

The biggest breakthrough came on February 15. TNLA leader Sengottavan, also known as Maaran, was arrested in the Siruvani jungles. In fact, he surrendered when he was cornered by an STF team. Soon after this, Krishnamurthy, an activist of TNRT and a new member of the Veerappan gang, was arrested in the Guttielathur jungles, near Satyamangalam. The police were confident that with their arrest, concrete clues to Veerappan's whereabouts would become available. But nothing has materialized so far.


THE WAR AGAINST VEERAPPAN has been going on for more than a decade. Police officers who worked with the STF have all returned to regular postings. SP Gopal Hosur, who very nearly died in the Rangaswami Oddu ambush on May 24, 1993, is now in Bangalore as DCP (Central) in charge of law and order.

Inspector Biddanda Ashok Kumar has lived with the disappointment of having failed to get anywhere near Veerappan, in spite of his best efforts. Ashok is currently an inspector in the Chickpet police station, Bangalore. He might one day return to the STF, now that operations have resumed.

Inspector Ahmed Bawa, another fine officer who never tired of devising plans to catch the bandit, has been promoted to assistant commissioner of police (ACP), in charge of the same Chickpet area.

SI Chandrappa, who survived the Hogenekal ambush in 1990 with bullet injuries, is currently posted to the City Crime Investigation Branch (CCIB), Mysore, as an inspector. He has taken to acting in his spare time, and can be seen now and then in Kannada films.

SI Srikantraje Urs, who survived the Chengadi shootout in which AHC Ponnappa met his end, is with the wireless section in Mysore. A highly committed policeman, Urs has been decorated with the prestigious President's Gold Medal—only the second Karnataka officer ever to be thus honored from the wireless section—and also the Chief Minister's Silver Medal for overall meritorious service.

SI Krishne Urs, who drove his colleagues to safety after the Hogenekal ambush, served in Channapatna near Bangalore before being shifted to the capital.

Ramapura SI Rachaiah, who witnessed the death of his colleagues during Veerappan's attack on the station in May 1992, is now an inspector at the Nallappathana traffic station in Mysore.

CI Mandappa, who served in Kollegala in the early 1990s, is now a DSP posted at Hunsur, close to Mysore.

SP (now DIG) Bipin Gopalkrishna, who went after Veerappan as the head of the Mysore district police, is presently Director (Vigilance), Karnataka Road Transport Corporation (KSRTC), and lives in Bangalore.

Former STF commander DIG Thimmappa Madiyal, during whose tenure Gurunathan was arrested, is now an IG, serving as commissioner of police, Bangalore.

"Rambo" Gopalkrishnan, who providentially escaped death in the Sorakaimadu bomb blasts, is now DCP (Law and Order) in Coimbatore.

Walter Dawaram, chief of the Tamil Nadu STF, has retired from service. Settled in Chennai, he still breathes fire. "Given a chance, I would go after him again," he says.

Driver Anwar Pasha, who spent fourteen days as the bandit's captive in the Bandipur National Park in 1997, along with Krupakar and Senani, was transferred after his release to the Nisana Begur range on the banks of the Kabini River, close to the famous jungles of Kakanakote. After serving there for a while, he was suspended from duty on charges of abetting deer poachers. He has since been reinstated, and serves in the Hediyala range, close to Bandipur. Pump operator Raju and cleaner Krishnappa, the other hostages, are still in Bandipur.

Krupakar and Senani, the wildlife photographers, wrote a book in Kannada titled *Sereyalli Idda Hadinalku Dinagalu* ("Fourteen Days in Captivity"), detailing their experiences as Veerappan's captives. They continue to work in Bandipur.

Dr. Satyabrata Maiti, the scientist with the Indian Institute of Horticultural Research in Bangalore, whom Veerappan chose to take hostage along with Krupakar and Senani, left Bangalore last year to take up a posting in Anand, Gujarat, as the director of the Indian Council for Agricultural Research.

The silver-haired forest guard Andani, who, being from the same area, has closely followed Veerappan's criminal career since the mid-1960s, is still in service and is now working in the Hanur range. The other guard, Vishakanta, also part of the hostage group, presently serves at the Kollegala government timber depot.

Forest watchers Dasa, Jadiya, Kumbha, Raju, and Nanjanayaka, all daily wage employees, who spent forty-four harrowing days as Veerappan's hostages, continue to serve in Gundal in the Bailur range from where they were taken hostage. The other hostage, watcher Mahadeva, also a daily wage earner, quit his job in March 2000.

Driver Basavaraju, who heroically drove his jeep through slushy jungle paths in the night to convey the news of the kidnapping to his boss, Vijay Kumar Gogi, is now in the Heggada Devana (HD) Kote range under the Mysore Forest Division.

Abdul Kareem, whose special leave petition in the Supreme Court turned the Rajkumar kidnapping drama on its head, continues to live in the quiet suburb of Yadavagiri in Mysore. His request for police protection was granted by the state government, and anyone wanting to meet him now will have to convince the gun-toting police constable at the gate. Kareem has become a celebrity of sorts in Mysore.

Rajkumar gradually went out of media focus after his release. His experiences as Veerappan's captive were serialized in a popular Kannada weekly called *Taranga*. He lives in his Sadashivanagar mansion in Bangalore, meeting only select people. His professed "understanding" and "affection" for Veerappan, whom he called "Thambi" ("Brother"), seem to have dulled the public frenzy for him.

Govindaraj and Nagesh have put their harrowing experiences in the jungle behind them. Govindaraj, who is also Rajkumar's son-in-law, is a producer of Kannada films and television serials. He has since gone back to work. Nagesh, who is also related to the Rajkumar family, is back in Gajanur. He looks after the family's estate there.

Nagappa Maradagi, who created a sensation by escaping from Veerappan's clutches, has become incommunicado. He is apparently not in Rajkumar's employ anymore, and lives in a village somewhere near Bangalore.

Police informers Muthuram, Nataraj, and Nagaraj, who helped the police in the early 1990s, have lost touch with each other. Muthuram, now in his early thirties, is married with a baby girl and continues to live in Dinnalli Satyamangalam. He has quite miraculously escaped Veerappan's wrath. A small-time political activist now, Muthuram is quite popular in Ramapura and the adjoining areas and is known to be a resourceful man. He takes up civil contracts on behalf of locally elected bodies like the Zilla Panchayat and Zilla Parishad. Nataraj, the wine store cashier, left Ramapura soon after Gurunathan's death, a disillusioned man. The police did not keep their promise of helping him. Tragically, he became a pauper after losing his job, and is said to be living somewhere near the small town of Sira in Tumkur district. The whereabouts of Nagaraj, the *coolie*, whose dalliance with the Veerappan gang galvanized Muthuram and Nataraj into action, are unknown. His last job was at the estate of Malavalli subinspector Yellappa's farm near Hassan.

Chandni, the Lambani girl who was lured into Veerappan's gang by the double-crossing police informer Kamala Naika, moved to Bangalore with the CRPF constable Puttamallachan, who had promised to marry her. She discovered too late that he was already married. He kept her in a house near his own, but soon after she gave birth to a girl, he abandoned her. Disillusioned and unhappy, she now lives in Marathalli near Bangalore airport and works in a garment factory for a salary of 2,500 rupees. Her child is being brought up by her mother in Dinalli Satyamangalam village, which has ostracized her. She has since changed her name to Shanthi. "Who will give me a job if I reveal my real name? My life was ruined by Kamala Naika, who was my close relative. I don't know what will happen to me in the future," she cries.

As Chandni and others like her struggle to come to terms with their lives, irrevocably changed by contact with the infamous bandit, the question remains: How will Veerappan's story end?

# Glossary of Selected Terms

AHC: Assistant Head Constable

AIADMK: All India Dravida Munnetra Khazhagam

AIYYA: "Older brother" in Tamil.

AMAVASYA: New moon.

AMMA: "Mother" in both Tamil and Kannada.

ANNA: "Older brother" in Kannada.

ANNAI: "Older brother" in Tamil, a respectful form of address.

APEX COURT: The Supreme Court of India.

APPAJI: A respectful form of address that means father.

ARRACK: A rum-like drink.

AVARGALE: A respectful form of address in Tamil, the equivalent of "mister" or "sir" in English.

BANDH: A Hindi word for a labor strike held to express solidarity for a cause.

BANIAN: A vest worn by men inside a shirt.

BASARI TREE: An indigenous tree found in the forests of south India.

BEEDI: A cheap, hand-rolled cigarette smoked by rural Indians.

BSF: Border Security Force

CENTRE: The central or Indian government

CF: Conservator of Forests

CI: Circle Inspector

CM: Chief Minister

COLLECTOR: A high-ranking district bureaucrat in charge of administration.

CRPF: Central Reserve Police Force

DACOITY: A word coined from the Hindi word "Dacoit," which means the act of committing large-scale robbery and looting.

DAR: District Armed Reserve

DCF: Deputy Commandant of Forests

DEVATHE: A Sanskrit word that means goddess.

DGP: Director General of Police

DHARNA: A Kannada word for a congregation of people who have come together to seek redress.

DHOOPA TREE: An indigenous tree found in the forests of south India.

DHOTI: A formal garment, invariably white in color, worn wrapped around the waist by south Indian men.

DIG: Deputy Inspector General

DISTRICT: A geographical portion of a state comparable to a county in the United States

DODDI: A cattle pen.

DOSA: A kind of rice pancake. A very popular snack in south India.

DSP: Deputy Superintendent of Police

FOREST CELL: State police department division that investigates forest-related offenses.

GYPSY: A four-wheel-drive vehicle.

HC: Head Constable

HONNE TREE: An indigenous tree found in the forests of south India whose wood has commercial value.

HUNDI: A receptacle placed in the temples of India into which offerings in cash and kind are made by devotees.

IDLI: A steamed rice cake that is a popular snack in south India.

IG: Inspector General

IPS: Indian Police Service

JAWAN: A Hindi word for soldier.

KARADI TREE: An indigenous tree found in the forests of south India.

KSRP: Karnataka State Reserve Police

LAGNA, MEENA LAGNA, MESHA LAGNA: Signs of the zodiac.

LTTE: Liberation Tigers of Tamil Eelam

LUNGI: An informal garment worn tied around the waist by south Indian men.

MAHA PURUSHA: "Great man" in Kannada.

MAHAZAR SHEET: An official report of a criminal incident as documented by the police or forest department officers.

MATHI TREE: An indigenous tree found in the forests of south India.

MIZO: A member of a community belonging to the state of Mizoram in northeast India.

MLA: Member of the Legislative Assembly

MM HILLS: Malai Mahadeshwara Hills

MP: Member of Parliament

MYSOREPAK: A popular candy in south India.

NAMASKARA: A Kannada greeting.

NAMASTE: A formal salutation that is done with palms folded.

NHRC: National Human Rights Commission

PATTA: Private land.

PATTI: "Village" in Tamil.

PERIAVARE: "Elder one" in Tamil.

POOJA: Traditional offerings of flowers and fruits made to God accompanied by the chanting of prayers.

PMK: Pakkali Makkal Katchi, a political party.

PRASADA: A portion of an offering made to God which is eaten reverentially by devotees.

RAF: Rapid Action Force

RAGI: Millet.

RAGI SQUAD: A group so named because its members carry millet flour as a form of sustenance.

RASAM: A traditional spicy soup eaten with rice in south India.

RFO: Range Forest Officer

RSI: Reserve Subinspector

SAHEBRU: A respectful form of address that means "boss."

SAMBAR: A thick soup containing lots of vegetables that is eaten with rice.

SAMBAR POWDER: A seasoning powder.

SAMPIGE TREE: A tree commonly found in south India whose flowers are extremely fragrant.

SAREE: A long, traditional garment with many folds, worn mainly by south Indian women.

SCHEDULED TRIBES: A term coined by the British and written into the Indian constitution; refers to the oldest inhabitants of the country.

SESSIONS JUDGE: A member of the judiciary.

SHORT EATS: An assortment of snacks.

SI: Subinspector

SLR: self-loading rifle

SP: Superintendent of Police

STF: Special Task Force

SUO MOTO: On the volition of the court.

TADA: Terrorist and Disruptive Activities Prevention Act

TALUK: A geographical division of a state, smaller than a district.

TATA SUMO: A multi-utility vehicle.

TEHSILDAR: A government official responsible for the administration of a taluk.

THATHA: "Grandfather" in Kannada.

TNLA: Tamil Nadu Liberation Army

TNRT: Tamil National Retrieval Troops

TRAX UTILITY VAN: A multi-utility vehicle made by the Hindustan Motor Company.

VANAVASA: exile

VIDHANA SOUDHA: The building housing the government Secretariat in Bangalore, the capital of Karnataka.

VRATHA: A religious vow.